RAINY BRAIN,
SUNNY BRAIN

Elaine Fox, born in Dublin, is a leading experimental psychologist and neuroscientist. Formerly Head of the Department of Psychology and Centre for Brain Science at The University of Essex, she is currently a Visiting Research Professor in the Department of Experimental Psychology at the University of Oxford. She has published widely in scientific journals and her work has been discussed in *The Economist*, *New Scientist*, *New York Times*, *Guardian*, *The Times* and others.

RAINY BRAIN, SUNNY BRAIN

The New Science of Optimism and Pessimism

ELAINE FOX

WILLIAM HEINEMANN: LONDON

Published by William Heinemann 2012

4 6 8 10 9 7 5 3

First published in Great Britain in 2012 by
William Heinemann
Random House, 20 Vauxhall Bridge Road,
London SW1V 2SA

www.randomhouse.co.uk

Addresses for companies within The Random House Group Limited can be found at:
www.randomhouse.co.uk/offices.htm

The Random House Group Limited Reg. No. 954009

A CIP catalogue record for this book
is available from the British Library

ISBN 9780434020171

The Random House Group Limited supports The Forest Stewardship
Council (FSC®), the leading international forest certification organisation. Our books
carrying the FSC label are printed on FSC® certified paper. FSC is the only
forest certification scheme endorsed by the leading environmental
organisations, including Greenpeace. Our paper procurement policy
can be found at: www.randomhouse.co.uk/environment

Printed and bound by CPI Group (UK) Ltd, Croydon, CR0 4YY

CONTENTS

At every single moment of one's life one is what one is going to be no less than what one has been.

– Oscar Wilde, *De Profundis*

A pessimist sees the difficulty in every opportunity. An optimist sees the opportunity in every difficulty.

– Winston Churchill

INTRODUCTION

ALVY'S PSYCHIATRIST

    How often do you sleep together?

ALVY

    Hardly ever. Maybe three times a week.

ANNIE'S PSYCHIATRIST

    Do you have sex often?

ANNIE

    Constantly! I'd say three times a week.

– Annie Hall

Psychological science has established a simple truth: how we view the world and how we interact with it change how the world responds to us. It's a compelling fact that's all too easily forgotten. Our way of being, our take on things, the attitude we bring to life, what I call our affective mindset, colours our world, affecting our health, our wealth, and our general well-being. Psychologists have developed several ways to measure different mindsets – pessimism and optimism – so that it's now possible to quantify the differences between these fundamental ways of thinking. Most remarkably, these differences – whether we turn towards the bright side of life or the dark – can be traced to specific patterns of activity in the brain itself. Bundles of nerve fibres connecting contemporary areas of our 'thinking' brain with ancient regions that control our most primeval emotions make up different aspects of our affective mind. The 'rainy' brain part highlights the negative, while our 'sunny' brain draws us towards the good things in life. Both are essential, and it's the checks and balances between these two systems that ultimately make you you and me me. It's our affective mind that gives meaning to our lives by tuning us in to what really matters.

For over twenty years, the diverse ways in which people interpret the world around them have been at the heart of my scientific work. My quest has been to try to illuminate, piece by tantalising piece, those parts of our brain that allow us to experience joys and fears, appreciate beauty, have fun, and worry to the point of existential despair. Affect infuses our mind with meaning, making us aware of what might harm us, alerting us to what might go wrong, drawing us towards what's good for us, and highlighting the pleasures and sheer joys of living. Across millions of years of evolution, ancient neural structures have reached out to forge links with more recent brain regions, developing circuits and networks that tune us in to what's important. Subtle differences in the reactivity of these affective brain circuits result in deeply divergent attitudes and outlooks on life – the heart of what I call our 'affective mind.' It is here that we will surely find the answers to why we differ so much from one another.

Our affective mind gives us soul, puts the fire into life. This capacity to experience and feel emotions, especially in how we react to pleasures and dangers, is shared with many other species, but when linked up with our enlarged cerebral cortex – that part of our brain that gives us our unique cognitive talents to speak, think, and solve problems – our affective mind allows us to transcend the rest of biology. This glorious intersection of thinking and feeling can lead us to be stopped in our tracks by the haunting beauty of a sunset or to be moved to tears by a simple sequence of musical notes or words.

The same combination of ancient and contemporary brain regions also has a downside, however, leaving us vulnerable to existential angst. All too easily, we can be overwhelmed by fears and worries and laid low by the sheer 'monstrous crying of the wind,' as W. B. Yeats so beautifully put it.

My own attempts to understand the affective mind in all its complexity has followed the path of psychological science itself, initially focusing on the negative before turning to the question of why some people flourish, seemingly resilient to all that life throws at them. For most of its history, psychology has been concerned with problems: anxiety, depression, addictions, compulsions have all been central topics. Over the years, thousands of research grants have been won and scientific papers written on why some people are prone to a pervasive pessimism that can slide into depression and anxiety, and armies of researchers have tried to figure out effective ways to alleviate the distress caused by all this negativity. A focus on the negative is understandable and appropriate, of course, given the devastation that anxiety disorders and severe depression can cause in people's lives.

My own approach to unravelling this mystery has been to probe the minds of the anxious and depressed with the traditional tools of cognitive psychology. Flashing positive and negative images on a computer screen, sometimes so fast that they are below the radar of consciousness, and then asking people to detect items that occur in the same location as quickly as they can, allows me to measure how quickly people react to different types of images – negative or positive – revealing a momentary glimpse of what captivates the unconscious mind. If your mind is drawn towards a negative scene, like the aftermath of a car crash, for instance, in preference to a happier image, then items appearing in that location will be found faster. The difference may only be hundredths of a second, but decades of research using techniques like this reveal that the anxious brain shifts imperceptibly towards the negative.

The tide within psychological science is gradually turning to what makes us happy and optimistic. And this unfolding story is telling us that the optimistic mind is drawn inexorably towards the positive, while simultaneously delicately turning us away from the negative.

The cognitive styles of those prone to pessimism and anxiety and those prone to optimism and happiness are, indeed, fundamentally different. Why? Do these deep-set biases play a *causal* role in why some people are pessimistic and anxious, while some are deeply hopeful and optimistic? In a nutshell, how and why does the affective mind differ so much among people?

Breathtaking developments in psychological science, alongside startling advances in the technology underlying neuroscience and genetics, give us an abundance of new evidence on these old questions. Most modern-day psychology departments house a variety of sophisticated brain-imaging machines that allow us to peer into the inner workings of our brains as never before. Combined with traditional methods, this new information throws fresh light on just how much our outlook on life is linked to processes taking place deep inside our brain.

The way we interpret and react to the things that happen has an incalculable impact on the kind of life we lead. Consider the following tale of two brothers I knew when I was a university student. Daniel and Joey were born a year apart in a small town in the west of Ireland in the 1960s. Their parents were reasonably affluent, with a small corner shop that both boys worked in when they were young. Both went to the local Christian Brothers' school and were actively involved in the local Gaelic Athletic Association club. Their lives were not marked by anything spectacular; nothing too bad, or too good, ever really happened in their small town. Today, Daniel is a multimillionaire, living in the United States with a string of successful businesses to his name. Joey is a schoolteacher in Dublin, struggling to pay his mortgage.

Right from the beginning the two boys were different. Always on the lookout for opportunities, Daniel began a paper route from the family shop at the age of seven, earning a per cent of the profits; a year later he began to deliver groceries on his bike to elderly people unable to come into town. Most of his customers gave him generous tips. All through his teenage years, Daniel ran errands here and there, often persuading Joey to help out. By the time he went to university in Dublin at the age of eighteen, Daniel had accumulated enough money to put a deposit down on a flat near campus. He asked Joey if he wanted to pool their money together, but Joey was worried that he might lose his savings and put it in the bank instead. Daniel continued to come up with small business ideas. By the time Daniel was finished with his degree, he was renting the flat out, using the income to pay the mortgage on another, bigger property he was now living in, while also renting out two rooms to lodgers, one of whom was Joey.

Joey was always the better student; scholarly and conscientious, he obtained top grades on his final exams and went on to postgraduate studies. He turned down several chances to get involved in Daniel's business ventures, his natural caution persuading him not to take the risk. This was often sensible, since many of Daniel's projects were spectacular failures. In the long run, however, Daniel was highly successful, and Joey, while not unsuccessful, lived a very modest life.

Most of us can see reflections of both Daniel and Joey in ourselves. Sometimes we plunge straight in, throwing caution to the wind; sometimes we're a bit more reluctant to take a chance. There are times we face the world with an open heart and an open mind, ready to relish all that life has to offer. Other times, we approach the world with a more timid mindset, apprehensive and on the lookout for problems.

The way Joey's life turned out, and how different it was from Daniel's, shows us the impact that one's outlook has on the things that happen. In spite of similar backgrounds, similar abilities, similar genes, the way their lives unfolded was poles apart. A simple difference in attitude resulted in divergent life trajectories.

From the extremes of anxiety and depression, where people are convinced that nothing will ever turn out well, to milder apprehension, pessimists highlight the dark side of life. Problems are seen as setbacks rather than opportunities. Optimists, like Daniel, are alert to every opportunity and tend to jump in, boots and all. Good scientific evidence tells us that these differences affect how happy we are, how successful we become, and how healthy we remain.

My probing and analysing of these two dimensions of our affective mind has led to a surprising conclusion: the roots of our sunny brain are embedded deep in *pleasure*, the parts of our neural architecture that respond to rewards and the good things in life, while the roots of our rainy brain lie deep among the ancient brain structures that alert us to danger and threat – our *fear* brain. Tiny variations in how our pleasure brain and our fear brain react and how well this foment is kept under wraps by higher control centres of the brain lead to the emergence, over a lifetime, of a network of connections that make up our rainy brain and our sunny brain.

All of us have these rainy-brain and sunny-brain circuits, in more or less the same regions, but the potency of these circuits varies markedly from person to person; some react instantly to pleasure and fun, and others take longer to warm up. Similarly, some people are highly sensitive to danger, worrying and fretting about the slightest threat, while others have a much higher threshold for fear. It is these differences, I believe, that form the bedrock of who we are.

In *Rainy Brain, Sunny Brain* we go on a tour of contemporary, cutting-edge science as well as explore the experiences of many optimists and pessimists. I will show you the staggering amount we have learned in the last couple of decades about what can strengthen and weaken the two crucial dimensions of our affective mind: our response to pleasure and to fear. We will see how science is beginning to unlock the mystery of what makes us who we are. It's not a simple story, with the answer lying somewhere among the boundaries of our genetic makeup, the constant flux of the things that happen to us, and, most importantly of all, how we learn to see and interpret those things that happen. Genes matter, yes, but the degree of influence they have is very much related to our environment.

We are all born with certain genetic strengths, as well as genetic vulnerabilities, but whether these inclinations ever emerge depends crucially on the nature of the world we inhabit.

Our story will traverse disciplines as diverse as psychology, molecular genetics, and neuroscience to see how the deepest mysteries of what makes us who we are are gradually being unravelled. To understand this area of science we must delve beneath the quirks and biases of how we think and venture deep into the cells and networks in our brains and even down to sets of particular genes that we now know underlie many aspects of our personalities. This is a fascinating story of how genes and the things that happen to us interleave in complex ways with chains of influence running in both directions. What's exciting is that we now know that optimism, just like pessimism, results from an intricate dance of genetics, life experiences, and specific biases in how each of us views and interprets the world around us. Beyond genetic vulnerabilities and strengths, it's what life throws at us that determines whether our genetic potentials are fulfilled and which brain circuits – positive or negative – are strengthened. It is this delicate ebb and flow of circuits deep in our brain that shapes the contours and valleys of our personalities. Whether we can gather ourselves together and emerge stronger from a crisis or whether we are bowled over by setbacks, ruminating endlessly on the negative, is influenced by whether our sunny or our rainy brain circuits dominate.

Knowing our vulnerabilities as well as our strengths is important and potentially useful. Being aware of what can elicit and even change these predispositions can help us protect ourselves and ultimately set us on the path to flourishing. The good news is that the brain circuits underlying our rainy brain and sunny brain are among the most plastic in the human brain. Prolonged stress or depressive episodes can result in structural changes in highly specific parts of our brain, just as prolonged periods of joy and happiness can transform our neural architecture. This tells us that our brains can and do change. Subtle variation in how we see the world – our biases and quirks of mind – can reshape the actual architecture of our brain, pushing us towards a more optimistic or pessimistic take on life. By changing the way our brain responds to challenges and joys, we can change the way we are.

I describe several techniques, based on strong scientific evidence, that are known to make real changes to how our affective mind operates. By modifying the checks and balances between our rainy brain and our sunny brain, we will see that we do not need to be resigned to a life of fearful avoidance, but instead we can take steps to change our outlook – and change our life.

CHAPTER 1

Rainy Brains and Sunny Brains

The Affective Mind

For there is nothing either good or bad,
but thinking makes it so.

– WILLIAM SHAKESPEARE,
Hamlet, Act 2, Scene 2

It was a cold, rainy day, and I was running late. I had forgotten just how busy the tube gets during the London rush hour. Hurrying down to the platform, jostling against damp people all rushing somewhere, I heard the announcement that the Central Line was momentarily suspended. A collective groan went up. Then came the news that the Central Line was entirely shut down because of a body under a train at Bond Street station. Everyone knew what that meant: another suicide on London's ancient underground system. I'm sure I wasn't the only one who felt guilty about my irritation.

I later found out that the man who threw himself under that train was Paul Castle, a wealthy property tycoon, polo player, and friend of

Prince Charles. From humble beginnings, he had made and lost two fortunes and currently owned properties in some of London's most exclusive areas, as well as a swish apartment in St. Moritz in Switzerland and a private plane to fly him there. What could have driven him to such drastic action? His friends couldn't explain it. 'It was out of character,' one said. His friend Stephen Brook said that Paul had had recent health problems and the recession had affected his business. We can only speculate that a moment of pessimism and despair had convinced him that it was not worth going on.

Late the previous night, on the other side of town, a young woman jumped off Blackfriars Bridge into the dark, freezing Thames. Apparently also intent on suicide, she panicked when she found herself in a busy boat lane and started shouting. Within seconds, Adan Abobaker, hearing her distress, grabbed and threw a life preserver as far as he could into the dark water. 'I realised it was nowhere near her,' he said later. Without hesitation, he stripped off his coat and sweater and jumped in. It took Adan more than two minutes to reach the young woman, but he managed to bring her back near shore away from the shipping lanes, where they were both rescued by the crew of a safety vessel who had seen what had happened. Both survived, following several hours of treatment for hypothermia at a nearby hospital.

Adan had recently fallen on hard times and was living in St. Mungo's hostel for homeless people. 'I just did what needed to be done,' he said, making light of his bravery. 'I just hope she's got a family. Life is worth living; it's not worth giving up.' If only Paul Castle had thought that.

Some people have an unshakeable belief that things will work out. Others can only imagine a future without hope. Wealth seems to have little to do with it. Adan Abobaker had nothing and yet risked his life because 'it's not worth giving up.' Paul Castle had wealth and success beyond what most people dream of, and yet he thought it was not worth going on.

Psychologists and neuroscientists have worked long and hard to devise ways to quantify such profoundly different takes on life. A first step is to ask what we mean by the terms *optimism* and *pessimism*. Loose vocabulary, while fine in everyday life, is not concise enough for a thorough, scientific analysis. To effectively quantify these mindsets, we need better definitions of the common words used to label them.

An important starting point is the distinction psychologists make between dispositions, or traits, and states, or momentary feelings. Think of some moments of happiness or despair you have experienced, such as when you won a prize or were offered an exciting job, or when somebody died. These experiences are *states* of happiness or sadness; they reflect the transient highs and lows of everyday life. A *trait*, on the other hand, is a more stable characteristic that endures across time. These are the emotional styles or ways of thinking that remain fairly steadfast across our lives. Mary has 'Mary-like' characteristics that remain fairly stable, just as Dave stays 'Dave-like' through thick and thin. Bubbly, happy babies tend to become adventurous, outgoing children who tend to become extroverted, sociable adults.

Scientific studies support this notion. In one study, the best predictor of happiness and optimism at the end of a nine-year period was happiness and optimism at the beginning of the study. In spite of major changes in life circumstances, optimists tended to stay optimistic, and pessimists tended to stay pessimistic.

The influence that our personalities have on our environmental experiences is illustrated in a study published in 1989 by Bruce Headey and Alexander Wearing of the University of Melbourne in Australia. They interviewed residents of the state of Victoria on several occasions over many years to see how life events and personality affected people's happiness. They wanted to know the extent to which a person's personality versus the things that happened to them affected well-being and happiness. Personality might account for, say, 40 per cent of happiness, whereas life events might account for 60 per cent. Alternatively, perhaps personality would turn out to be more important.

It didn't take the researchers long to realise that they had made a fundamental mistake. As their study progressed, it was clear that the same kind of things kept happening to the same people over and over again. Lucky people were lucky again and again. Likewise, people with lots of bad experiences, like relationship breakups and job losses, seemed to encounter one bad thing after another. Their assumption that personality and life events would have separate influences on happiness was wrong. Instead, personality itself had the strongest influence on what happened to people. The optimists had more positive experiences, while the pessimists had more negative experiences.

Subsequent studies have confirmed that our personality, or our affective mindset, has a profound impact on the life events that we experience, and this does not tend to change too much over time. Picture a bubbly, outgoing child who is warm and friendly. People are much more likely to respond to this child with smiles and physical affection than they are to a withdrawn, unsmiling child. If he behaves consistently, the social world of the happy child will inevitably be more positive than that of the frightened child. There's no luck involved: the emotional style of the child is playing a part in the kind of social world she inhabits. How we act in the world changes the kind of environment we experience and hence the range of opportunities and problems likely to come our way.

Optimism and pessimism, then, just like other features of our personality, can be thought of as traits or dispositions as well as states. Dispositional optimists are often upbeat and happy, with sunny dispositions that can infect those around them. Dispositional optimism is not just about being happy and upbeat, however; it's more about having genuine hope for the future, a belief that things will work out, and an unshakeable faith that we can deal with whatever life throws at us.

Optimists are not naïve – they don't believe that nothing will ever go wrong – but they do have a deep-seated conviction that they can cope. Similarly, dispositional pessimism is not about being constantly sad and anxious but about being apprehensive about the future, aware of potential dangers, more alert to what might go wrong rather than what might go right. These are the people who err on the side of caution. Rather than take a risk, they will play it safe, although even the most pessimistic among us are likely to have times of great joy and happiness and hope for the future.

The scientific evidence that these fundamentally different mindsets come with costs and benefits is now overwhelming. One of the most important findings to emerge from the scientific literature, however, is that the real benefits of optimism only come when an optimistic mindset is linked with a healthy dose of realism. Blind optimism, and a belief that nothing will ever go wrong, is unlikely to be of any real benefit.

I discussed this with Michael J. Fox, the actor who was diagnosed with Parkinson's disease at the age of twenty-nine and is, by his own admission, an irrepressible optimist. The escalating movement problems caused by Parkinson's forced him to leave his highly successful movie and television career behind. Eighteen years after diagnosis, he was making a documentary with the unlikely title *Michael J. Fox: The Adventures of an Incurable Optimist*. I was involved because Michael was interested in the scientific take on where optimism comes from and whether it can be measured in a reliable way.

Chatting after filming was complete, I saw that Michael fulfilled all the key characteristics of a dispositional optimist. An illness that would get most of us down had, it seemed, left him still upbeat, enjoying life. 'Don't think that I'm not aware of risk or what might go wrong,' he told me. 'I'm actually very good at assessing risk, but I know that I will be able to deal with whatever happens. Over the years, I have learned that I can deal with any difficulty. I don't necessarily like it, but I generally feel I can deal with it.'

He explained that one of the most difficult things for him in the early days was the shift from people seeing him as 'Michael J. Fox, the actor' to 'Michael J. Fox, the actor with Parkinson's' to finally 'Michael J. Fox, the guy with Parkinson's.' 'It really was tough,' he said, but he had often wondered why he did not get depressed.

This was a real puzzle to him, as he wasn't in any doubt from an early stage that Parkinson's would end his flourishing acting career. Yet, apart from a couple of bouts of understandable frustration, he had always managed to stay hopeful about the future. It's this type of resilience, an optimism that doesn't put its head in the sand, that science has shown makes a real difference to our lives.

This type of optimism seems to occur naturally and is found in the most unlikely of places. When I was a teenager, I remember being profoundly shaken by the power of Italian author Primo Levi's *If This Is a Man*, recounting his experiences as a young chemist from Turin in a German concentration camp during the Second World War. In pared-down, unsentimental language, Levi chronicles the horrific story of a year at Auschwitz. The horrors of that year were to become the defining moment of his life. However, Levi never seemed to lose sight of the resilience of the human spirit, in spite of all the evidence to the contrary. In many ways, his book rendered one of human history's darkest hours into a force for good in the world.

Levi attributed his survival largely to his capacity to perceive his fellow inmates, as well as himself, as people and not as objects. Holding on to this perspective allowed him to avoid the demoralisation, or what he called the 'spiritual shipwreck', that engulfed so many others.

In a later book, Levi describes his long trek to freedom marching across eastern Europe and Russia, where the 'vigorous people full of the love of life' rekindled in him the joy of living that the camps had almost extinguished. Levi's account gradually unfolds as a story of hope, echoing the experiences of many who have come through great adversity. Sometimes this optimism stems from a belief in a higher being – God – with the anticipation of a better life elsewhere; sometimes it comes from a deep-set belief in the innate goodness of humankind.

The original meaning of *optimism* is much closer to this notion than to the 'rose-tinted glasses' or 'sunny-side-up' ideas that we currently associate with optimism. The original sense comes from the Latin word *optimum*, meaning 'the best possible,' and the word was first coined by the German philosopher and mathematician Gottfried Wilhelm Leibniz (1646–1716). Leibniz argued that God had created the best possible world and that this optimum world could not be improved upon. In other words, optimism had little to do with notions of 'the bright side' or the 'glass half full'; instead, it referred to the idea that the world was already the best possible and couldn't get any better.

Optimism, then, has a lot to do with accepting the world as it is – both good and bad have their place – and the trick is not to allow notions of evil and negativity to overwhelm us. Primo Levi and Michael J. Fox are realists who are fully aware that there will be problems and setbacks and that they need to be flexible and creative in finding solutions to their problems, but overall they have an unshakeable belief that things will work out in the end. And things invariably do, not because of random luck, but because optimists take control of their own destiny. These are the people who take steps to solve their problems.

The trait of pessimism is almost the polar opposite. The mind of the dispositional pessimist becomes infused with negativity, and every setback is taken as further evidence that the world is against them. Derived from the Latin word *pessimus*, the philosophical perspective of pessimism views this world as the worst of all possible worlds and assumes that everything ultimately gravitates towards evil. In psychological science, however, pessimism, just like optimism, is viewed more as a dispositional trait or an emotional style – our typical way of dealing with the world. Pessimists are convinced that their problems are beyond their control and will never go away. 'Bad things just happen, and you can't do anything about it; you just have no control over it,' as one pessimist I interviewed told me. Believing that good things happen to other people is a hallmark of this mindset. Such feelings of powerlessness frequently lead to an enduring passivity and lack of motivation, which are other key components of pessimism and its darker cousin, depression.

Optimists, in contrast, feel that they have some control over what happens to them, tackling problems as temporary hitches rather than as ongoing difficulties. They have a natural tendency to accept the world as it is but believe that the way you deal with things determines who you are. If Primo Levi had taken the construction of the concentration camps *personally*, his experiences would have overwhelmed him. Instead, he managed to distance his thoughts by keeping in mind the humanity and decency of most of the people around him. Likewise, there was no descent into despair for Michael J. Fox when he was diagnosed with Parkinson's disease. Instead, he came out fighting and set up a foundation that is now raising millions of dollars each year for research into the disease.

Optimism and pessimism reverberate throughout our lives, leading to very different life experiences. Psychologists have come up with several ingenious ways to estimate the core characteristics of these mindsets. One option is to simply ask people, Are you an optimist or a pessimist? Psychology departments around the world are sinking under the weight of scales and questionnaires that probe and assess every attribute you can think of. Are you clever? Are you happy? Are you tough-minded? If it differs between people, there's sure to be a questionnaire to measure it.

Several well-established scales are available that tell us how we rate compared to other people. One of the simplest and most reliable is called the Life Orientation Task (LOT), developed by Charles Carver at the University of Miami and Michael Scheier at Carnegie Mellon University.

A revised version called the LOT-R is presented below. Self-report measures like the LOT-R have been a mainstay of psychology

The Life Orientation Task–Revised

	Agree a lot (A)	Agree a little (B)	Neither agree nor disagree (C)	Disagree (D)	Disagree a lot (E)
1. In uncertain times, I usually expect the best.	☐	☐	☐	☐	☐
2. It's easy for me to relax.	☐	☐	☐	☐	☐
3. If something can go wrong for me, it will.	☐	☐	☐	☐	☐
4. I am always optimistic about my future.	☐	☐	☐	☐	☐
5. I enjoy my friends a lot.	☐	☐	☐	☐	☐
6. It's important to me to keep busy.	☐	☐	☐	☐	☐
7. I hardly ever expect things to go my way.	☐	☐	☐	☐	☐
8. I don't get upset too easily.	☐	☐	☐	☐	☐
9. I rarely count on good things happening to me.	☐	☐	☐	☐	☐
10. Overall, I expect more good things to happen to me than bad.	☐	☐	☐	☐	☐

for many years and are at the heart of telling us how we feel relative to others. Fill it out now to find out how optimistic or pessimistic you are. It's important to fill out each question honestly; try not to let your answers to each question be influenced by those that came before. There are no correct or incorrect answers. The important thing is to answer each question according to how you really feel and not by what you think other people might say. Once you have completed the questionnaire, you can turn to the notes at the back of the book to see how to work out your score.

If you are like most people, you will have scored around 15, which is mildly optimistic. Very low scores reflect a pessimistic outlook, whereas scores moving up towards 20 and above reflect a highly positive outlook on life. The LOT-R gives psychologists a quantifiable indication of a person's core outlook on life. Our take on life will change to some extent from time to time, of course, but deep down there is a consistency to these characteristics over time. In other words, if you fill out this questionnaire again in a year's time, your score is likely to be similar.

A sole reliance on what people tell us, however, is fraught with difficulties. The problem is that many things affect how we respond: if you're attracted to the cute psychologist scoring your questionnaire, you might present yourself in a more positive way than you actually feel. Other times people may simply lie. Most difficult of all are the times when we don't have an intimate knowledge of our own mental processes. This, in fact, is most of the time. Research tells us that we are completely unaware of the vagaries of our mental processing. If I ask you whether you generally notice positive rather than negative information in the news, you almost certainly won't know. You may think you're fairly positive, but studies that measure what type of information our brain zones in on show that these natural tendencies operate well below the radar of consciousness. Therefore, to thoroughly quantify the distinctions between optimism and pessimism, it's essential to move beyond asking people about their outlook on life.

One approach is to capture the complex patterns of how our brain reacts to the good and the bad, or how enigmatic cognitive processes can draw attention to either the negative or the positive side of life, providing us with vital information about the roots of our affective mindset. Startling developments in brain-imaging technology allow us to dig below what we say and measure the brain circuits underpinning optimistic or pessimistic outlooks in great detail.

Some of the most exciting new insights come from studies using functional magnetic resonance imagery (fMRI). This brain-scanning machine is essentially a large magnet that provides a visual image of the flow of blood around the brain. When people are thinking positive thoughts or looking at pleasant pictures, we can see which brain regions become more active as they become engorged with blood. When a part of the brain is needed for a particular task, it sparks into life and uses up lots of energy. The consequent depletion of energy sends out a signal to the rest of the brain to dispatch more oxygen as quickly as possible. Oxygen is then rapidly transported to the needy area via the bloodstream, and it's this extra oxygen in the blood that's detected by the fMRI machine.

The flow of oxygen around the nooks and crannies of our brain uncovers previously hidden processes to give us a covert view of the brain in action, and the fMRI allows us to pinpoint the specific regions of the brain linked with optimistic or pessimistic mindsets. It turns out that these patterns of brain activity are also relatively enduring. If I measure which part of your brain is active when you win a prize, the same brain circuit will light up if measured again six months later, when something else good happens. Another region may light up when you hear bad news, and this same region will again respond to disappointment in a year's time. Just as with responses to questionnaires like the LOT-R, the way our brain responds to positive and negative events measures an enduring aspect of our affective mind. This gives us a unique insight into our typical reactions to emotional events.

A real advantage of direct measures of brain activity, like fMRI, is that it's much more difficult to fake your responses or tell the researchers what you think they want to hear. This is why brain-imaging technologies are an essential part of the scientific tool-kit to uncover the source of our outlook on life. To quantify a person's level of optimism or pessimism in a more precise way, we can ask them (subjective level), or we can measure the brain circuits associated with these different mindsets (neural level).

A third way to probe the inner workings of our affective mind is to examine our way of looking at the world – our deep-rooted biases and quirks of imagination that lie at the heart of who we are. These cognitive processes lie somewhere between what people say and the spikes of activity of individual cells, or neurons, deep in our brains. Our cognitive biases – subtle shifts of mind towards the good or the bad – cannot be measured by asking people, because we are simply not aware of these subterranean mind shifts. Similarly, brain-imaging techniques cannot fully uncover the subtleties of memory, imagination, and interpretation that emerge from neural activity.

These states of mind – our cognitive biases – are best accessed by the traditional methods of cognitive psychology. For example, imagine you are walking along the street and see an acquaintance whom you have not met for a long time. While you are ready to greet him, he walks right by without acknowledging you at all. You might assume that he's being rude, does not like you, doesn't want to talk, and has, in fact, deliberately ignored you. Alternatively, you can conclude that your acquaintance was busy and preoccupied and so simply didn't notice or recognise you. Perhaps he couldn't remember your name and didn't want to embarrass himself. Social situations like this are highly ambiguous, illustrating why our *interpretations* have such a big influence on how we feel. A more positive interpretation of events – he was preoccupied – maintains and nourishes an optimistic mindset, whereas a negative interpretation – he doesn't like me – can spiral into negative thoughts and a pessimistic mindset.

Biases in how we interpret things are at the core of our affective mind. Our brains contain a multitude of such biases, operating well below our radar of consciousness and ultimately leading us to having a particular slant on things. This tendency of our affective mind to zone in on the good or the bad, or to interpret ambiguous social situations in flattering or gloomy ways, is the basis of how we experience the world around us.

How do these slants of mind come about in the first place? A large part of the answer has to do with how we select what to focus on from the confusion of sounds and sights bombarding us at every moment. In a world containing an endless stream of information, what we notice is becoming ever more important, and this selectivity has crucial implications for our emotional stability. This aspect of mind – what cognitive psychologists call *selective attention* – forms the kernel of our affective mind.

To see how selective attention operates, stop reading for a moment, and concentrate on what you can hear. I bet lots of things now come into focus that you didn't notice before – the hum of the central heating, a distant plane, birdsong outside, children playing in the street, a distant radio. You may also now feel the weight of the book (or e-reader) in your hands, the pressure of the chair at your back. You may suddenly remember something you need to do later. All of these sensations and thoughts were there all the time; you just weren't paying attention to them – they were in the background. This habit of our brain to bring into focus what is immediately relevant, and to screen out the rest, is vital. Without this ability we would be overwhelmed by information overload. This same selectivity, however, filters out what our brain considers to be irrelevant and therefore is the starting point in the construction of our affective mind and what it learns to highlight and to ignore.

As a cognitive psychologist, I am intrigued by this ability of our brain to focus on some things more than others, to absorb and remember specific facts and experiences, and then weave them into a coherent narrative coloured by our personality and by our life experiences. This surely has to be one of the most fascinating stories in contemporary science. We now know that each and every one of us has a mind permeated by a myriad of biases that colour how we see the world and how we remember our past. From the moment we are born, smells, sights, sounds, and textures bombard us from every direction. Capturing the essence of this internal turbulence, William James, the founder of scientific psychology in the United States, described the infant's impression and experience of the world as a 'blooming, buzzing confusion.' This 'confusion' has to somehow be made sense of, and it's our brain's job to achieve this complex task. From the multitudes of things we take note of, our brain has to somehow make sure that we notice the important things and not pay too much attention to those that are less relevant. Things that might injure us (dangers) or those that might sustain us (pleasures) are understandably the strongest magnets for this affective energy, whereas details like the colour of pictures on the wall aren't critical and can therefore be safely ignored. This is why our mind is infused by an affective energy that guides all of our mental processes.

When I was a young girl, we had an elderly neighbour named Mr Graham, whom I regularly helped out. Mr Graham must have been in his eighties, and his tall, athletic build was beginning to become fragile. He had run on the cross-country team for Trinity College in his youth, but a serious leg injury sustained in the First World War, in addition to his advancing years, had left him slow and weak. His beloved wife had died a few years before, and while he could still hobble around his treasured garden, he now found it difficult to get out to the shops. I used to do some shopping for him and occasionally made him lunch, although this fiercely independent man was reluctant to accept much help.

We lived in a beautiful area about twelve miles from Dublin City, surrounded by stunning coves, beaches, and coastal scenery. On sunny summer Sundays, the crowds of North Dublin descended on the beaches and walkways of Howth. Unfortunately, the Irish weather is rarely sunny, and for many months of the year the dark clouds, dank fog, and bitter winds that swirl in from the sea can make life challenging. But even on those darkest days, Mr Graham's optimistic outlook was remarkable. On bitter frosty mornings, he would point out to me the first signs of a new bud breaking through the hard soil. 'Won't be long before the daffodils are out,' he would say. He told me stories of the war, and although they were peppered with tragedies and dark moments, he seemed energised by happy memories of camaraderie and deep friendships.

He was not unaware of tragedy; he was sometimes very sad and clearly felt intensely the loss of his wife of more than fifty years. But he always looked on the bright side. He seemed to notice the good things, and the bad just didn't get him down too much. I remember one cold morning waiting at the bus stop outside his house on my way to school, watching him struggle up the steep hill to the road to put out his rubbish. I knew from experience that there was no point in offering to help. He finally dragged his bin to the gate and, breathing heavily, looked out over the raging cold sea barely visible through the grey mist. 'How lucky we are to live in such a beautiful place,' he said.

Our affective mindset sets the course that our life will take. Think of the ambiguity of a half smile on your boss's face as you arrive a little late for a meeting. Is she pleased to see you, or is she annoyed that you are late? How you interpret that smile affects how you would feel about being given extra work. The positive take – *she is relieved I am here* – might make you think that this is important work and your boss has faith that you will do it well. The negative interpretation – *she is angry that I am late* – is likely to make the extra work feel like a chore or even a punishment.

A tendency to pay more attention to danger or negativity, however slight, can result in a pessimistic view of a world filled with constant dangers and disappointments. A partiality for pleasure and positivity, like Mr Graham's, can give the impression of a world overflowing with success and good things. How does our brain achieve this feat? How do our unique personalities and ways of looking at life translate into how much we notice and remember about the world? More importantly, how does the way in which we view the world influence our emotional style and outlook?

The Pull and Push of Pleasure and Fear

To begin to answer these questions, we need to pare away all the complexities of life and get back to the most primitive aspects of our behaviour. Our most fundamental behavioural tendency is, of course, to move towards positive things and away from nasty things. Good things pull us in, bad things repel us.

The American psychologist T. C. Schneirla spent a lifetime observing animals and humans and became convinced that it is this simple principle that unites all species. For any living creature, the best way to maximise survival is to approach good things like food and sex, and to avoid dangerous things like predators and poisons. The rest of our behaviour and all the complexity of our lives are rooted in these two fundamental tendencies.

Schneirla joined the psychology department at New York University in 1927 and remained there and at the American Natural History Museum until his death in 1968. One of the strongest advocates of field research at the time, he was convinced that psychologists needed to be out and about observing animals in their natural, wild environments. This brought him into frequent conflict with his NYU colleagues, who believed that animal behaviour was best understood under the more controlled conditions of the laboratory. Even today, this is a source of debate among psychologists. Do we aim for the naturalness of the 'real world' with all its complexities, or do we shoot for the rigour of the laboratory? In Schneirla's time, the dominant ambition was to develop very general and comprehensive theories that could explain *all* of animal as well as human behaviour. In those days of grand 'theories of everything,' only large-scale explanations cutting across all species were taken seriously.

An unfortunate downside of this view was that psychologists became obsessed with the similarities, rather than the differences, among species. Ever wonder why the white laboratory rat emerged as the model to explain the behaviour of *all* species? The fixation on similarities is a large part of the reason. The humble rat became the focal point to explain the actions, memories, perceptions, and emotions of all creatures, including us. This may seem a bit bizarre to us now, but it shows how scientists, like anybody else, can get carried away, often leading them to miss the obvious. And the obvious, as Schneirla realised, was that species do differ from one another in profound ways. While there are obvious similarities between rats and the pigeons – they both respond to a reward, and the pattern of how they learn and forget is often remarkably similar – there are also deep-rooted differences. As my PhD supervisor made clear many years ago, just try to train a pigeon to find its way through a maze, or a rat to respond only to red circles and not to blue squares. Pecking something they see comes naturally to pigeons, so psychologists can capitalise on that. Rats are much more driven by their sense of smell, so trying to train a rat to respond to squares versus circles results in a traumatised rat as well as a traumatised psychology student.

This is what Schneirla realised back in the 1920s. While he certainly did not deny the value of laboratory research, from his very first field trip to the Panama Canal to study army ants in 1932, he became convinced that the wonders and excitement of animal behaviour could only be appreciated and understood by observing normal behaviour as it unfolds in the wild. In an ironic twist, despite the problems he had with the 'grand theorists' of his day, it was Schneirla who came up with a general principle that is now widely accepted. From all of his observations and experiments, both in the lab and in the wild, he recognised that what unites all living creatures is the urge to find food and shelter (approach reward) and not get eaten (avoid danger). Whether we are a pigeon, a rat, a horse, or a human, *approaching* a reward and *avoiding* a threat are the great motivators.

This selectivity in what we notice is at the heart of our being from the very moment we enter the world, and it is why we have both a rainy brain *and* a sunny brain. Some of our selectivity is innate, and some is picked up over a lifetime. In spite of the worries of many parents, babies who are able to crawl rarely tumble off sheer edges, for even at the age of just two months they are able to distinguish depth. We can see this in a series of classic experiments in which infants were placed on solid glass over a 'visual cliff' apparatus. Underneath one-half of the glass was a sheer drop, and under the other was a shallow space. Even though the babies could feel the solidity of the glass beneath them, nothing would persuade them to venture over the deep part, not even the enticement of their own mothers on the other side. That innate fear provides the human infant with the ability to avoid potentially harmful falls. Even the draw to move towards the protection and warmth of your own mother is not enough to risk the danger of the visual cliff.

Watching an antelope sip nervously from a stream while keeping an eye on a lion resting nearby gives you the sense of the uneasy anticipation that these *approach-avoid* situations instil. In such classic pull-push situations, we are torn between pleasure and danger. Danger generally wins the battle, but there are clear differences between people in how far they will go to achieve pleasure in the face of danger. Some babies may venture part of the way over the visual cliff, whereas some will keep well away from the edge. The tug of pleasure is stronger for some of us, while the fear of danger exerts a stronger push for others. These divergences, while often quite subtle, can have a profound influence on our outlook as they are played out hundreds, if not thousands, of times throughout our lives.

It is these great motivators that have led over evolutionary time to the development of circuits and connections embedded deep in our brain that make up our *fear brain* and our *pleasure brain*. The fear brain is constantly on the lookout for danger and keeps us safe in an unpredictable world. The pleasure brain has the job of ensuring that we seek out those things that are good for us. Both sides are essential and drive the set of wider brain processes that I call the rainy brain and sunny brain.

Our rainy brain and sunny brain are constantly monitoring the world, ensuring that we tune in to the dangers as well as the pleasures of everyday life. My research over many years has forced me to conclude that it is the reactivity of our rainy brains and sunny brains that is the primary source of our selective perceptions. Deep within the neurological networks and chemical and genetic mixes of the brain lurk volcanic-like shifts and movements that reverberate and echo. This ebbing and flowing between our sunny brain and rainy brain, over time, leads to the fundamental biases and quirks of mind that form the primary elements of our affective mind.

Such a quirk of mind, or tendency to notice certain types of things more than others, is what psychologists call an *attentional bias*. Think of how often you are drawn to stories in the news about your favourite sports team. Your mind seems to effortlessly ignore lots of less interesting details in order to pick out exactly what interests you. Those things that we notice – our biases – are the things that mean the most to us.

We can see how this selectivity in attention works by looking at the well-known 'Cocktail Party Effect' discovered by the British psychologist Edward Cherry in 1953. He realised that in a crowded room in which lots of different conversations are being conducted simultaneously, you still notice if someone mentions your name. Your brain somehow screens out all the cacophony of sounds and zeroes in on that one person who is talking about you. To figure out how we do this, Cherry designed special headphones so that he could play two different messages to each of his volunteer's ears at the same time. The volunteer could hear both messages but was instructed to follow only one of them. It's pretty easy to dampen down the background noise and listen to only one voice. Lots of experiments show that volunteers aren't aware of what's going on in the ear they are not paying any attention to, unless their own name is spoken – then they notice. As Schneirla would have been pleased to know, words relating to danger and pleasure also get noticed.

The intriguing thing is that we are not at all aware of these biases. As we go about our normal day, our brain continues to analyse and probe what's going on around us like a radar spiralling in circles, ensuring that we don't miss out on the things that are of most interest to us. Think of the chocolate lover trying to stick to a diet: all she seems to notice are billboards and posters with chocolate and candy. When you're on a diet, the world seems to gang up against you, as people enjoy cakes in every café on every street corner. They're not, of course, and this illustrates the real power of our biases. It just seems that way.

When cognitive biases are turned towards emotional information, this has a powerful influence on our outlook. The optimist tunes in to the bright side, while the pessimist looks towards the dark. It's difficult to measure these biases, as they happen with lightning speed, and, to make matters worse, our brains zone in on the good or bad news well below our conscious radar. However, cognitive psychologists have invented some ingenious techniques that provide us with accurate and subtle measures of what our brain is noticing when we are looking the other way. Cherry's dichotic listening task allowed him to see how well people could select one ear over the other, and this principle has now been extended to what we see as well.

A technique called the *attentional probe task* is most commonly used to reveal such biases in vision. We can do this by showing people pairs of pleasant, nasty, or neutral photographs on a computer screen and then see which grabs their attention. These pairs of pictures – perhaps a snarling dog with an image of a playful puppy – are presented rapidly, usually for less than half a second, and volunteers are asked to press a button if they see a small triangle (the probe) on the computer screen when the pictures disappear. Two images flash up for half a second – one on the right and one on the left; they disappear, a triangle appears on the left or the right, and then you have to respond as fast as you can. The computer records the time it takes you to press the button, giving us a reaction time. It turns out that people are much faster detecting the triangle when it follows a picture that appeals to them or captures their attention,

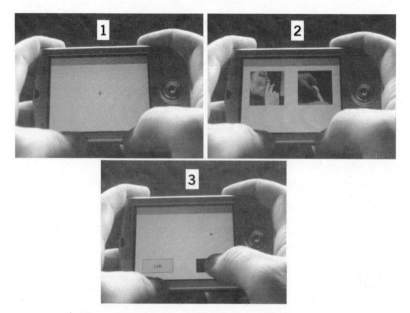

FIGURE 1.1 Diagram of a sequence of events in an attentional probe task. (1) The fixation cross is presented for five hundred milliseconds on a PDA. (2) The two pictures – one smoking, one neutral – are displayed. (3) The probe to which the participant must respond is presented. *Source:* en.wikipedia.org/wiki/File:Visual_Probe _Task_on_a_PDA.jpg.

providing a crafty way to measure their cognitive bias. Imagine that a picture of a luscious apple pie is presented on the computer screen alongside a picture of a rather less appealing sandwich. The two images disappear, and then a small triangle appears where the picture of the desirable apple pie had been. If your brain has already zoned in to that location – which seems likely – then you will be quicker to press the appropriate button than if the probe had appeared where the less appealing sandwich had been.

This is just one of the many sophisticated ways that allow us to sneak up on the brain as it reveals the complexities of its twists and turns. One fascinating fact discovered more than twenty years ago is that anxious and pessimistic people are drawn towards negative things while avoiding positive scenes. Think of a news report or your local newspaper in which lots of good and bad news is presented on a daily basis. The more anxious among us will filter out the positive – they won't even notice that it is there – and zoom in like a cruise missile on the negative stories.

In my own research, I was keen to find out how and why negative information exerted such a pull on the minds of the anxious. One thing I noticed early on was that my control volunteers, those who were chosen because they were less anxious and generally more optimistic, were not unbiased. I was expecting them to be fairly balanced, paying more or less equal attention to the positive and the negative. Not so. This was a surprise at the time, since the theory predicted that anxious people were anxious precisely *because* they filtered out the positive and tuned in to bad news, while those who were not prone to anxiety gave equal weight to both the good and the bad.

Study after study told us, however, that those who were not anxious showed a strong bias to *avoid* negative information. When a nasty picture or word was flashed up, they shifted their attention away instantly. Just as the anxious were drawn to bad news, the low anxious avoided it. All of our volunteers were completely unaware of these biases. Most said that they noticed that lots of pictures were being presented but were concentrating so much on reacting to the probes that they didn't pick up on any relationship between the nature of the pictures and the location of the probe. They were incredulous when I showed them that the speed with which they detected the probes was influenced reliably and consistently by whether the preceding pictures were positive or negative.

When I gave this same test to Michael J. Fox, he said the same thing. 'I knew there were pictures flashing on and off, but I was concentrating on pressing the buttons and not making any mistakes.' It came as no surprise to find that his attention was drawn towards the positive – his speed to detect the probe following positive pictures averaged about 490 milliseconds (less than half a second), while he took about 560 milliseconds to notice the probes following negative images. Like most optimists, his attention was drawn subconsciously towards the pleasant pictures. A difference of 70 milliseconds (less than one-hundredth of a second) may seem immaterial in everyday life, but in brain time this is an age.

Our affective mind not only influences what we notice but also determines what we remember. To test this out, ask a bubbly, happy friend to tell you five things that happened to him before the age of twelve. It can be anything: a party he went to, a favourite pet, parents divorcing, going to school, anything. Now do the same with a more downbeat friend. Don't prompt; just ask for anything that comes to mind. My bet is that the optimist will come up with mainly happy, upbeat memories, and the pessimist will recall sadder, darker events.

The effect of different mood states on what we remember was studied first by the Stanford University psychologist Gordon Bower in the 1980s. In his experiments, Bower used hypnosis to put people into either happy moods or sad moods and then asked them to re-member some event that had occurred during the last year. The happy folk reported lots of positive memories, and the sad people were more likely to remember more negative and sad things.

There is an obvious problem in studying such autobiographical memories, however. While they are the most interesting kinds of memories, we don't have any real knowledge of what has actually happened to someone. When a depressed patient says to a psychol-ogist that things are always going wrong and that every time she tries to start a conversation, people rush off saying they are busy, we don't know if this is true or not. Uncertainty about the veracity of autobiographical memories makes controlled laboratory studies especially important.

For this reason, Bower again used hypnosis to shift his volunteers into a happy or a sad mood and presented them with a stock list of words, some of which had a positive feel to them (e.g., party, happy, joyous), while some related to more negative things (e.g., cancer, death, failure). The results couldn't have been clearer: the group in the happy mood recalled more positive words; the sad people re-membered more of the negative words.

Bower's experiments tell us that rather than presenting us with an honest and accurate account of the past, our memories provide us with a highly selective version of events that fit neatly with our particular outlook and interests. It's hard to overestimate the impor-tance of this point. Our memories are filtered through our own per-spective, ensuring that we cannot rely on them to give us an accurate picture of the past.

Selective remembering offers an important clue as to why some people are happy and optimistic while others tend towards depres-sion and sadness. Negative and dark memories encourage the for-mation of a pessimistic outlook on life, just as positive and happy memories generate an optimistic outlook. But it's important to re-member that the link between our outlook and our memory is a two-way street. A good mood can lead to happy memories, but happy memories can also lead to a good mood.

To see this for yourself, try to remember a time when you were extremely happy – perhaps when you passed an important exam, got married, got your first job, went out on a first date with someone you had been interested in for ages. Imagine all the details as vividly as you can, including how you felt at the time. After a few minutes, you will find your mood lifting as you re-experience the same happy feel-ings that you are recalling. Many psychology experiments have shown the same thing; our memories affect our current moods just as our current mood influences what comes into our minds. Like the proverbial chicken and egg, this circular relationship between what we remember and the mood we're in makes it tricky to work out whether it's the mood or the memory that comes first.

There are two main reasons why subconscious biases in our at-tention and our memory are important. First, these slants of mind lie at the heart of differences in how we experience life. Second, what we notice and remember plays a disproportionate role in shaping what we believe. It's not that the optimist sees every single thing as rosy, just as the pessimist does not see everything as bleak. Instead, it's the emphasis of one over the other that, over time, makes a difference.

What psychologists call the *confirmation bias* is a great example of how low-level biases – the stuff of our affective mindset – can shape our beliefs. If you are convinced that women are worse drivers than men, then you will confirm this belief by noticing lots of examples of bad driving by women. What you miss are the examples of poor male driving or good female driving. Things that don't fit with your core belief don't get noticed. Our belief system determines what we notice about the world around us, but at the same time our beliefs are determined to a large extent by what we notice in the first place.

Mark Snyder, a psychologist at the University of Minnesota, has run many studies confirming that beliefs really can turn out to be self-fulfilling prophecies. If you meet someone for the first time and have been told that he is nervous, then aspects of his behaviour that seem apprehensive will become salient. To prove this, Snyder linked up pairs of volunteers and asked some of them to figure out whether their partner was extroverted and others whether their partner was an introvert.

If your assignment was to find out whether someone was an extrovert, and you were allowed only a couple of key questions, what would you ask? If you are anything like the volunteers in Snyder's study, you would ask things like, 'What would you do to liven up a party?' or 'Do you enjoy meeting lots of new people?' When you think about it, these questions are not very informative because they can only *confirm* the question. On examining the videotapes of interactions between his volunteers, it was obvious to Snyder that people always veered towards these kinds of questions. Those in the 'introverted' group would ask things like 'Are there times that you wish you were more outgoing?' As Snyder says, 'We tend to seek out only confirming evidence,' when what we really need is *discon-firming* evidence.

Biases and quirks of the mind play an important role in consolidating our beliefs, but they are also said to influence how happy and how healthy we are. Can a belief really lead to physical changes in our body, even to the point of illness? The answer from studies in psychology and neuroscience is a resounding yes. There are also persuasive examples from medical practice showing that what we think and believe can make us sick. Dr Clifton Meador graduated from medical school in 1955 and spent many years practicing medicine in Alabama and elsewhere. In his early years, he accepted without question the dominant 'biomedical' model, which stated that physical problems caused physical symptoms and that treating the core physical problem would cure the symptoms.

However, Meador's experiences with many patients gradually convinced him that medicine had to take a wider view. Time and time again he came across cases where people became sick because they *believed* they were ill, even though nothing was actually wrong. He recounts the story of one patient who was diagnosed with terminal liver cancer and given just months to live. The patient became weak and frail and died within the expected time frame, yet a postmortem revealed that the doctors had got it wrong: the patient did not have cancer. He died because he 'believed he was dying of cancer.' His belief was so powerful that it induced death.

Meador recounts the even more dramatic story of Vance Vanders, who was a patient of Meador's medical mentor, Dr Drayton Doherty. In the spring of 1938, Doherty admitted a sixty-year-old black man to what was then a completely segregated black hospital on the outskirts of Selma, Alabama. Vance Vanders had been ill for several weeks, was not eating, and had lost a lot of weight. Cancer was suspected, but test after test failed to reveal what the problem was. Eventually, as he went into decline and death seemed inevitable, Vance's wife told Doherty that several weeks earlier Vance had been summoned to the cemetery at midnight by a local witch doctor. Voodoo and 'black magic' were common among the black community in Alabama at the time. She was not sure why, but an argument had broken out, and the witch doctor had waved some foul-smelling liquid under Vance's nose, saying that he had 'voodooed' him and that he would die very shortly. 'You are doomed to die,' the witch doctor boomed. 'Not even the doctors can save you.' Vance staggered home in shock and had not eaten since.

Upon hearing this, Doherty thought long and hard about what to do. The next evening he called all of Vance's family to his bedside. Ten or more people surrounded the dying man. He then announced in the most authoritative voice that he could summon that he had lured the witch doctor back to the cemetery under false pretences and demanded that he lift the curse. At first the witch doctor just laughed at him, he said, but then Doherty recounted how he had 'grabbed the witch doctor by the throat' and forced him to tell what he had done. 'It turns out,' he said to Vance, 'that the witch doctor had rubbed lizard eggs into your skin and that some had managed to crawl down into your stomach where they hatched out. All have now died except for one large lizard that is now eating up all your food and the lining of your body.'

He then summoned his nurse, who made her way through the shocked crowd with a large phial of liquid.

'We must get rid of the lizard,' he said dramatically as he injected what was in fact a strong emetic into Vance's arm. Within a few minutes, Vance was vomiting profusely, and at just the right moment – unnoticed by all in the room – Doherty produced a large green lizard that he had hidden in his bag.

'Look, Vance, look what has come out of you! You are now cured. The voodoo curse is lifted!'

Apparently, Vance's eyes rolled, and he leapt to the back of the bed. Amid the moaning and groaning of his relatives, he fell into a deep sleep. More than twelve hours later, Vance woke up ravenous and wolfed down a large meal of bread, milk, and meat. He went on to live for another ten years, eventually dying from normal old age.

'It is very clear,' writes Meador, 'that Vance believed at the deepest level that he was cursed and doomed to die.' Mere words had the power to induce death, and indeed mere words had been able to bring him back from the brink.

The well-known *placebo effect*, from the Latin 'I will please,' is the finding that people can feel better and gain benefits from a drug or medical treatment if they believe that it will do them good, even if that 'drug' is just a sugar pill. The placebo's lesser-known, and darker, twin is the *nocebo* effect, from the Latin 'I will harm.' This is what almost killed Vance Vanders. Put simply, people get worse because they believe they'll get worse. Arthur Barsky, a professor of psychiatry at Harvard Medical School, has reviewed the scientific and medical literature and concluded that nocebo effects are usually vague symptoms directly caused by the suggestion or belief that something is harmful.

One of the first laboratory studies of the nocebo effect was conducted at the University of California in 1981. Volunteers had several electrodes strapped onto their heads and were told that the study was about the effects of a mild electric current on brain function. They were warned that the electric current might cause severe headaches but that there should be no other adverse effects. More than two-thirds of the thirty-four volunteers did report severe headaches. The researchers later revealed that not a single volt of electricity had been produced. Expectation alone had made healthy people ill.

Jon-Kar Zubieta and his colleagues at the Molecular and Behavioural Neuroscience Unit at the University of Michigan in Ann Arbor have provided crystal-clear evidence that our beliefs can indeed have a direct effect on our brains. They persuaded twenty healthy volunteers to take part in two twenty-minute pain challenges. On one occasion, people were told that they had been given a drug that had strong analgesic effects. A week later, they were told that the drug was a sugar pill and would not help the pain. In both cases, no drug was given, but the effects in the brain were striking. Some volunteers showed a strong placebo response in that they said that their pain had decreased, and there was a surge of dopamine and opiates – happy chemicals – in their brain. In marked contrast, a strong nocebo effect, in which people reported an increase in pain, was linked with a reduction in the amount of dopamine and opioids being released. This is startling evidence that what we expect and believe produces neurochemical changes at the very heart of our pleasure-seeking brain.

It's one thing to induce headaches by belief alone, but can our beliefs influence our physical health for better or for worse? Can it really be the case that our minds can influence life and death? Like Vance Vanders, can we really be 'scared to death'? Evidence from the large-scale Framingham Heart Study suggests that the answer is yes. This study began in 1948 and followed the fortunes of 2,873 women and 2,336 men. Taking care to account for all known risk factors for heart disease – obesity, high cholesterol levels, high blood pressure, and so on – a report by Rebecca Voelker in the *Journal of the American Medical Association* in 1996 reported that women who *believed* that they were more prone to heart disease were four times more likely to die than women who did not believe.

CHAPTER 2

Sunny-Side Up

Investigating Optimism

I still have vivid memories of David, a boy I knew in school. In a sea of Irish faces, he stood out with his shock of blond hair. He was also the first person I ever met whose pleasure brain seemed to be stuck on overdrive. He would light up a room as soon as he walked in, exuding an infectious sense of fun and happiness. Everyone loved David. He was bright, attractive, and one of life's risk takers; by the age of fifteen, he had fallen off cliffs, crashed his father's car, experimented with drugs and sex, and otherwise pushed himself to the far edges of excitement. Fear for David was fun. What he seemed to crave more than anything was the rush of adrenaline, which drove him to seek out danger. At sixteen, he tried to leap from the roof of one city building to another but missed his target and fell to his death. As our parents and teachers wondered about suicide, we teenagers knew that depression was a million miles from David's experience. What killed him was having too much fun.

David's experience gives us a glimpse into the life of the sunny brain, with all its ups and downs. My theory is that the spark at the source of the sunny brain is the pleasure centre deep in the ancient regions of our neural tissue. All of us crave pleasure, but for some of us, like David, it verges on an addiction. Think of the satiated pleasure you feel after an excellent meal or the triumphant pleasure after a win by your favourite team. Now imagine sitting down after a long day and unwrapping that bar of chocolate that you have been thinking about. As you bite into the smooth and silky surface, the taste and aroma fills your senses as only a rich, dark chocolate can. Feelings of pleasure like this are caused by our pleasure-seeking brain, which allows us to react to the good things in life. This hedonic cone, or pleasure centre, is the engine room that propels our wider sunny brain. The sunny brain, in turn, drives an optimistic mindset. To understand the roots of optimism, then, we need to understand in more detail how the pleasure brain works.

The function of our pleasure system is to entice us into doing things that are biologically good for us. This is why delicious food, enjoyed in the company of family and friends, is one of the great pleasures of life. In ancient times, just as now, a supportive network and a ready supply of food were vital to our well-being and survival. Our pleasure brain tunes in to all those things that enhance our survival prospects. Thus, the sensory appreciation of tastes, odours, sights, sounds and touches are at the very heart of feeling good. The sensual caress of a lover, the smell of coffee, the freshness of a sea breeze can all lift our spirits in a chain of events that eventually leads to a rosier view of life. Even seeking out a warm log fire on an icy day is biologically meaningful and gets the attention of the pleasure brain, sparking neurological reactions that make us seek them out over and over. For many, sensory pleasures are what make life worth living. If we cannot stop and smell the roses (or the coffee or the chocolate), it's difficult to feel alive, happy, and positive.

Ironically, it is scientific research on depression that is now providing new evidence for this view. Andy was a young man who took part in one of my studies on optimism and pessimism. For several years, Andy suffered severe depression. Endless varieties of drug and talk therapies had little impact on his persistent black moods. Andy's main complaint, however, was not the dark moods and pervasive pessimism; his 'inability to feel joy' is what really bothered him. 'I used to enjoy life,' he said. 'Simple, everyday pleasures would give me a real boost.' However, as his depression crept back, it was usually the lack of pleasure that he first noticed. 'The edge is taken off things. I lose interest in everything. Life just seems dull.'

Andy's gradual loss of interest in meeting friends, having sex, and even the simple pleasure of going to a movie or out for dinner has been difficult for successive girlfriends to deal with. Technically called *anhedonia*, this inability to experience pleasure forms a crucial part of depression and is a close companion of pessimism. Neuroscience research tells us that the pleasure brain is underactive in depression. It's hard to imagine an optimist, deeply engaged with life, unable to experience and enjoy pleasure. Optimists usually have great enthusiasm and energy, and they are eager to relish all that life has to offer. Savouring pleasure, whether it's sensory experiences like the bliss of a cold beer on a hot day or the more abstract joy of being captivated by a wonderful painting, is central to optimism and to feeling good.

The Pleasure Centre

Psychologists and neuroscientists are now beginning to learn more about the parts of the brain that ensure that some experiences or objects will be highlighted so that they seem rosier, or shinier. By painting such a 'pleasure gloss,' or what is called a *hedonic tone*, on some experiences, the brain makes sure that some things are viewed through rose-tinted glasses. Nature has devised this cunning way to make sure we seek out those things that are good for us. Pleasure, in other words, is the currency that keeps us coming back for more.

It's important to appreciate, however, that pleasure is something more than a sensory experience. As the Dutch psychologist Nico Frijda puts it, pleasure is the 'niceness gloss' that's painted onto our sensations, and it's this gloss that nudges us towards useful objectives like seeking out food, water, and sex. Without these motivations we probably wouldn't survive for long, and so pleasure forms one of the great driving forces – seek out pleasures – alongside the other great motivator of avoiding danger or pain. The ancient Greek philosopher Epicurus, who lived from 341 to 270 BCE, defined pleasure as the 'absence of suffering.' The eighteenth-century English philosopher Jeremy Bentham also claimed that pleasure and pain are the two 'masters of mankind,' believing that humans were designed by nature to seek out pleasure and to avoid pain. Modern science continues to view pleasure and pain as important motivating forces, and much effort has been spent on figuring out ways to measure pleasure and to find its source in our brain.

These research efforts tell us that the pleasure-seeking brain's core is a tiny structure called the *nucleus accumbens* (NAcc). This ancient structure sits underneath the cortex, right at the front of the brain. As with many fundamental discoveries in science, the uncovering of the brain's 'pleasure centre' came about by accident.

Back in the 1950s, two young Canadian psychologists named James Olds and Peter Milner were trying to figure out how the brain controls the sleep-wake cycle. After working on this problem for some time, they realised that implanting electrodes deep into the brains of rats might help find the answer. When activated, electrodes deliver a tiny pulse of electricity directly into a specific part of the brain. The resulting effect on the animal's behaviour could then be observed. The procedure is painless, since the brain does not contain any pain receptors, and the electrodes are implanted surgically under a general anaesthetic. When the animal wakes up after the operation, it can move around freely, unaware of the electrode inside its head.

Olds and Milner had a good idea of which brain area might be involved in arousal, and they hoped that by stimulating this region they would get the final proof. Their plan was to place the electrodes in a part of the brain called the *midbrain reticular formation*, located along the midline of the brain. Previous studies had indicated that this region was probably the one that controlled the sleep-wake cycle. Luckily for the science of pleasure, however, their aim was not very good, and they inserted the electrodes a short distance away from the intended target. Thus, when they stimulated the electrodes, the rat's level of arousal did not change at all. What did happen, though, was that the rats seemed to be drawn to the location they were in when they were stimulated. Running around the cage, the rat would stop in its tracks and return to the precise spot where it had been when the electrode was activated. The rats gave every sign that they craved more of the stimulation.

Realising they were on to something, Olds and Milner then conducted the now famous experiment where the rats were given free rein to press a lever that activated the electrode as often as they liked. The results were astounding. The rats couldn't get enough of the tiny jolt of electricity and would press the lever over and over again, sometimes up to 2,000 times in an hour. The rats even gave up opportunities to eat, drink, or have sex for another hit.

Olds and Milner eventually discovered that instead of inserting the electrodes into the midbrain reticular formation, as they had intended, they had in fact implanted them in the NAcc. This tiny region was soon heralded as the 'reward centre' or the brain's 'pleasure zone.' It wasn't long before electrodes were implanted in humans to see whether activating this newly discovered pleasure zone might help people struggling with depression or pain. If people like Andy were unable to experience pleasure, then perhaps zapping their pleasure centre over and over would kick-start the system, eventually lifting the dark clouds of depression.

In what was to become one of the most controversial research programs ever conducted in psychiatry, Dr Robert Heath at the Tulane University Medical School in New Orleans began implanting electrodes deep in the brains of patients with a variety of mental health problems. His view was that a dysfunction in the pleasure response was the root cause of many mental illnesses, such as depression and schizophrenia. If only the pleasure centre could be switched back on, Heath thought, we might be able to cure a variety of mental problems.

One of his patients, labeled B-19, was a typical example. Tortured by depression for several years, the twenty-four-year-old confided that he was troubled daily by thoughts of suicide. Inspired by the work of Olds and Milner, Heath implanted a scattering of small electrodes deep into B-19's brain. When the patient recovered from surgery, the research team stimulated each electrode in turn and asked B-19 what he felt. Most electrodes had little effect, but when the electrode in the NAcc was stimulated, B-19 reported an immediate hit. 'It was pleasurable and warm,' he said, making him want to masturbate and have sex. Just like Olds and Milner's rats, this young man stimulated this particular electrode over 1,500 times in one three-hour session and complained vigorously when it was taken away.

News soon spread about the new techniques, and patients in other hospitals began to report similar feelings. The Spanish neuroscientist Jose Delgado, who was working at Yale University, described several experiments on the implantation of electrodes into a variety of species, including humans. Perhaps most famous for stopping a charging bull in its tracks by stimulating an implanted electrode, Delgado also found that stimulating the NAcc in humans could lift depression, at least temporarily. This transience, however, turned out to be a problem. Stimulating electrodes in the NAcc undoubtedly had intense effects, but the effects never lasted very long, which is why implanting electrodes in the NAcc never became a viable cure for depression.

The fleeting nature of pleasure makes a lot of sense. The urge to eat, drink, and reproduce are all critical for the survival of our species, but once we have eaten, quenched our thirst, or had sex, there's little need for the pleasure brain to linger. Hence, the pursuit of happiness *only* by means of pleasure is generally a futile exercise. There's little doubt, however, that stimulating the NAcc does lead people to want more. Before we can see how this works, we need to digress a little to see how communication takes place within the brain.

A Little Anatomy

There are a number of ways to look at the brain. It is made up of two halves, which are mirror images of each other. We can also divide the brain into three parts from bottom to top. At the bottom, where the brain and spinal column connect, sit a number of structures that are essential for life. These are the parts of the brain that ensure that we keep breathing, keep blood pressure and body temperature well balanced and generally sustain life. Up a step is the middle part of the brain, which contains many of the core areas for emotions and memory, among other things. These are often called *subcortical* (below the cortex) and are much older in evolutionary terms than the upper part of our brain, the cortex. Indeed, many of the brain parts we find in this midbrain region – often with exotic sounding names like amygdala, nucleus accumbens, hippocampus – are similar to those we find in the brains of other creatures with whom we share this planet. Our cortex, however, is different. It has grown so big that it has been forced to fold over and over to fit inside the skull; hence, the familiar convoluted appearance of our brain. The cortex encases the middle brain regions and is responsible for many of the attributes we consider uniquely human, like language, reasoning, and imagination.

The various regions of the brain need to be able to communicate with one another so that actions can be coordinated. This is achieved by means of dense networks of connections that allow all areas of the brain, from bottom to top, to 'talk' to each other. To see how such brain networks develop, let's look at how internal communication takes place. Among the several types of cells found in the brain, the most important for sending and receiving messages are the nerve cells, also known as neurons. Each neuron is made up of three parts. The dendrites are treelike branches whose main function is to receive input from other neurons. The soma, or cell body, contains all the important things that the cell needs to stay alive, including its DNA. The third part is the axon, which is like a living electrical cable that carries electrical impulses at lightning speeds towards the dendrites of other neurons. Most axons in the brain are extremely short, while others, like those that run down our legs, can reach up to six feet in length.

While estimates vary, most neuroscientists agree that there are more than 100 billion neurons in the human brain, and that each one can contact up to 10,000 other neurons. This leads to a bewildering complexity of communication. In the early days of neuroscience, the belief was that neurons 'talked' to each other by means of electrical impulses that sparked from one neuron to the next. This view changed dramatically when a crucial experiment was conducted in 1921 by Otto Loewi (1873–1961), a professor of pharmacology at the University of Graz in Austria. Around Easter that year, he wrote in his diary that he had had several sleepless nights. He had become absorbed with the idea that electrical communication might not be the only way that messages were transmitted. Perhaps, he thought, chemicals might also be involved. During one fretful night, he awoke frequently and wrote down several ideas that came to him in a dream. The next morning he could not remember anything of the dream and was unable to read his hastily scribbled notes. Describing the next day as 'desperate,' he knew that he had dreamed something important. On waking from the same dream again the following night, he went straight to the laboratory.

Let's see how he worked this out. Loewi knew that the vagus nerve controls the speed at which a heart beats and that stimulating this nerve slows down the heart. But was this because an electrical impulse jumped from the nerve to the heart? Or was there a chemical that seeped from the nerve to the heart? In an ingenious experiment, he removed the hearts of two frogs with the vagus nerve still attached and, with the hearts still beating, placed the first heart in a solution. He then stimulated the vagus nerve of this heart and, as expected, the heart slowed down. He quickly placed the second heart in the same solution and to his joy saw that the beating of the second heart also began to slow down. In this eureka moment, Loewi had discovered that chemicals *must* be involved in the transmission of information from one neuron to the next. How else could the second heart have slowed down? We now call Loewi's discovery *neurotransmission*, and he shared the 1936 Nobel Prize with his long-term friend and collaborator, the British scientist Sir Henry Dale, for this work.

While Loewi discovered the chemical basis of neurotransmission in 1921, it was another twelve years before the precise chemical, acetylcholine (Ach), was identified. Since then, more than fifty other neurotransmitters have been discovered. We now know that at the end of each axon there are tiny sacks called *synaptic vesicles* that contain a specific neurotransmitter, such as dopamine. When an electrical impulse arrives down the axon, this causes the synaptic vesicles to move to the edge of the neuron and spill their contents out into the tiny gap between neurons. These chemicals then drift across the synaptic cleft and are detected by receptors on the walls of the dendrites of the next cell.

Just like a lock and key, if the neurotransmitter has the right shape, it will fit the receptor on the next neuron. This will cause that neuron to send an electrical impulse down its own axon, which will in turn release its own neurotransmitter and continue the process. If the neurotransmitter does not have the right shape, then it will not stimulate the next neuron.

FIGURE 2.1 Diagram of a synapse: An illustration of neurotransmission. An electrical impulse stimulates the neuron to spill small amounts of neurotransmitter into the small space between neurons (synaptic cleft). The neurotransmitters then drift in the fluid, and if appropriate receptors are positioned on the dendrites of another neuron, the neurotransmitter will cause this cell to fire and so the chain of messages continues. *Source:* www.wpclipart.com/science/experiments/chemical_synapse.png.html.

The chemical messengers most active in our sunny brain are dopamine and the opioids – the endogenous brain variety of opiates. The NAcc is filled with cells that contain either dopamine or opioids, and it is the action of these neurotransmitters that facilitates our enjoyment and desire for a wide range of experiences. I believe that these chemicals, the oil in the engine room of our wider sunny brain, are one of the principle sources of optimism.

When a rat is given something good to eat, like sugary water, the level of dopamine in its NAcc increases instantly, as it does when it engages in sex. The same thing happens to humans. When an electrode implanted in the NAcc is activated, as with B-19, the NAcc becomes flooded with dopamine. Fun activities also kick-start our dopamine systems.

Matthias Koepp, a neuroscientist at the Institute of Neurology in London, conducted an intriguing study using student volunteers who played a battle-tank video game when lying inside a brain scanner. Whenever they destroyed an enemy tank or collected a flag, the students won money. Whenever this happened, an immediate burst of dopamine could be seen in the volunteers' NAcc.

It has been shown, however, that the story of pleasure is much more complex than dopamine alone. Kent Berridge, a psychologist at the University of Michigan, made the crucial discovery that the opi-oid chemicals are also critical for the functioning of the pleasure brain. Stimulating different areas of the NAcc in a large number of rats, he found that when neurons containing opioids were activated, sweet things tasted even sweeter. In other studies, rats were found to work very hard, happily learning to jump through all sorts of hoops, just for the reward of a shot of angel dust (PCP) – another activator of the opioid receptors – directly into their NAcc.

Berridge then tested people who used cocaine recreationally. Cocaine increases the amount of dopamine released in the brain; this fact had long been thought to be the reason why cocaine makes you feel good. However, by artificially suppressing the typical surge of dopamine when taking cocaine, Berridge made a remarkable discovery: the pleasure from the cocaine did not decrease in the slightest. What did change was people's *desire* for the drug; it still felt great, but the desire to take more was reduced. These findings led Berridge to the crucial insight that dopamine is involved in wanting something but not necessarily for liking it. Wanting and liking are different aspects of pleasure, with different neurotransmitter systems involved. It's the opioids that paint the pleasure gloss on our experiences, while dopamine keeps us coming back for more.

When stimulated by pleasure – whether it's through having sex, taking drugs, eating chocolate, playing games, or activating an implanted electrode – the NAcc becomes flooded with dopamine and opioids. This shows us that cells communicate with one another by means of chemicals, and it is the sweeps and waves of these neurotransmitters on which brain circuits are dependent. If the same neurons talk to each other over and over again, pathways develop that form links among different brain areas. Just as a stream carves a channel through the sand, the flow of synapses among groups of neurons can establish entrenched pathways. Once laid down, these pathways ensure rapid communication between areas of the brain that may be very far apart. In this way wider circuits, like the sunny brain, begin to develop. Modifying the activity of neurotransmitters to even a small extent can therefore have profound effects on the responses of entire networks across the brain with a resulting impact on our personality and temperament.

Circuits that make up the sunny brain consist of neurons in the NAcc that form links with neurons in particular areas of the prefrontal cortex (PFC), which is the part of the cortex that sits right at the front of our head above our eyes. The whole architecture of this network begins when the NAcc begins to form links with nearby subcortical structures involved in emotion and pleasure. Gradually connections are made with more distant areas like the PFC. Among many duties of planning, reasoning, and problem solving, the PFC also plays the vital role of inhibiting more ancient parts of the brain, like the NAcc. Imagine visiting your local bakery and savouring the colourful array of cakes on display. Your NAcc will instantly sense reward and send out the signal to eat; the PFC, however, can assess the situation and send signals back that there's no need to panic, you are not starving. Like an accelerator and a break, the NAcc drives us towards pleasure, while the PFC inhibits our more primal impulses. Information is sent back and forth along these pathways in repeating loops, allowing these brain areas to respond as a unit.

The network of connections running upward from the NAcc to the PFC and downward from the PFC to the NAcc is a vital circuit that controls our response to positive and rewarding situations. The dynamics of the links between the ancient pleasure centres and the more recent control centres in the cortex are crucial, one pushing us to act, the other dampening down our impulses. In the right balance, these brain circuits nudge us towards happiness and optimism.

Is the Sunny Brain More Active in Optimists?

Andy's experience tells us that the absence of pleasure can often be more difficult to deal with than the sadness that goes with depres-

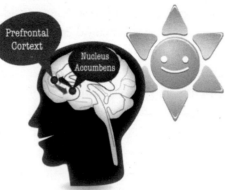

Sunny Brain

FIGURE 2.2 A schematic illustration of the sunny brain showing the links between the PFC and the NAcc.

sion. Neuroscientists are beginning to realise that this anhedonia – the inability to appreciate the simple pleasures of life – is the forgotten side of depression. There is, however, growing scientific support for the notion that the sunny-brain circuit does indeed differentiate between those who are depressed and unable to experience pleasure and those who are happy and optimistic.

Richard J. Davidson, a psychologist at the University of Wisconsin–Madison, tested this theory with twenty-seven people who were depressed and nineteen healthy and happy control volunteers. To simulate the ups and downs of everyday life, all the volunteers were shown a series of pictures that depicted positive as well as negative scenes while their brains were being scanned in an fMRI machine. Each picture was presented on a screen just above the person's head as he lay in the scanner during a session that lasted about forty minutes. In the early part of the session, the NAcc of the volunteers became active when the pleasant positive images were viewed. This is what we would expect. What was more surprising was that the depressed and happy groups were very similar. The NAcc of the depressed jumped into action just as much as the pleasure circuits of the control volunteers.

Something very different happened during the second half of the session. Now, when happy volunteers viewed positive images, their NAcc continued to stay active, but the pleasure brain of the depressed slid back to baseline. The depressed people were unable to sustain the firing of their pleasure brain after its initial activation. Pleasure is always short-lived, but it's far more fleeting in the depressed.

A closer look at the data from this study tells us that it is not just the pleasure centre but the entire sunny-brain circuit that's involved. Early on in the session, when the NAcc responded to positive images, so did the PFC. But during the second half of the session, when activity in the NAcc declined for the depressed group, so did activity in the PFC.

This study suggests that it's not so much that depressed people cannot feel pleasure, but that they just cannot sustain it. In fact, the depressed patients for whom activity in the NAcc declined most sharply also reported the most difficulty in experiencing pleasure and happiness. This is strong evidence that the functioning of the brain in depression makes it difficult to sustain positive feelings and that the sunny-brain circuit is vital to enhancing pleasure and happiness.

Is there evidence that the sunny-brain circuits are important for optimism? Studies that measure brain activity tell us that the sunny-brain circuitry is indeed involved, not only in feelings of happiness and pleasure but also in the desire to *approach* rewards. And approaching rewards is one of the important components of optimism. We can measure the electrical activity of the brain by strapping an array of electrodes on a person's scalp. The electrodes pick up the activity generated by the millions of synapses that occur at any moment in the brain. Every time a neuron fires, it generates a tiny electrical pulse that is detected by these highly sensitive electrodes. Using such electroencephalography (EEG) techniques, researchers have discovered that merely approaching positive things is associated with a higher degree of activity in the left half of the cortex in healthy people. Thus, if you are looking at a picture of a stunning sunset or a luscious box of chocolates, the neurons in the left half of your brain will fire more vigorously than those on the right. We don't fully understand why this is the case, but there's little doubt that a leftwards asymmetry in cortical activity is associated with approaching pleasurable things.

The activity of the brain when it's resting tells a similar story. When people are sitting quietly, there is a baseline difference between optimists and pessimists. Pessimists show substantially less activity in the left half of their brains, while optimists show much more activity in the left half relative to the right half of their brains. This reduction in the normal leftwards asymmetry is a neural marker of the lack of pleasure that we see in depression.

The same cerebral asymmetries are seen in monkeys, with happy healthy monkeys showing much more activity in their left cortex compared to fearful and apprehensive monkeys, which show relatively more activity in the right side of their brain. Whether these asymmetries originate in subcortical or cortical areas is not fully understood as yet, but it is clear that these asymmetries are linked with the propensity to approach or avoid rewards, and people with a marked leftwards asymmetry are happier and more optimistic than those with a more rightward asymmetry.

Fundamental brain differences like this show us that the roots of optimism can be traced to the functioning of the brain circuits that make up our sunny brain. The anatomical links and connections between the NAcc and the cortex also tell us that greater happiness and an optimistic mindset are associated with ancient pleasure circuits in the brain. It was no surprise that Ruut Veenhoven, a sociologist at Erasmus University in Rotterdam, found in an extensive review of the literature that those who enjoyed life and regularly experienced simple everyday pleasures were consistently happier than those who took a more ascetic stance on life.

To verify that optimists really are keener to seek out pleasure, I set up a study at the University of Essex. The idea was to measure optimism as well as a trait known as *sensation seeking*, which is the degree to which a person pursues sensory pleasure and excitement. High-sensation seekers crave vigorous, intense experiences. They will take risks just for the intensity of the moment. Low-sensation seekers prefer quieter, slower, and inherently less risky experiences, perhaps a dinner party with excellent conversation, over a hell-raising party with loud music.

Like other personality traits, sensation seeking lies on a spectrum, with most people being somewhere in the middle. About 10 per cent of people are at the highest end of the scale, and 20 per cent fall into the low-sensation-seeking part. Men score a bit higher than women, and those under twenty years of age score higher than those over thirty.

To find out where you stand on this spectrum of sensation seeking, you can fill out the questionnaire below and then turn to the notes at the back to work out your score. Check the box that most accurately describes you for each of the following questions.

I had two hundred students fill out the Brief Sensation Seeking Scale shown on the next page as well as the LOT-R that we saw in Chapter 1. I wasn't surprised to find that those who reported a more upbeat outlook were also more inclined to seek out and experience pleasure. I was more intrigued to see whether the patterns of brain activity would relate to these self-reports of optimism and sensation seeking.

I selected two groups of people who reported either very high or very low scores on optimism/sensation seeking. When I examined the patterns of brain activity of these two groups using EEG, the brains of the optimists/high-sensation seekers showed the telltale leftwards asymmetry. Cortical activity in the pessimists was primarily in the right half of the brain.

Other research demonstrates that the brains of high-sensation seekers contain higher levels of circulating dopamine relative to low-sensation seekers. In other words, high-sensation seekers, who are more likely to be optimists, have a highly active pleasure brain. In

The Brief Sensation Seeking Scale

	Disagree a lot	Disagree	Neither disagree nor agree	Agree	Agree a lot
1. I would like to explore strange places.	☐	☐	☐	☐	☐
2. I get restless when I spend too much time at home.	☐	☐	☐	☐	☐
3. I like to do frightening things.	☐	☐	☐	☐	☐
4. I like wild parties.	☐	☐	☐	☐	☐
5. I would like to take off on a trip with no preplanned routes or timetables.	☐	☐	☐	☐	☐
6. I prefer friends who are excitingly unpredictable.	☐	☐	☐	☐	☐
7. I would like to try bungee jumping.	☐	☐	☐	☐	☐
8. I would love to have new and exciting experiences, even if they are illegal.	☐	☐	☐	☐	☐

one study, a team of psychologists at the University of Kentucky led by Jane Joseph showed high- and low-sensation seekers a series of photographs while their brains were being scanned. When highly stimulating pictures were shown, the pleasure brains of the high-sensation seekers went into overdrive with almost no activity in the PFC. For the low-sensation seekers, the most active part of the brain was the PFC, the area that inhibits and controls emotions. This pattern of neural activity means that the high-sensation seekers not only derive a bigger hit from excitement but are also less able to regulate that excitement.

This tendency to be highly responsive to rewards has many benefits, but it also has some downsides. Because the experience of pleasure is fleeting, the pursuit of pleasure can all too easily spiral out of control, sometimes tipping into dangerous risk taking and addictions. But if kept under control, experiencing pleasure is the spark that strengthens the circuits and networks that make up the sunny brain. And one of the great benefits of the sunny brain is the optimistic mindset it nurtures, which is not only about feeling joy and happiness, or even just about feeling good or thinking positively about the future, but also about sticking with tasks that are meaningful and beneficial. Our sunny-brain circuits help us to stay focused on the things that bring us rewards, and this keeps us engaged on important tasks.

This is a central insight, backed up by anatomical evidence, of how our sunny brain works. Optimism is about more than feeling good; it's about being engaged with a meaningful life, developing resilience, and feeling in control. This dovetails nicely with psychological research showing that the benefits of optimism come from the ability to accept the good along with the bad, and being prepared to work creatively and persistently to get what you want out of life. Optimistic realists, whom I consider to be the true optimists, don't believe that good things will come if they simply think happy thoughts. Instead, they believe at a very deep level that they have some control over their own destinies.

As the University of Kentucky psychologist Suzanne Segerstrom puts it, 'Optimism leads to increased well-being because it increases engagement with life's goals, not because of some miracle happy juice that optimists have and pessimists don't.' This deep-rooted mindset and propensity to act sets off a chain of events that leads to all of the benefits that can come with a genuine form of realistic optimism. In the face of difficulties, optimists don't give up. Instead, they redouble their efforts and try to figure out a way of dealing with their problems.

This type of optimism is different from the 'happy thoughts will solve all our problems' approach that fills many self-help books.

Thinking positively or negatively is important, but there's much more to dispositional optimism than wishful thinking. Journalist Barbara Ehrenreich in her book *Smile or Die* presents a devastating critique of what she sees as the cult of positive thinking that pervades contemporary society. She realised how mindless this cult had become when she was diagnosed with breast cancer and was immediately deluged with positive messages on how this would 'make her,' would allow her to 'find meaning in life,' would even help her to 'find the divine.' Faced with a devastating illness, she was horrified at the suggestion that she should be grateful and that all she needed to do to get better was think happy thoughts. With a clear-eyed view, Ehrenreich demolishes the notion that the power of positive thinking is the solution to all of our problems. She's absolutely right. The scientific research tells us that optimism often has more to do with what people *do* and how their brain responds, rather than what people *think* at a superficial level.

What's perhaps most surprising is just how optimistic we are. Even in the darkest of times, we are able to find hope and think positive thoughts about the future. When two airliners flew into the World Trade Center on September 11, 2001, I was at work in the University of Essex. People gathered around a TV that had been set up in a corridor to watch the surreal events unfold. Nobody spoke much. As we watched the towers crumbling to the ground, one after the other, there was a sense of the world, as we knew it, ending forever. 'America Under Attack' screamed the headlines. I wondered about one of my best childhood friends, who worked near the crash site in lower Manhattan. Many of our students and staff were American and were unable to contact their families and friends back home. As we all stared at the TV screen, the phone lines between England and America were silenced. The events were both personal as well as distant and surreal.

What emerged over the next few weeks was remarkable. The 'self-centred,' 'rude,' and 'impatient' stereotype of the hard-boiled New

Yorker seemed to crumble, as a gentler, more community-spirited New Yorker emerged. A CBS News/*New York Times* survey of 1,008 people one year after the attacks found that 82 per cent of people felt that the city had profoundly changed for the better. While there was still fear and unease, many respondents said that New Yorkers were less arrogant and nicer, with a stronger sense of community and unity. Many had made real changes in their own lives, such as spending more time with family and friends. Several likened it to the spirit of London during the Blitz.

Gary Tuchman, a CNN reporter, credited the September 11 attacks as a turning point in New York's character. There's now a 'more humane' and 'civil' atmosphere in the city, he claimed.

When I spoke to my childhood friend Anne, whom it turned out had been just a couple of blocks away at the time of the attack, she said this was absolutely true. 'People are talking to each other on street corners now,' she told me. 'For the first time since living in New York, I'm regularly chatting to complete strangers.'

Survey after survey confirm that, even in the darkest moments, people are usually positive about the future. Take the following findings from a survey conducted by the United Kingdom's National Lottery in 2009. Overall, 75 per cent of the British people questioned described themselves as optimists, while 58 per cent said that being around optimists was infectious and made them feel happy. The United States is no different. Following the election of Barack Obama as American's first African American president in 2008, a wave of optimism swept across the nation, according to newspaper reports. Even though the country was in one of the deepest economic crises it had ever experienced, national polls reported that 71 per cent of Americans believed that the economy would soon start to improve. In terms of their own personal financial situations, 63 per cent of Americans thought that things were about to get better, and an impressive 80 per cent said that they were strongly optimistic about the next four years.

It was not only in the United States that optimism was surging following the election of Barack Obama. A survey of 17,356 people in seventeen different countries found that citizens in fifteen out of these seventeen countries were convinced that the world would become a better place. On average, 67 per cent of people believed that the Obama presidency would lead to improved relations between the United States and the rest of the world.

What is the reason for such irrepressible optimism, especially in the face of so many global problems? The answer is both complex and intriguing. One part of the puzzle is that our brain is wired to ensure that we remain hopeful for the future. As we have seen, our sunny brain also plays an important role in keeping us engaged with ultimate rewards. Optimism is a crucial survival mechanism, honed by nature, to keep us going even when everything seems to be going wrong. Psychologists call this the *optimism bias*, and almost all of us have fallen prey to its appeal at some point.

An Optimism Bias

The optimism bias, or what's often called the *positivity illusion*, is the finding that people consistently overestimate the likelihood of good things happening to them. Answer the following: What do you think are your chances of earning a higher salary than average? Be honest – what do you really think? Over your lifetime, do you think you will earn more than the norm, about average, or a bit less? Chances are you will say 'more.' But if you think about it for a moment, it's impossible for everyone to earn more than average, yet almost everyone believes that they are the exception. Living longer than average or having a great marriage and great kids is no different. In his book *Irrationality*, the British psychologist Stuart Sutherland reported that 95 per cent of drivers surveyed claimed that their driving was better than the norm. We all expect to drive better and live longer, healthier, wealthier lives than average.

The same thing happens when we ask about bad events: How likely are you to get a serious illness? Most people consistently underestimate their chances.

Why are our brains biased in such an optimistic way? One reason is that it's simply what makes us get up in the morning. It's essentially a cognitive trick that helps us stop worrying about all the things that might go wrong and being overwhelmed by possible problems and pitfalls. The potential downsides are real, though, since an overly rosy view may lure us into ignoring potential dangers. A woman ignoring a lump in her breast because she believes that she will never get cancer is putting herself in real danger.

Because the optimism bias is so common, it must have been highly adaptive, and, from an evolutionary perspective at least, there must be some survival benefit to this mindset.

Science gives us several clues as to how the optimism bias might be of benefit. Take the tendency of men to overestimate how appealing they are to women to see how this adaptation works. Frank Saal, a psychologist from Kansas State University, paired up forty-nine males and forty-nine females who hadn't previously met and got them talking to each other individually for a few minutes. Following this interaction, other groups of men and women observed the conversations on videotape. Women almost always said that the woman in most of these interactions exuded an air of general friendliness, but the men usually thought the woman was displaying sexual interest. In two subsequent studies, where male managers interacted with their female employees, or male professors interacted with students, men consistently mis(interpreted) female friendliness as a sexual come-on.

Martie Haselton, a psychologist from the University of California, Los Angeles, claims that these effects are predictable. He and David Buss developed the error management theory, in which they argue that because men are limited in the number of people they can mate with from an evolutionary perspective, there's a high cost to missing out on an opportunity, while the pain of rejection is short-lived and not overly costly. Therefore, it pays for men to overestimate how appealing they are to women, and so the seeds of optimism – realistic or otherwise – are sown.

An inbuilt optimistic bias has real benefits in our everyday life as well. For one thing, our belief that things will be good in the future makes us feel happier and more satisfied with life at the moment. Countless surveys, such as those conducted by the University of Illinois psychologist Ed Diener, have shown that people say they are happy and satisfied with life most of the time. Diener and his colleagues developed the simple Satisfaction with Life Scale (SWLS) back in 1985, which is still used to see how content we are with our lives. Have a go below to find out how you compare to others, and then turn to the notes at the back for information on scoring the SWLS.

If you are like most people, you will have scored fairly high on this simple scale. In agreement with international surveys on optimism, Diener finds that most of us say we are fairly satisfied and happy with most areas of our lives.

The Satisfaction with Life Scale

Below are five statements with which you may agree or disagree. Using the 1–7 scale below, indicate your agreement with each item by placing the appropriate number on the line preceding that item. You need to be open and honest in your responding. The points in the scale are: 1 = strongly disagree, 2 = disagree, 3 = slightly disagree, 4 = neither agree or disagree, 5 = slightly agree, 6 = agree, 7 = strongly agree.

_____ 1. In most ways my life is close to my ideal.

_____ 2. The conditions of my life are excellent.

_____ 3. I am satisfied with my life.

_____ 4. So far I have gotten the important things I want in life.

_____ 5. If I could live my live over, I would change almost nothing.

Optimism, no matter how we measure it, is very common, and the brain states that underlie this optimistic mindset are rooted in the pleasure centre of the brain, with the NAcc at its core. A close look at this hedonic core reveals that there are two key parts to the pleasure brain: feeling good and desire. Wanting is the unsung side of pleasure, coordinated by a complex network of dopamine-containing neurons that guarantee we stay engaged and focused on things that are of ultimate benefit to us.

The distinction between 'wanting' and 'liking' is crucial to understanding the sunny brain. Self-help books generally focus on the good feelings that come with liking something, along with the idea that positive thoughts will bring a range of benefits. It's this 'positive-thinking mafia' that generated Barbara Ehrenreich's scepticism. The story, however, turns out to be much more complex than 'happy thoughts will solve everything.' Wanting and liking are separate and equally important components of pleasure, and it's the former that, in my view, spawns many of the benefits of optimism.

We can see this effect in one of the most obvious characteristics of optimists, which is the ability to stick with a task in spite of setbacks. When you speak to optimists like Michael J. Fox, one of the things that strikes you is their refusal to give in to difficulties. Optimism is not a passive mindset; it's about being actively engaged with life.

Armed with a better knowledge of what optimism is and the brain circuits associated with it, we can now examine whether there are major benefits to optimism. Startling claims have been made for optimism, or at least for the power of positive thinking. All that's required, according to the creed, is to think positively, and good things will start to happen. Your cancer will be cured. You will get that job you have always wanted. The perfect partner will suddenly appear in your life. As Ehrenreich reminds us, much of this descends into magical thinking, completely divorced from reality.

While thinking alone is not as effective as many gurus would have us believe, there is solid evidence that optimism is associated with actions that do bring advantages. An accident survivor, paralysed from the waist down, who believes that she can still have a high quality of life is likely to go to the gym to work on her upper body strength, and get out and about to enjoy an active social life. Someone who believes her life is over will probably not do these things. The difference in quality of life has less to do with the power of positive thinking and more to do with the power of positive actions. The two are not unrelated, but it's the actions that reap the rewards of optimism.

With this in mind, a careful look at the scientific evidence shows that there is a case for at least three major benefits to an optimistic mindset: better health and well-being, the ability to pick ourselves up after a crisis, and greater success in life.

The Benefits of Optimism

While there has been much unsubstantiated hype, there are many scientific studies that suggest that a positive mindset, like optimism, is associated with better health and well-being. This is almost certainly due to the link between an optimistic mindset and beneficial *actions* rather than any magical power of thoughts. Most dramatic of all is the assertion that optimism can make us live longer.

In a now famous study, Deborah Danner and her colleagues at the University of Kentucky examined the handwritten diaries of 180 Catholic nuns from all over the United States, describing their lives from the moment they joined their convents in 1930. The average age of the novices was twenty-two when the study began, and Danner's team managed to track all these nuns down almost sixty years later, when the nuns' ages ranged from seventy-five to ninety years old. The diaries were carefully examined for signs of how the nuns responded to life events and were coded as to which nuns showed an optimistic outlook and which a more pessimistic view of life. This is not an ideal way to measure optimism and pessimism, but it was the best the researchers could do with the data at hand. In spite of the rather crude measure, this was a great study because the nuns all lived in fairly similar and sheltered conditions for most of their lives, and their diet and daily activities were also similar.

When the nuns were contacted in the 1990s, 76 of the 180 had died. Over 50 per cent of the nuns had exceeded their life expectancy, which was not particularly surprising given their abstinent and healthy lifestyles. The notable finding was that the optimistic nuns lived the longest. Those who had written upbeat diaries in their youth outlived their more negative sisters by an average of ten years. When we consider that giving up smoking is estimated to add maybe three to four years to your life, an extra ten years for a rosy outlook is remarkable.

So how does this work? If optimism really does help us to live longer, what could the mechanism possibly be? Is it because optimism makes us live in different ways, or could the happy thoughts themselves make a difference?

The fact that people who are buoyantly optimistic also tend to be resilient in the face of adversity provides one clue as to how optimism is associated with longevity. Barbara Fredrickson, a psychologist at the University of North Carolina, has found that resilient people use optimistic thoughts and positive emotions as a way to cope with difficult situations. She explains why this is effective with her 'broaden and build' theory. The central concept is that positive emotions *broaden* the range of ideas we have for dealing with adverse situations. In a typical experiment people were given a temporary boost of 'positivity': they were given a bag of brightly coloured candy or shown funny video clips. When then asked to write down what kinds of things they would like to do if they had a spare half hour, those in a positive mood came up with far more ideas than those who had watched a scary movie. This makes sense, since one of the functions of negative emotions like fear is to narrow our attention down to a potential threat. In contrast, positive emotions tend to ex-

Sunny-Side Up

pand and widen our attention, and they generally lead us to more creativity. The message here is that if you want a successful brainstorming session, get people into a happy and relaxed mood first, and the ideas will flow far more easily.

I find support for this broadening effect of positive emotions in a simple experiment we run in laboratory classes. We raise or lower our students' mood states by showing them short clips of either a comedy or a sad movie. Following the video clip, everyone is given a range of puzzles and problems. Those in a positive mood are usually better at solving the puzzles than those in a darker mood. Put simply, when we are feeling positive emotions, like joy and happiness, our thoughts get more expansive, and this enables us to become more creative, enabling us to 'think outside the box.'

This broadening effect of positive emotions can be very useful in helping us deal with difficulties in a more creative way. This can be seen in the burgeoning of compassion and togetherness that occurred in the aftermath of the September 11 attacks in New York City. Fredrickson interviewed several people immediately after the attacks and found that, while there was grief and sadness, there was also a profound thankfulness to be alive. Indeed, she noticed that people who were able to express at least some positive emotions were more resilient and far less likely to slip into despair than those who were overcome by negativity.

Apart from the immediate benefits, according to Fredrickson, this aspect of good moods also allows us to *build* a range of personal resources that help us to cope with adversity in the longer term – good friends, hobbies, a pleasant physical environment, and so on – all of which are crucial when the bad times dawn. This is why optimistic people fared better following the 2001 terrorist attacks and almost certainly why Danner's optimistic nuns lived an average of ten years beyond their gloomier sisters.

Prospective studies that follow people for a number of years also find that optimism is linked with better health and stronger

~ 57 ~

resilience in a crisis. A study led by Mika Kivimaki and colleagues at the University of Helsinki in Finland assessed levels of optimism and pessimism in 5,000 people and then followed them for about three years. Some people experienced a major trauma, such as the death or serious illness of a family member. The levels of optimism people reported *before* the life-changing event turned out to be one of the best predictors of health and well-being *afterward*. The more optimistic we are, then, the healthier we are.

Anecdotal evidence supports this view. Take the example of Thomas Edison, who got a phone call in the early hours to say that his factory was on fire, with £120 million worth of equipment and building already destroyed. Even worse, his insurance company was quick to point out that it could cover only a small portion of the loss. Far from being distraught, Edison invited his friends and family to join him watching his beloved New Jersey factory and laboratories go up in flames. Friends were incredulous that he seemed calm in the face of the rapidly unfolding disaster. Once he had established that no one had been injured and that life was not in danger, he even seemed to be enjoying the spectacle. Edison saw the blaze as a fantastic opportunity to set about redesigning a new and better site.

Following the disaster, Edison quickly gathered a team together to redesign the factory along with a new suite of research labs. Reconstruction began just weeks after the fire, and within a year the new factory was up and running and making a profit. Proving Churchill's dictum, he saw opportunity rather than disaster. Resilience and an ability to keep going in the face of disaster is a hallmark of optimism that stems directly from a sunny-brain style.

This affective mindset also comes in handy when dealing with the normal problems of everyday life. In tough financial times, such as during economic recessions, people often find it difficult to make basic decisions: Do we sell our house now or wait for things to improve? Should I take some extra courses and wait for the job market to improve? If we allow ourselves to get overwhelmed by self-doubt and pessimism, we tend to get stuck, unable to do anything. Optimists take problems like this in their stride and look to the future with hope and confidence.

The evidence is growing that this is not just down to thinking positively, but also because optimism leads us to engage in activities that put us in the way of opportunity, which in turn gives us the resilience not to accept defeat.

Madam C. J. Walker is an example. Born in 1867 on a plantation in Louisiana, this daughter of former slaves was orphaned by the age of seven, married at fourteen, and divorced by the time she was twenty. Against all the odds, she became America's first self-made millionaire and was an inspiring social activist dedicated to improving the lot of both women and black people in America. She founded a successful company that made hair-care products, and she was in many ways a pioneer of the modern cosmetics industry. As beautifully told by her great-great-granddaughter, Madam Walker's rags-to-riches story was fuelled primarily by her irrepressible can-do attitude. Setbacks were tackled head-on with tireless energy. Friends and colleagues said that she would brush aside the deep-seated racism and sexism she encountered throughout her life. She walked a path paved with a deep-seated and unshakeable belief in the goodness of people and hope for the future. Her story reminds us that optimism is not so much about feeling happy, nor necessarily a belief that everything will be fine, but about how we respond when times get tough. Optimists tend to keep going, even when it seems as if the whole world is against them.

It's difficult to measure this kind of persistence in the lab, but Suzanne Segerstrom, a University of Kentucky psychologist, figured out a clever way of doing this with her graduate student Lise Solberg. Using the LOT-R, they measured dispositional optimism in fifty-four students and then presented them with eleven anagrams to solve in a twenty-minute period. The trick was that the first anagram (GGAWIL) was impossible to solve, and then it was followed by ten anagrams that varied in difficulty from moderate to very difficult. This maximised the early perception of difficulty. These are exactly the conditions under which we would expect optimism to have the strongest effects on persistence. The results were notable: the pessimists stuck with the first anagram for about a minute before giving up, but the optimists spent twice as long, trying to work out the impossible anagram for more than two minutes before giving up and moving on to the next.

Intriguingly, the team also found that this greater persistence on the task was also related with a surge of stress hormones and increases in physiological arousal. These costs muddy the water with regard to the links between optimism and better health. How can increased physiological stress be reconciled with the notion that optimism has benefits for our health?

The answer comes from another study conducted by Segerstrom. Testing large numbers of law students in their first year of study, she found that the optimists had greater physiological stress and poorer immune system functioning. This turned out to be due to the optimistic students being more likely to engage in conflicting goals. Law school is highly demanding, and socialising and making new friends often conflict with spending long hours studying in the library. Optimists were far more likely to do both and therefore burn themselves out, with the inevitable adverse consequences on their health.

The intriguing finding, though, was that these short-term costs disappeared in the second year of study, when the students' immune functioning returned to normal. As a result of their increased engagement during the previous year, those who had worked the hardest now achieved the most, not only in their exams but also in building a supportive network of friends and colleagues. The short-term costs followed by longer-term gains helps to reconcile the apparently complex pattern of results on optimism and physical health. This is supported by the results of a meta-analysis –

a study of studies – that was completed in 2009 and found strong evidence that optimism is associated with better physical health in the longer term.

Given optimists' greater persistence, it comes as no surprise to find that optimism is also linked with success. In the business world, optimism is advantageous, since the ability to deal with failures is often required. While it might seem strange to link optimism with failure, without optimism it's virtually impossible for budding entrepreneurs to put their plans into action. Setting up a business is all about maintaining a belief that things will work out, even though there are likely to be many hurdles and obstacles to overcome. Former British prime minister Winston Churchill, no stranger to adversity himself, said, 'Success is the ability to go from failure to failure without losing your enthusiasm.' This is why Thomas Edison, whose optimism was magnetic to those around him, constantly encouraged his workers to never give up. On one occasion, having realised that he had tried out more than 10,000 different ways to develop an electric lamp, he famously proclaimed: 'I have not failed. I've just found 10,000 ways that won't work.'

All these traits can be seen in abundance in the story of Amazon.com founder Jeff Bezos. Back in 1994 he had a eureka moment when he stumbled on a website that said the use of the web was growing by more than 2,000 per cent a year. *There must be a way of making money out of such growth*, he thought. Going through many options, it dawned on Bezos that an online bookstore was perfect. While there is a physical limit to how many books can be stored in a bookstore or warehouse, an online store has the advantage of no limits – millions of books could be made instantly available with pictures and excerpts. And so Amazon.com was born.

Start-up costs were high, and the naysayers soon began to gather. Even though the online bookstore took off quickly, it was several years before Amazon started to turn a profit. Commentators warned Bezos that the company would fail. When Barnes & Noble entered the same market a couple of years later, most thought that Amazon was finished. A prominent investment analyst firm even declared the company 'Amazon.toast.' Bezos himself was undeterred.

With a dedication to making Amazon an easy-to-use and completely customer-focused website, the company has gone from strength to strength. According to Bezos himself, one of his best assets, and the key to his success, is a sense of optimism. 'Optimism is an essential ingredient for doing anything hard,' he says. This is why optimists, who cope better with failure, are often the most successful.

An optimistic mindset brings more than individual benefits; it can also be highly infectious and is frequently the instigator of social change. Instead of meandering meekly along the course that one's background and family set out, an optimistic outlook often impels people to break boundaries. Nelson Mandela, who spent twenty-seven years in a South African jail, never gave up hope. While no one could accuse him of being unrealistic, he also had a deep sense of optimism. He just knew deep in side himself that apartheid would crumble. Where most of us would have lost heart and given up, he never lost faith that justice would one day be done. Eventually it was, and people all around the world joined together to watch black South Africans vote for the first time ever and give Mandela a landslide victory in the presidential elections.

Another unlikely world leader, also fuelled by optimism, addressed the US Democratic National Convention in 2004 and challenged delegates to aim for a politics of hope rather than a politics of cynicism. He pointed out that he himself was the most unlikely of senators. His father had been a goat herder in Kenya, eventually emigrating to study in the United States, where he married the daughter of an oil worker. He was not talking about 'blind optimism,' he said, or 'the almost willful ignorance that thinks unemployment will go away if we just don't talk about it.' He was painting a larger canvas in thinking about the 'hope of slaves sitting around a fire singing freedom songs; the hope of immigrants setting out for distant shores; the hope of a young naval lieutenant bravely patrolling the Mekong Delta; the hope of a millworker's son who dares to defy the odds; the hope of a skinny kid with a funny name who believes that America has a place for him, too. The audacity of hope!'

That skinny kid with the funny name has now made it to the White House, and alongside Barack Obama's many abilities, there's little doubt that his constant hope and optimism played a part in getting him to where he is today. A friend of mind was at Obama's presidential acceptance speech in Chicago in November 2008, and he recounted the energy that seemed to pervade the crowd. 'The excitement and sense of hope was palpable,' he told me. 'Everybody was swept along on a wave of togetherness and a real optimism that things finally really were getting better.' International surveys conducted at the time showed that this wave of optimism not only swept around America but also engulfed the entire world.

Optimism is infectious because hope against the odds is one of the most inspirational characteristics of the human spirit. Shirin Ebadi is a case in point. Growing up in Tehran in the 1950s, her childhood was spent in a family that she describes as 'filled with kindness and affection.' Studying law at Tehran University, she was the first woman in Iran to be appointed a judge. Following the Islamic Revolution in February 1979, she was dismissed along with all other female lawyers in the country and assigned to secretarial work, since, according to the Revolutionary Council, woman were 'not suited' to such roles. Unemployed for many years, Ebadi never gave up. She finally regained a license to practice law in 1992. She took on many controversial cases and continues to tirelessly pursue social justice for the women and children of Iran. Awarded the Nobel Peace Prize in 2003, she is now one of the leading human rights campaigners in the world, even though she still remains unappre_ ciated by her own government.

The kind of optimistic mindset, and ability to act, that unites such disparate people as Shirin Ebadi, Nelson Mandela, Jeff Bezos,

Thomas Edison, and Michael J. Fox is what drives the human race forward. It's this sense of hope and resilience that's likely to have helped us walk out of Africa and spread around the globe millions of years ago, the only species to thrive in almost every climate. Without the ability to persist, it's hard to imagine how human societies could bounce back from disasters. Think of the devastation following the tsunami in Japan, or the floods in New Orleans, or the bombed-out cities lying in ruins across Europe after the Second World War. The rebuilding efforts that take place after these catastrophic events are based on people working together in a spirit of hope and optimism that allows human societies to flourish.

CHAPTER 3

The Rainy Brain

Why Optimism Is
More Elusive Than Pessimism

I first experienced the effects of raw fear growing up in Dublin in the 1970s, during a period when our school would regularly take in girls from Northern Ireland. This was at the height of what we called The Troubles, and it was considered a good idea to get these girls away from the bomb blasts and shootings of Belfast, some two hours' drive across the border, to the peaceful environs of Dublin suburbia. On one occasion a couple of us were walking home for lunch with a Belfast friend called Sandra, who had already spent a couple of weeks at our school. As we were walking and chatting, we suddenly became aware that Sandra was no longer beside us. We looked around to see her about ten yards back, lying flat on the pavement. It turned out that a car had backfired and – completely unnoticed by the rest of us – she had hit the deck. Somewhere deep in her emergency brain, an alarm signal had been sent out. In the Belfast of the day, sounds like cars backfiring indicated trouble. The fear and trauma she had experienced back home had been reignited by a simple sound. Sandra's instant reaction illustrates the emergency brain in action.

The emergency brain operates in lightning-quick time and etches dangerous events indelibly into our memory. I'm sure that gunfire was far from Sandra's mind as we walked home from school that sunny day, but as soon as the car backfired, her emergency brain sprang into action, taking control. When threat is present or imminent, this system, embedded deep in the ancient regions of our brain, releases adrenaline into our bloodstream, increasing our breathing and heart rate, and making us sweat. These physical symptoms allow us to react when we are in danger, preparing us to either run for our life or stand and fight – the classic 'fight or flight' response.

Millions of years of evolution have provided us with this potent system. This is the brain's panic button, which alerts other parts of the brain to impending danger, bringing the potential threat into our consciousness so it can be assessed in greater detail. At the same time, the emergency brain dampens down all other processes, thus ensuring that our attention zones in on the source of danger without being distracted by less relevant details. When faced with immediate threat, our fear brain makes sure that we take notice, giving us every chance of getting out of harm's way fast.

Once fired up, the fear system dominates everything else. Several years ago, I took part in a demonstration of how deeply embedded such primal fears can be. In a moment of madness, I agreed to have a large python draped around my neck to see firsthand the effects of this ancient fear. I was kitted out with sophisticated sensors on my hands and chest to measure the reaction of my body when the snake was placed around my neck. I knew that the snake was from the local zoo, had no venom, and was well used to these stunts. In fact, the keeper told me that the snake usually got bored and fell asleep during these demonstrations. None of this meant anything to my emergency brain. As soon as I saw the snake, my heartbeat began to increase, and my breathing got a bit faster. When the snake slid across my shoulders, I could feel my heart pumping and my hands become sweaty. As he moved around a little, I had a moment of near panic, and the sensors showed that my heart rate escalated dramatically. Even when the snake was taken away, it took me some time to calm down. Although my conscious, or rational, brain knew I was perfectly safe, my fear brain had gone into overdrive.

Given that most of us nowadays live in safe environments, the fact that fear remains a driving force in our lives remains an interesting question. In developed societies, the chances of being attacked by animal or human being are remote. Nevertheless, we worry about a range of disasters and personal disappointments. It is not just the primal fears of natural dangers that besiege us, but also the more enduring anxieties and worries of what others think of us. Are we popular? Will we be successful in life? All of these fears are perfectly understandable, but why are we still afraid of things that rarely pose a threat to us nowadays?

The well-worn answer to this question is that the ancient parts of our brain that we share with most other species evolved during a period in which our ancestors were threatened by a range of natural dangers, such as violent storms and predators. This ancient structure – the amygdala – still burns bright when we are confronted by these dangers. There's plenty of evidence that the dangers that threatened our ancient ancestors still activate the ancient parts of our emergency brain, which in turn control many other regions of the brain – stopping us in our tracks so that the danger can be dealt with. Thus, even though we rarely encounter snakes, they, and other threats to our forebears millions of years ago, still cause dramatic fear reactions. In this way, our fear brain dictates much of what we are afraid of. This is why fears of enclosed dark places, open spaces, spiders, and snakes are still the most common intense phobias to appear in psychologists' clinics. Clearly, ancient dangers continue to have a powerful hold on our fear brain.

Arne Öhman, a professor of psychology at the Karolinska Institute in Sweden, conducted intriguing experiments on this subject.

He discovered that our brains are especially tuned in to dangers from our evolutionary pasts. In one study, arrays of photographs were flashed on a large screen for a fraction of a second, and volunteers had to press a button on the left if all the items in the display were 'the same,' or a button on the right if one item in the display was 'different.' The idea was that people had to respond as quickly as they could while trying not to make too many mistakes. So if a display contained nine pictures of mushrooms, or nine pictures of snakes, the volunteers had to press the left button as quickly as they could. The more interesting cases occurred when one of the items was different from the rest, such as a snake among eight flowers. Then the button on the right had to be pressed.

When Öhman and his team examined the pattern of reaction times across hundreds of trials, a clear pattern emerged. If the *different* item in a display was a snake or a spider, rather than a flower or a mushroom, people were much faster to respond. For example, people were much faster reacting to a display of nine mushrooms and one snake than to a display of nine mushrooms and one flower. The threatening item was noticed much faster than the less threatening picture. This subtle difference in response time gives us a glimpse into our evolutionary past and shows us that, even today, our brain still pays more attention to the dangers that confronted our ancestors. This leads us to the conclusion that those of our ancestors who were good at noticing and avoiding snakes and spiders stayed around long enough to produce offspring with more efficient threat-detection systems. Our brains still retain this ancient memory. As those twenty-first-century Swedish students sat in Öhman's Stockholm lab pressing buttons in response to pictures, the wisdom of their ancestors who lived thousands of years previously drove their reactions.

To understand how this fear system operates and the role it plays in the wider rainy brain, we need to examine the physical seat of fear in the brain in more detail.

The Anatomy of Fear

Just as with the pleasure brain, the emergency brain is made up of a number of separate, but highly interrelated, structures. Most of these are buried deep within subcortical parts of the brain that have rich connections to each other as well as to different parts of the cortex. While all are important for shaping our fear response, there's little doubt that the tiny, almond-shaped structure called the *amygdala* is central. The size of a thumbnail, the amygdala is made up of at least thirteen separate sections, each of which may serve a different function. This is a startling feat of biological engineering. The sheer elegance and complexity of this wondrous nodule has been uncovered by hundreds of inventive and painstaking experiments that have led to an explosion of knowledge about the science of fear. We now know more about fear than any other emotion, and knowledge about the amygdala and fear, and the influence they have on our lives, is flowing in from labs all over the world on an almost daily basis.

New York University psychologist Joseph LeDoux has been at the forefront of the science of fear. His work, primarily with rats, shows that the amygdala sits at the heart of the fear system. In an important breakthrough, he discovered that there are *two* routes from the senses to the amygdala, one fast and one slower. He called the faster pathway the 'low road,' or the 'quick and dirty' route, and the other the 'high road,' a more leisurely trail on the highway of fear. To appreciate how this works, consider what happens in our brain when we are in the presence of danger. Everything starts at one of the five senses. We might see something alarming like a snake, or hear something like a fire alarm, or smell a hint of smoke in the dead of night. This information, whether it's something we see, hear, smell, feel, or taste, is swept to an area of the brain called the *thalamus*, which sits more or less in the middle of our head, just above the brain stem. The thalamus is like a relay station, gathering information about the world outside and then shunting this sensory information off to the most relevant part of the brain for further analysis.

As all of this sensory information streams in via the thalamus, the job of the amygdala is to scan it for even the faintest hint of danger. If any threat is perceived, then the amygdala operates at breakneck speed. When danger lurks there's no time for delay, so the quick and dirty route shunts scary sensory information straight from the thalamus to the amygdala, literally firing before we have time to think. When we're faced with a possible snake on the pathway, even a second's thought can be deadly.

The so-called slower route is still fast, but the information is sent from the thalamus to the cortex for more detailed analysis before being redirected to the amygdala. This route allows for a more detailed assessment of the information by the higher, more rational areas of the brain. The visual cortex, for example, can analyse the potential danger in more detail to figure out whether it might be a snake or an innocuous piece of wood lying in the grass.

The amygdala acts fast and also has to operate outside our conscious awareness. As we are busy getting on with other things, this ancient brain region is constantly scanning our surroundings for danger. Once danger is noticed – from whatever route it comes – the amygdala signals the rest of the brain to stop whatever else it is doing and concentrate. A friend of mine who worked in a bank was held up at gunpoint many years ago and still remembers how he froze when he saw the gun aimed at his head; his entire attention was consumed by the gun. Afterwards, when the police asked him to describe the robbers, he couldn't even remember whether they had been wearing masks or not. The main threat, the weapon, had completely captured his attention.

Convincing evidence that the amygdala is the primary player in human fear comes from work by Ray Dolan, a neuroscientist at the forefront of research on how the human brain reacts to fear. He runs a leading neuroimaging laboratory at University College in the centre of London. He realised that while research with animals showed that the amygdala was central to fear, we did not know much about the biology of human fear. His technique was to scan people's brains when they were in fearful situations to see whether the amygdala is also crucial for human fear. Because we cannot ethically terrify people in the laboratory, the typical technique is to present volunteers a series of scary photographs. In Dolan's study, people were asked to lie in the brain scanner while several different faces with varying emotional expressions were shown on a screen just above them. Some of the faces were friendly and smiling, some were angry, some were sad, and some looked afraid. When Dolan and his team examined the huge amount of data that emerged from the brain scanner, it became clear that the amygdala became most active when a fearful expression was shown and was more subdued when people were looking at a happy expression. Notably, people taking part in this experiment did not *feel* scared, but their amygdala was still tuned into any hint of danger.

We humans are social creatures, with an uncanny ability to pick up emotions from others quickly. If we see someone looking afraid, that's a pretty good clue there might be danger around. Several studies have now confirmed it is the reaction of the amygdala, deep in our emergency brain, that allows us to notice such signals of potential danger.

Dolan, along with his colleague John Morris, also from UCL, and Arne Öhman from the Karolinska Institute in Sweden, wondered whether the amygdala would react to *unconscious* threat, danger signals that we are not even aware of. In his Stockholm lab, Öhman had already discovered that flashing subliminal pictures of spiders and snakes could produce a stress response. He rigged people up with sensors to detect sweat on their palms and flashed up various pictures of snakes, mushrooms, flowers, and spiders so quickly that people were not able to tell what the pictures were. Technically known as *masking*, this technique involves presenting pictures very rapidly and then – just a few milliseconds later – replacing the image by a picture of random squiggles and lines. A picture of a snake might be presented for just fourteen milliseconds, and then the mask (the squiggles) is presented for about half a second.

All you see in this type of experiment is a brief flash and then the image of the squiggles; it's impossible to make out the pictures behind the mask. The giveaway was the sweatiness of the volunteers' palms. Even though they could not see it, when a picture of a snake or a spider was flashed up, the volunteers' palms got sweaty; when pictures of flowers or mushrooms were shown, they stayed dry. This momentary physiological reaction tells us that danger had been noticed even though the volunteers couldn't see anything at all.

The three scientists realised that fMRI gave them a unique opportunity to see what was happening inside the brain in these experiments. Following Dolan's original study, a series of faces with different emotional expressions were projected onto the screen. Each face was masked, just as in Öhman's studies. Unbeknownst to the participants, sometimes the squiggles were preceded by a fearful face and sometimes by a neutral face. Even though they could not see the faces, the amygdala was alert to the danger signal. Again and again, when a fearful expression was presented, the amygdala would light up on the brain scans, a telltale sign that the emergency brain was sitting up and taking notice, even at this most subtle hint of danger.

This ability of our emergency brain to detect threat can even help apparently blind people to 'see' danger and other emotional signals. I first became aware of the startling ability of people with severe brain damage to pick up emotional signals several years ago, when I conducted a series of tests on a gentle old man called JB. In his mid-seventies when I first met him, JB had had a severe stroke a couple of years previously, which had left him with some mild difficulties with movement. The most unusual problem that still lingered stemmed from the fact that he had had a stroke in the parietal lobe on the right side of his brain, which gave him what neurologists call *spatial neglect*, which simply means that JB was unaware of anything on the left side of space. This is fairly common after injury to the right side of this area of the brain. When eating dinner, a victim will eat food from only the right side of the plate, completely ignoring what's on the left. Or when asked to cancel out letters on a page, the person will only notice the letters on the right. This is a problem of attention, not vision, since, if you tap the plate on the left, the person will become aware of the uneaten food.

Because JB had a severe form of this spatial neglect, I realised that this provided an opportunity to test the hypothesis that danger signals, like a fearful facial expression, could be detected in the absence of awareness. I presented various pairs of items to JB at the same time, one on the right and one on the left, and asked him to tell me what he saw. I might hold up an apple on the right and an orange on the left, and JB would say, 'apple.' Even when I asked whether there was anything else, he would look carefully but again say he could see just one thing, an apple.

The really interesting results came when I held up pictures of faces with different emotional expressions. Again, JB generally missed the items on the left, but not always. Sometimes he would notice the face on the left as well as on the right. It turned out there was a pattern to this. When the face on the left was *emotional*, with a happy or fearful expression, he was much more likely to notice it. When the face had a neutral expression, it almost always slipped by unseen. This told me that JB's brain was tuned into emotional signals. The surprise was that I could find no evidence that his brain was more tuned into the fearful expressions compared to the smiling faces, as I had expected.

Realising that fearful body language is a clear sign of imminent danger, Marco Tamietto and Beatrice de Gelder from the Cognitive and Affective Neuroscience Laboratory at Tilburg University in the Netherlands conducted a similar experiment with three patients who had spatial neglect like JB. They showed pictures of body language instead of facial expressions. Crouching fearful postures were shown alongside positive images of people dancing and having a good time. The fearful body language was detected much more frequently in the neglected visual field than positive postures.

The team at Tilburg studied an even more surprising condition known as blindsight. The area at the back of the brain – the primary visual cortex – is responsible for conscious vision. When this area is damaged, people are unable to see. Even though their eyes are fine, the brain damage renders them effectively blind. Investigations of people with this type of brain damage have discovered remarkable abilities to 'see' unconsciously. De Gelder studied a patient known as TN, who had extensive damage to his primary visual cortex and was effectively blind.

'We were amazed,' said de Gelder, when 'TN was able to make his way along a cluttered hallway without colliding into anything at all.'

When the team questioned TN, he said that he had no idea how he had managed to navigate his way around many unseen objects.

In 2009, de Gelder and her team conducted further studies with two other blindsight patients, DB and GY, and found further evidence of how well emotional signals could be processed. They capitalised on a phenomenon known to psychologists as 'emotional contagion,' which is the finding that we instinctively synchronise our facial expressions with those of others. In other words, if someone smiles or scowls, we tend to follow suit. This is a very subtle effect and can only be detected by placing small electrodes around the face that pick up the slightest hint of the muscle movements that go with smiling or frowning. What de Gelder and her team discovered was that, *even though they could not see* the photographs, both GY and DB demonstrated emotional contagion when shown pictures of emotional faces. A smiling face elicited the beginnings of a smile even though the patient could not see. The same thing happened with emotional bodily expressions; a crouching fearful stance induced a hint of a frown. Once again, unseen fearful images produced stronger effects than positive expressions, showing the priority of fear over pleasure. This tells us that the ancient emergency brain bypasses cortical vision, helping us to notice danger in less than the blink of an eye.

It's not just those with brain damage who are better able to 'see' fearful emotions. For those with normal vision it has also been found that fear can improve our ability to see. The flared nostrils, wide eyes, and open mouth of a frightened face are instantly recognizable. Even back in the days of Charles Darwin, scientists assumed that this distinctive expression had to do with social communication. As soon as we see a frightened face, we know that something's up, and we take precautions. Adam Anderson, a psychologist at the University of Toronto, has given us a rather different take on the evolutionary significance of a fearful facial expression. Along with his colleague Joshua Susskind, they discovered that the typical contortions of the fearful face allow for an increased flow of air through the nostrils as well as increasing the range of vision. The volunteers' peripheral vision improved when they pulled a fearful face but got worse with they pulled a disgusted expression. Fear, it seems, might help us to see danger coming.

NYU psychologist Liz Phelps has also found that simply seeing someone with a frightened face can improve our vision. Her team presented volunteers with a difficult task of working out whether a series of light grey lines were tilted or vertical. The contrast between the lines was very small, making this tricky work. If a fearful expression was flashed up on the screen fifty milliseconds beforehand, however, the volunteers were better at the difficult visual task, compared to when they had seen a neutral face. This is almost certainly due to the fearful face activating the amygdala, which then activates the visual cortex. Seeing fear in others sends the visual part of the cortex into overdrive, allowing us to see more clearly. Fear, then, not only prepares us for action but also improves our vision, making us sharper and more alert to our surroundings.

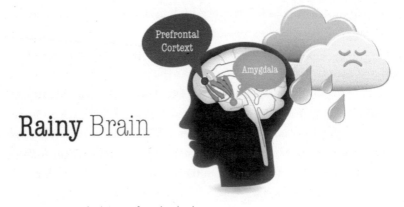

FIGURE 3.1 An image of a rainy brain.

The amygdala is central to our fear response and is at the heart of the emergency brain, but there is also a network of other brain regions that make up our rainy brain. One key discovery in the science of fear is that the amygdala has far more connections reaching out into various parts of the cortex than the cortex has back down to the amygdala. Think of it like this. Imagine a water pistol fight between a team of ten (amygdala) and a team of four (cortex). For obvious reasons, the smaller team is always going to get a soaking: an anatomical reality that explains why we can so easily be overtaken by feelings of fear even when we know there's no real danger. So someone with a fear of open spaces might freeze in terror in the supermarket, even though she is well aware that there is no real danger.

Fear's capacity to hijack the system like this is nicely illustrated by the experience of Colin Stafford Johnson, a cinematographer working on a documentary in India for the BBC's Natural History Unit. One hot day, Colin was walking alone along a dried-out Indian riverbed. Turning a corner, he came across a group of tiger cubs playing with their mother. The mother tiger immediately charged him, stopping dead about fifteen feet away from him and letting out a deafening roar. Logically, Colin knew that the tiger was not going to kill him because he had witnessed tigers carrying out such threat charges towards other tigers many times before. This, he knew, was the tiger's way of shouting 'back off – or else.' Nevertheless, he recounts, 'there was that primordial terror there. I was quite literally rooted to the spot. It took my body about two hours to recover.'

Inside Colin's head his amygdala blasted out an alarm signal telling the rest of his brain there was an immediate danger and all other processes should stop. Even though the higher cortical areas of his brain were sending another message – *this is OK; the tiger is not going to attack* – his primal fear response could not be stopped.

From the examples given so far, we can see that the role of the amygdala is primarily to help us detect and react to potential danger. Whether it's fighting, freezing, or fleeing, fear gets us out of harm's way as quickly as possible. Such episodes of extreme fear not only prepare us for action but also lay down enduring memories that have ongoing effects on our thoughts, judgements, behaviours, and feelings. These play an important role in making us who we are.

When I give lectures on fear, people usually ask about the role of feelings in all this. According to Joseph LeDoux, feelings are something of a red herring in the science of fear. He makes the point that the fear system is all about survival and that feelings are no more important than any other outcomes of the fear response, like sweaty hands, increased adrenaline, pumping heart, and so on. Feeling only comes about when the fear system has already taken the best course of action. Evolution, according to LeDoux, has designed an emergency brain that helps us survive direct threats, and in these situations it's action, not thinking or feeling, that counts.

Clearly, we do feel fear. We all know the unpleasant feelings we get when a vicious dog rushes towards us with hackles up or the dread we feel when waiting for an important test result. Back in the 1800s, William James, the founder of scientific psychology in the United States, proposed that emotions like fear are experienced only as a *result* of our bodily sensations. Hence, his famous dictum 'We are afraid because we run,' not the other way around. This conjecture leads to an interesting prediction. If our feelings really do come from our bodily sensations, then the stronger the reaction of our body – and the more aware we are of these sensations – the stronger our experience of fear should be.

In a clever experiment to test out this hypothesis, Ray Dolan and his team presented people with what is known as the *heartbeat detection task*. While lying in an fMRI scanner, volunteers could hear a sequence of tones triggered by their own pulse. Sometimes the tones were presented immediately, while other times there was a short delay before the sequence was presented. The trick was to judge the timing of your own heartbeat relative to the tones. I've tried this myself, and it's not easy.

Dolan and his team found that some people really excel at this task and some are really bad. The intriguing result was that those who were good at judging their own heartbeat also reported much stronger feelings of anxiety and fear. Supporting James's original theory, those who had a heightened awareness of their bodily reactions also experienced stronger emotional feelings. Interestingly, the region of the brain that was most active when people were doing this task was another ancient part of the brain called the *insula*. This implies that, while the amygdala might be crucial for orchestrating the defensive and protective aspects of the fear response, it is the insula that plays a role in translating these primal fear reactions into what many call fear: the conscious feelings of being afraid.

In addition to subcortical areas of the brain, like the amygdala and the insula, we now know that more modern parts of the brain, especially the cortex, play a powerful role in our fear responses. In particular, activating specific parts of the prefrontal cortex can dampen the response of the amygdala in an interplay between amygdala and cortex reminiscent of Freud's epic struggle between the 'primal id' and the 'superego.'

Just as with the pleasure brain, there is a brake as well as an accelerator. Yet the cortex cannot entirely switch off the emergency brain's warning signal, and the anatomy tells us why. The vast number of amygdala-cortical connections – outnumbering those going in the opposite direction – allows the emergency brain to unduly influence the more advanced cortical areas. This is why Colin was rooted to the spot even though he knew that the tiger was not going to attack. It's also why such primal emotions as fear play an essential role in what we notice and remember.

Our emergency brain is not democratic and naturally prioritises danger-relevant information. This automatic protection system is crucial, maximising our survival chances at every turn. Such a powerful and difficult-to-control system also comes with a downside. Frequent activation of the alarm centres at the heart of our emergency brain can sensitise and imbalance the rest of the rainy brain, with its numerous connections running between subcortical and cortical regions. As the emergency brain becomes stronger and inhibitory centres weaken, we are gradually nudged towards a more pessimistic mindset, on the lookout for the worst. It's this gradual emergence of negative thinking with developing biases to highlight the bad rather than the good that can ultimately lead to the development of gloomy thoughts and even escalate into more enduring anxiety disorders.

This is the dark side of our defensive system. The neurobiology of fear explains how our emergency brain can take over our mind and why this makes pessimism a common – and potentially dangerous – outlook on life. The ancient parts of our emergency brain ensure that we are drawn inexorably to potential danger. No surprise, then, that bad news sells: the attraction of danger is enduring and not easily overcome. Newspapers, TV, and radio all bombard us with negative stories – financial meltdowns, recession, global warming, swine flu, terrorism, war. The list is endless, and alongside the natural tendency of our brain to zone in on bad news, this pessimism can be overwhelming. A cursory look at any news source tells us that the media is infused by a pervasive attraction to pessimism.

We can now see why. Our emergency brain highlights danger-laden information, relegating the potentially pleasurable to second place. Even the faintest hint of threat is picked up instantly, putting a halt to all other processes in order to concentrate on the danger. Such a proclivity to notice the negative rather than the positive makes it more difficult to be optimistic. As politicians and priests have shown through the ages, it's far easier to frighten people than to calm them. Once the fear brain is activated, logic tends to get shut down for a while, and in many modern situations this can be a real problem. Not only do the effects of fear make it more difficult to experience pleasure and develop an optimistic outlook, but they can also lead to more pervasive anxieties and worries that can take the lustre off life.

Emory University psychologist and political commentator Drew Westen illustrated how the effects of alerting the fear system can linger with the story of the notorious 'daisy ad' run by Lyndon Johnson's presidential campaign in 1964. The ad turned the tide against conservative Barry Goldwater, even though it never named him or discussed his policies. At the time, the Cold War was at its peak, and the fear of nuclear catastrophe was pervasive. Goldwater was a supporter of nuclear weapons, and Johnson wanted to get the message across that Goldwater could not be trusted with a weapon of mass destruction. The ad opens with a pretty little girl plucking petals off a daisy one by one, charmingly counting and confusing her numbers as birds sing in the background. Suddenly we are startled by a louder male voice beginning a countdown, 'TEN, NINE, EIGHT . . .' The little girl looks up into the sky, face filled with apprehension, as the camera slowly zooms in on the pupil of her eye, which gradually is replaced by the vivid image of an atomic bomb detonating and a mushroom cloud spreading across the screen.

'These are the stakes,' says Johnson's steady voice. 'To make a world in which all of God's children can live, or to go into the darkness.' The ad ends with 'Vote for President Johnson on November 3rd' written across the screen in white letters against a black background.

People did, and by all accounts the daisy ad was a crucial factor in swinging the election Johnson's way. Because our fear system is so easy to ignite, the ad instantly concentrated people's minds on the threat of nuclear annihilation to the exclusion of anything else. Moreover, once activated, the resulting anxieties were difficult to switch off, and these fears were now subtly associated with Johnson's rival. By manipulating ancient circuits in the brain designed to detect danger, the ad unconsciously persuaded people to avoid a particular political candidate.

This is a typical upshot of arousing our emergency brain: fear unleashed in an instant can lead to lingering anxieties. On top of that, the memories we form when we are scared are difficult to shake, and such a negatively infused mind can nudge us towards a pessimistic outlook. The constant reminder of dangers and bad things that have happened makes it difficult to see the world as a rosy place. This is the price we pay for our emergency brain. We would not survive for long without such a powerful fear system, but this system also makes it hard to become more optimistic. Whether it's the fear of stepping out of our comfort zone, apprehensiveness about taking a risk, or the apprehension that maybe we aren't good enough, it's our fears and anxieties that frequently hold us back, turning us towards the darker, more negative side of life. In other words, the ultimate obstacle to an optimistic life is fear itself, our emergency brain.

What if we could switch off our emergency brain and banish fear from our lives? Would this lead to a happier, more fulfilled life?

To find an answer to this question, we can study people who have sustained damage to their amygdala, which leaves them without fear. In spite of this, people with amygdala damage generally lead remarkably normal lives. Linda had severe epilepsy from a very young age; at one point, she was experiencing violent seizures up to eight or nine times a day, and she had become nervous and embarrassed about going out. Epilepsy is characterised by a surge of electrical activity that spreads across the brain, usually starting at a specific location. This location differs for everyone, but in Linda's case her electrical surges always started in or around her left amygdala, right at the heart of her emergency brain.

At the age of thirty, Linda agreed to have surgery to remove her amygdala along with part of the left hippocampus – an area important for memory – to control her seizures. The surgery was successful. When I first met Linda, she was in her early forties and had experienced virtually no seizures in the ten years since the operation. The surgeon's worries about inducing amnesia proved to be unfounded, probably because her right hippocampus was untouched. However, the removal of her left amygdala had left Linda without a core part of her fear brain.

Meeting Linda, you wouldn't know that anything was wrong aside from an occasional awkwardness of manner and a slightly strange pattern of eye contact. She is happily married and leads an otherwise normal life. There was one catch. Like others with amygdala damage, Linda has no problems recognising a smiling face as 'friendly' and a frowning face as 'threatening,' and facial expressions like disgust or surprise similarly don't pose her any problems. But show her a frightened face, and her response is blank. 'No emotion,' she says, 'seems neutral.' I showed her photo after photo of fearful facial expressions, and she always struggled to identify the emotion being shown. It turns out that this is a classic finding: those with amygdala damage seem to lose the ability to recognise fear in others.

I spoke about Linda to Andy Calder, a psychologist based at the Medical Research Council's Cognition and Brain Sciences Unit (CBU) in Cambridge. Andy has studied several people with amygdala damage. When I told him about Linda's difficulty with fearful expressions, he confirmed that this specific problem is typical. 'When we show photos of primary emotions like happy, surprised, or dis-

Identifying Emotions

Type of Emotion	Performance of Controls (average correct out of 20)	Performance of DR (number correct out of 20)
Happiness	16.33	15
Sadness	16.00	15
Anger	14.33	5
Fear	16.33	6
Disgust	18.25	20
Surprise	17.58	18

Performance of control volunteers (ages fifty-four to sixty) and DR (age fifty-two) in recognising sounds relating to different emotions. *Source:* Sophie Scott et al., 'Impaired Auditory Recognition of Fear and Anger Following Bilateral Amygdala Lesions,' *Nature* 385 (1997): 254–257.

gusted faces,' he said, 'most people, including those with amygdala damage, have no problem.' Pictures of fear and anger are a different story. 'They just can't recognise fearful expressions and often cannot distinguish between fearful and angry-looking faces.'

Andy and his team have also found that the inability to recognise fear is not restricted to facial expressions. They prepared snippets of sounds that reflected different emotions, like laughter for happiness, retching for disgust, screams for fear, and so on. In the Identifying Emotions table, you can see how DR, a woman with no amygdala, fares against normal volunteers in identifying emotional signals.

I confirmed these findings in further talks I had with Linda, who doesn't recognise a wide range of common danger signs. She will happily try to pat a growling dog, walk out in front of moving cars, or pick hot coals up with her bare hands. Her husband reported that she frequently injured herself in the first two years after her surgery. She eventually relearned to be aware of the various dangers, but as she said, she does not feel any fear or apprehension.

Linda's husband also told me, 'Linda is now overly trusting. She can't imagine that anyone might con her or steal from her.' He said,

Evaluating face trustworthyness

Scientists perform an experiment showing some computer generated faces to different subjects and asking them to tell if they look trustworthy.

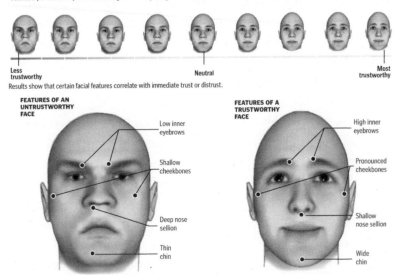

Less trustworthy

Neutral

Most trustworthy

Results show that certain facial features correlate with immediate trust or distrust.

FEATURES OF AN UNTRUSTWORTHY FACE

Low inner eyebrows

Shallow cheekbones

Deep nose sellion

Thin chin

FEATURES OF A TRUSTWORTHY FACE

High inner eyebrows

Pronounced cheekbones

Shallow nose sellion

Wide chin

FIGURE 3.2 Prototypical faces rated as 'untrustworthy' and 'trustworthy' as developed by Nicolaas Oosterhof and Alexander Todorov at Princeton University. *Source:* Javier Zarracina for the *Boston Globe*, www.gettyimages.co.uk/detail/news-photo /evaluating-face-trustworthiness-news-photo/134260600.

'She would give her PIN number to a complete stranger without considering the risk.'

Ralph Adolphs, the Bren Professor of Psychology and Neuroscience at the California Institute of Technology (Caltech), has found that amygdala damage leads to real problems in judging others, especially when it comes to trustworthiness. We read a lot into faces, judging how reliable or trustworthy a person seems – often with no evidence other than how they look. Alexander Todorov and his colleagues at Princeton University have worked out the characteristics that lead us to make these snap judgements. An upturned mouth, wide open eyes, and distinct cheekbones tend to be rated as trustworthy, while downturned mouth and eyebrows and superficial or even concave cheekbones are considered to be untrustworthy (see Figure 3.2).

Ray Dolan and his colleagues at University College London have found that the amygdala, among other brain areas, reacts strongly to such untrustworthy faces, activating our alarm system and making us feel threatened. This natural caution disappears if our amygdala is damaged.

Adolphs studied a patient called SM; unlike many amygdala-damaged patients who have one functioning amygdala, SM has none. Neither her left nor her right amygdala is intact. SM has no difficulty in identifying familiar people as well as many emotional expressions, but she is completely unable to recognise fear and trustworthiness in the faces of others. She is also overly friendly and approaches people, including complete strangers, in a way that slightly violates social norms, making people feel uncomfortable. The natural caution that regulates our usual social interactions seems to be absent.

Adolphs and his colleagues conducted a clever gambling experiment to see whether the amygdala might play a part in helping us to evaluate risk. Most of us are unlikely to take a gamble if the difference between winning and losing is very small or, alternatively, if the potential loss is very high. Imagine you are on *Who Wants to Be a Millionaire?*, and you have correctly answered the £500,000 question. You are now faced with a stark choice. With no lifelines left, you can tackle the final question. Get it right, and you win £1 million; get it wrong, and you walk away with just £32,000. Most of us would bank the £500,000 and not take the risk.

Adolphs's team tested SM as well as another patient with amygdala damage on a similar risky choice. They gave all their volunteers – twelve controls and the two patients – £50 at the beginning of the experiment and then asked them to gamble on the outcome of the flip of a coin. While the chance of heads or tails was always fifty-fifty, the experimenters varied the amount of money that could be won or lost on each flip. On some occasions the gamble could lead to a £50 win or a £10 loss, while on others the potential win was £20, but the loss would be £15. Like most of us, the control volunteers were less willing to take on the latter kind of gamble, a phenomenon called *loss aversion*. Both of the amygdala-damaged patients showed no signs of loss aversion. Instead, they were completely uninfluenced by the disparity between the potential gains and the potential losses. Even though SM and AP understood the potential gains and risks perfectly, they still took a chance even when the potential loss was greater than the potential gain. The amygdala, it seems, is important for inhibiting risky behaviour, especially when the outcome might go against us.

As I discovered with Linda, people with amygdala damage are not reckless, but they don't perceive the typical risks and dangers of everyday life. Noticing that SM was overly friendly and tended to stand a bit close for comfort, Adolphs provided further evidence that the amygdala is important in orchestrating social interactions. He used what is called a *stop-distance technique*, in which a volunteer is asked to stand a set distance from the experimenter and then walk towards him, stopping at a point that they feel comfortable. Most people, including twenty control volunteers tested by Adolphs, stop about .64 meters away, around 2 feet. SM stopped at just .34 meters, about 1 foot. Indeed, she never felt uncomfortable, even when standing nose-to-nose with a stranger. Amygdala damage eliminates a sense of personal space.

Without an emergency brain, we are left open not only to physical dangers but also to social risks. Without the cautionary brake that the amygdala applies, we are vulnerable to every scam and con artist going. Although the emergency brain nudges us towards a pessimistic mind-set, its utility would seem to outweigh any potential disadvantages.

Variation in the Reactivity of the Rainy Brain

Differences in the reactivity of our fear brain determine how we respond to all sorts of situations and are at the heart of who we are. These fundamental differences start early. Some infants are highly reactive, giggling and laughing when tickled. When they're a bit older, they readily approach people and are happy to play. Others are shy and nervous and need to be coaxed. People with very reactive sunny brains respond strongly to positive stimulation. Those with a highly sensitive rainy brain will avoid situations that seem risky, tending to focus on the potential downside of situations. A friend of mine was always reluctant to ask someone out on a date because of the fear that he might be rejected or embarrassed. Similarly, many people are hesitant to take on difficult challenges because of a fear of failure or getting hurt.

Psychologists typically refer to this type of rainy-brain personality as *neuroticism* or *trait anxiety*. The idea is that aspects of our personality dictate how we respond to a range of situations. If I go to the dentist, I might get anxious, as many do. Some people also get nervous about going to the movies, or driving on the highway, or even going to the store. Frequent episodes of situational, or state, anxiety like this are a marker of high levels of a more enduring form of anxiety that psychologists call *trait anxiety*. It's normal to feel anxious when in a new or threatening situation, such as when waiting to enter an exam room to take an important test. For those with high levels of trait anxiety, their state anxiety becomes elevated in all sorts of situations, many of them fairly innocuous.

Richard Davidson, the University of Wisconsin psychologist, has captured the neural essence of this personality style by using electroencephalography (EEG). Infants who cry a lot and are anxious, he discovered, have more activity in the right side of their frontal cortex relative to the left side. This right-sided asymmetry is also seen in adults. I have tested several people who report different levels of trait anxiety, and again and again I see the telltale right-sided asymmetry. Even monkeys show marked differences in cerebral asymmetry, and those with an extreme right-sided asymmetry – substantially more activity in the right than the left – also show much higher levels of circulating cortisol in their bloodstream compared to monkeys with an extreme left-sided asymmetry. Cortisol is a hormonal giveaway, revealing stress and fearfulness.

Measuring people's brain activity is fairly difficult, requiring specialised equipment. Most psychologists therefore measure neuroticism or trait anxiety by means of simple questionnaires. Several questionnaires to measure anxiety have been produced, but the most common is the State-Trait Anxiety Inventory (STAI) designed by Florida State University psychologist Charles Spielberger in the 1960s. This instrument has been used all around the world and consists of twenty questions measuring how people feel *right now* – their state anxiety – in addition to twenty other questions to get an idea of someone's trait anxiety – how they *generally* feel.

One item on the trait-anxiety scale is 'I lack self confidence.' People have to respond:

Almost never
Sometimes
Often
Almost always

I use the STAI routinely in my own research to categorise people into 'high' and 'low' trait-anxious groups. In my lab group, we also give a short questionnaire to students just before a lecture to get a quick sense of those likely to score high or low on the STAI. Try answering the questions below to get an idea of how neurotic, or trait-anxious, you are.

People who score high on scales like this generally have rainy brains that react more strongly to negative situations compared to those with low scores. If you scored higher than 35 on the questions below, chances are your cortical activity would show a strong right-sided asymmetry, and you would almost certainly show a clear bias towards negative pictures or words on the attentional probe task. Words like *cancer*, *attack*, and *rape* would readily capture your attention.

Essex Neuroticism Scale

Read each of the following items carefully, and then circle a number for each item on the table to show your answer. Please respond to all the items, and look in the notes at the back of the book to see how to score the questionnaire.

Items	Strongly disagree	Disagree	Neither agree nor disagree	Agree	Strongly agree
1. I often get a knot in my stomach.	1	2	3	4	5
2. I often feel jittery.	1	2	3	4	5
3. I often get discouraged and give up easily.	1	2	3	4	5
4. I worry a lot.	1	2	3	4	5
5. I am a very calm person.	1	2	3	4	5
6. Sometimes I feel very blue.	1	2	3	4	5
7. Worries about the future don't usually bother me.	1	2	3	4	5
8. I often feel very nervous.	1	2	3	4	5
9. Most people would say I am very reliable.	1	2	3	4	5
10. I rarely have difficulty sleeping.	1	2	3	4	5

The fear brain ensures that all of us are drawn towards genuinely threatening situations so that rapid action can be taken. It's not a good idea to ignore a predator or a car skidding towards you. What marks someone with high trait anxiety, though, is the tendency to be hypervigilant in situations that represent a fairly mild threat. Karin Mogg and Brendan Bradley, two psychologists based at the University of Southampton, put this idea to the test in an attentional probe task that varied the intensity of threat represented in various photographs. Some were highly negative and threatening, like mutilated bodies and murder victims, while others were mildly threatening, like a soldier holding a gun. They had people rate hundreds of photographs so that they had the perfect set of very scary, mildly scary, and neutral photos.

They found that everyone was oriented towards the very-high-intensity scenes, but with the milder threat, only the high trait anxious showed a bias. This tells us that it's the *threshold* that's important; everyone responds to severe threat, but the high trait-anxious have a lower threshold than most to switch into a vigilant mode. A sensitive and reactive rainy brain like this can easily lead to an escalating impression of a dangerous world by making people more aware of danger.

In a study reminiscent of the blindsight studies described earlier, I have used a task called the *attentional blink test* to see whether normal variation in trait anxiety – we are not talking about extreme fear here – can make a difference in how much people notice hidden danger. We brought people into the lab and presented them with a superficially easy task. Volunteers were told that all they had to do was look at a series of faces presented one after the other on a computer screen and say whether an emotional face was present or not. Most faces had neutral expressions, but occasionally there was a single emotional (happy or fearful) expression embedded in the stream. Once people got used to the speed at which the fifteen or so photos flashed by, they found the task fairly easy. On some streams, though, things got difficult – two tasks had to be attended to. First, if a nonface item – either a flower or a mushroom – popped up in the stream of faces, our volunteers had to say which it was as well as try to spot an emotional face. If the emotional face appeared less than half a second after the flower or mushroom, most people missed it completely. In fact, everything in this critical half-second time window is missed. Our attention really does blink, rendering us momentarily blind.

Figure 3.3 gives you an idea of what a single stream on this task looks like. Keep in mind that each image is flashed up for just 110

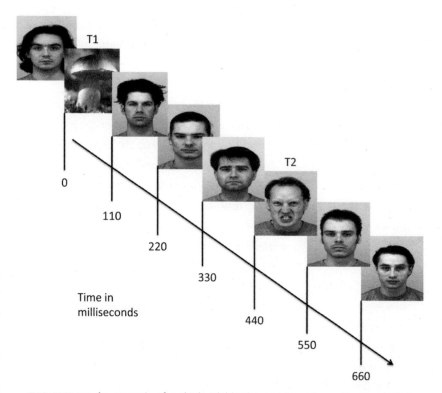

FIGURE 3.3 An example of a single trial in the emotional face attentional blink task. All the faces were presented one after the other for just 110 milliseconds each. T1 refers to the first target to be reported (either a mushroom or a flower), and T2 refers to the second target to be detected (Was an emotional face present? – yes or no). The emotional face could appear in *any* temporal location after the flower or mushroom picture (i.e., at any point up to 770 milliseconds later). *Source:* E. Fox, R. Russo, and G. Georgiou, 'Anxiety Modulates the Degree of Attentive Resources Required to Process Emotional Faces,' *Cognitive, Affective, & Behavioural Neuroscience* 5 (2005): 396–404.

milliseconds, so that all the items flash by in under a second, all in the same location on a computer screen.

Each of our volunteers was subjected to hundreds of these trials; sometimes no emotional face was present, but other times there was an emotional face that was either fearful or happy. When a happy or scared face appeared at least 550 milliseconds after the mushroom or flower picture (T1), everybody noticed it. If it appeared within half a second (500 milliseconds) of the flower/mushroom, then almost everybody missed it – a classic attentional blink effect.

However, when we then split people into low and high trait-anxiety groups – based on their scores on the STAI – a fascinating picture emerged. The anxious people were more likely to notice a fearful face. They still missed many, but, just like blindsight patients, they picked up far more of the fearful expressions, a pattern that was not seen in the low-anxiety group. There was no difference for happy faces; these were missed almost every time. The higher the level of anxiety, the more the fearful face somehow managed to sneak through the attentional blink – a sure sign of a more vigilant emergency brain.

Direct evidence for this phenomenon comes from a study that I conducted with Andy Calder and Mike Ewbank at the CBU unit in Cambridge. We asked people to lie in the brain scanner and showed them pictures of faces with angry, fearful, or neutral expressions. Just as Ray Dolan and others have found, we saw the amygdala light up when the fearful or the angry expressions were shown. The twist in our study was that we measured people's level of trait and state anxiety on the STAI by having faces that looked directly towards them or had an averted gaze. Given what we had learned from Karin Mogg and Brendan Bradley's work, we realised that this would be a way to vary the threat value of the faces. An angry face looking straight at you is the most threatening, whereas a fearful face looking either away or towards you is somewhat ambiguous. In contrast, an angry face looking away puts people more at ease, but when an angry person stares straight at you, there's a clear threat. State anxiety made a real difference to how strongly the amygdala – the emergency brain – fired, especially in response to the most threatening images. When the angry person looked directly at the volunteer, the amygdala and associated areas – the emergency brain – jumped into

DIRECT ANGER > AVERTED ANGER

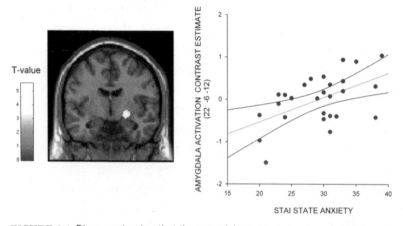

FIGURE 3.4 Diagram showing that the amygdala reacts more strongly to an angry expression when a person is looking directly at you compared to when they are looking away. The observer's level of anxiety also makes a difference in how vigorously the amygdala responds. *Source:* M. P. Ewbank, E. Fox, and A. J. Calder, 'The Interaction Between Gaze and Facial Expression in the Amygdala and Extended Amygdala Is Modulated by Anxiety,' *Frontiers in Human Neuroscience* 4 (July 2010): Article 56.

action, and this reaction was stronger the higher the level of state anxiety the volunteer had reported (see Figure 3.4). As we had suspected, normal variation in self-reported anxiety reflected real differences in the reactivity of the emergency brain.

Sonia Bishop and her colleagues at the CBU have also found that anxiety affects how well people can inhibit this activation. Using fMRI, they found that those reporting high trait anxiety could not activate the inhibitory areas of their prefrontal cortex as quickly or as effectively as those with lower levels of anxiety. This means that, for anxious people, not only does the emergency brain (amygdala) fire more quickly and strongly, but the inhibitory centres (prefrontal cortex areas) charged with dampening down this reaction are also slower to respond. On both fronts, the rainy brain of the high anxious is more reactive to potential danger.

The emergency brain is designed to help us deal with danger. Its reactivity differs markedly among people; some react instantly and for prolonged periods, whereas others have a calmer, more easygoing temperament with a fear system that only responds to a red alert. These differences are due to the vicissitudes of life and our genetic makeup, both nudging and pushing each other in subtle ways that eventually determine who and how we are. The fear system is powerful and can stop all other brain processes in their tracks as soon as danger is sensed. This is why it is so easy to activate fears and worries, as the daisy ad illustrates, and why the rainy brain can be a potent obstacle to developing a sunnier, more optimistic disposition.

CHAPTER 4

Optimism and
Pessimism Genes

Are There Genes for the Way We Are?

'Surely it's all in our genes.' So started a radio interview I was giving about a paper I had just published, which was widely reported in the media as heralding the discovery of the 'optimism gene.' The interviewer was pushing a point that many believe: there's a gene for everything; it's only a matter of finding it. Even our affective mindset, whether we are optimistic or pessimistic, might be due to a single gene. Indeed it was this idea – that hidden away in each of our cells might lurk an optimism gene or a pessimism gene – that motivated my initial studies to see whether differences in specific genes would lead to different outlooks on life.

It's a highly seductive idea. As I discovered in interview after interview, the notion that our genetic dispositions make us who we are is a story that many find appealing. It seems we have a great need to believe that it's all in our genes and therefore we can't do much about it. The techniques of modern molecular genetics now allow us to delve into the biology of our affective mind with great precision. We know that common variations in certain genes influence the functioning of brain circuits, which opens up the possibility of un-covering the genetics of who we are. It's an exciting area linking the sciences of genetics, neuroscience, and psychology. This approach allows us to get under the skin of brain circuits, to directly examine the sweeps and waves of neurotransmitters – the brain's chemical messengers – upon which they are dependent.

New facts emerge from this fast-growing science almost every day. But it turns out that asking whether our personality is down to nature or nurture really doesn't make much sense. It's a rather old-fashioned and very limited question. As unpalatable as it may be, re-search now tells us that there is no single gene for optimism or for pessimism. Instead, individual differences in our outlook emerge from an ocean of complex and multiple interactions in which our en-vironment unleashes or shuts down genes and in which genes them-selves can affect the kind of environment we experience. These processes are complex and not yet fully understood, but we have made startling advances in our knowledge of how optimistic and pes-simistic dispositions emerge. Genes matter, yes, but it's clear they don't operate in isolation. This means that our genes alone do not hold the key to the cornerstones of our personalities.

A number of different techniques have been used to figure out how our genes and environments work together in the development of our outlook on life. Twin studies have been the bread and butter of traditional genetic investigations. If we compare large numbers of identical twins (who share 100 per cent of their genes) to nonidenti-cal twins (who share 50 per cent of their genes) in terms of how pes-simistic or optimistic they feel, we can work out what proportion of their outlook is genetic. If the identical twins are more alike in terms of how pessimistic they say they feel than are nonidentical twins, then we know that, given fairly similar home environments and up-bringing, this difference has to be down to their genes.

In one of the largest studies of its kind, almost 46,000 twins and their relatives were quizzed about their level of 'neuroticism,' a key marker of the rainy-brain circuit. The genetic contribution – technically known as the *heritability* – of this personality trait was 41 per cent for women and 35 per cent for men. This means that over a third of the differences among people in how neurotic or anxious they felt was due to their genes.

I had the opportunity to test the heritability of optimism in collaboration with the Twin Research Unit at Kings College in London. Tim Spector has set up a register of more than 8,000 pairs of twins living all across the United Kingdom. In November 2009, we sent out the LOT-R questionnaire to almost all of these twins. About seven months later, the results showed that the identical twins reported more similar levels of optimism than did the nonidentical twins. Just like the results for neuroticism, the heritability of optimism turned out to be about 40 per cent.

A profound difficulty with twin studies, however, is that they don't tell us anything about the specific genes that might be important for different mental outlooks. They tell us only that genes in general play an important role.

In order to work out the exact genes involved, a logical starting point is to identify genes that affect particular neurotransmitter systems, like dopamine and serotonin, which we already know are intimately involved in the rainy- and sunny-brain networks. This is one of the big contemporary questions in neuroscience and psychology, and it received an enormous boost by the revelation of the complete human genome in 2005. This development generated great excitement and hope that we could finally pinpoint the specific genes that make us who we are. But, much to the surprise of many scientists, a host of specific genes for specific things has not been discovered. Instead, a more complex and much more intriguing story has emerged.

To get a handle of what's happening in this field, we first need to understand what a gene actually is. Originally it was seen as a unit of heritable material, but since the discovery of DNA by Francis Crick and James Watson in 1953, modern geneticists now think of a

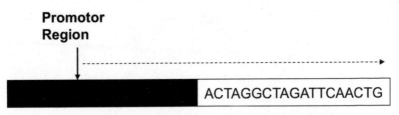

FIGURE 4.1 As shown, genes consist of a sequence of DNA consisting of C, T, A, and G bases preceded by a promotor region of DNA (the black bar).

gene as being a specific sequence of DNA. Information in DNA is stored as a code made up of four chemical bases called nucleotides: adenine (A), guanine (G), cytosine (C), and thymine (T), which are the elemental building blocks of life. When they join up with each other (e.g., A with T and C with G) these nucleotides form base pairs that are the core structure of DNA. What we call a gene is a particular sequence of these pairs preceded by what's known as the *promotor* region of DNA, as shown in Figure 4.1. DNA is passed on from generation to generation; with rare random mutations, the sequences remain constant.

Since the foundation of molecular genetics in the 1980s, geneticists have been uncovering more and more information about what genes are, how they work, and how they influence a large range of human traits and characteristics. This is science on a grand scale, and the unravelling of the complete human genome sequence in 2005 was a landmark moment in human history. If we are to journey into the bedrock of our personality, we need a road map. Until the sequencing of the human genome, this seemed like an insurmountable feat.

Many genes have normal variations that produce different effects in the body and brain. Called *single nucleotide polymorphisms*, or SNPs (pronounced 'snips'), these variations can provide vital clues to how likely someone is to develop a particular disease or even a personality trait. SNPs (see Figure 4.2) on those genes that influence

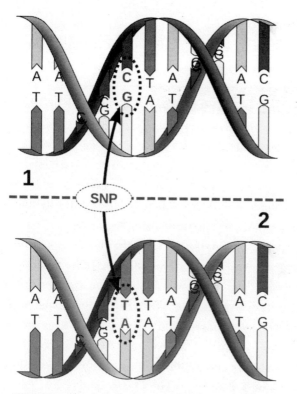

FIGURE 4.2 A diagram showing SNP. *Source:* Wikipedia.

the production of neurotransmitter systems will certainly influence how likely we are to become optimists or pessimists.

It turns out that several genes have SNPs that affect specific neurotransmitters, like serotonin and dopamine, which are involved in the functioning of the affective mind. The best known is the *serotonin transporter gene*, which modulates the level of serotonin in the brain and is associated with how resilient we are in times of stress. The *dopamine D4 receptor gene* is another gene that affects brain dopamine levels; a particular SNP on this gene is associated with the urge to do pleasurable things, like drinking alcohol or eating chocolate.

The more I learned about the startling developments in molecular genetics, the more I realised that combining the kind of psychology and neuroscience experiments I conduct in my lab with these advances in genetics was an obvious next step in unravelling the mystery of why some of us are incurably pessimistic and some are incurably optimistic. I soon discovered, however, that I had stumbled into the firing line between warring factions of molecular geneticists, with very different views on the best way forward for genetic science.

With passionate and powerful characters on both sides, the two camps of genetic science hold deeply entrenched views that they are reluctant to relinquish. In a nutshell, one camp argues that we should be guided by neurobiology and study specific genes that we know affect particular neurotransmitter systems. This is known as the *candidate gene approach*. The other camp argues that we don't know enough about the intricacies of the biology to identify the right genes to study, and therefore we should measure every single gene in a large number of people to try to identify the specific genes that predispose people to illness and disease. This is the *genome-wide association study* camp.

The search for 'vulnerability' or 'susceptibility' genes is time-consuming, costly, and difficult. The idea behind a vulnerability gene is that people who carry a particular SNP on a gene are at higher risk of developing a disease. A vulnerability gene for lung cancer, for instance, would put people at a higher risk of developing lung cancer, especially if they are exposed to cigarette smoke. Likewise, a vulnerability gene for anxiety would make people more likely to develop serious anxiety-related problems if they experience a major trauma.

In the first big breakthrough for the candidate gene approach, Danny Weinberger, an experimental psychiatrist at the National Institute for Mental Health (NIMH) in Bethesda, Maryland, studied a gene called COMT, which influences the production of dopamine in the brain. Like all neurotransmitters, dopamine is not a one-trick pony but instead involved in many functions in the brain. One of its major roles is to keep the pleasure system active; therefore, it's important for the sunny brain. But we also know that too little dopamine can cause movement problems, such as in Parkinson's disease, while too much dopamine is common in people with schizophrenia.

Weinberger and his team capitalised on the fact that schizophrenia is linked with high levels of dopamine in the brain to study a gene that varies naturally in healthy people. They knew that COMT breaks down the amount of dopamine in the brain to ensure a healthy balance but that some people have a particular version of the COMT gene that is inefficient. For people with this variant, their COMT gene works, but it's not as effective as it could be in breaking down dopamine, leaving them with relatively higher levels of dopamine in the brain, not as much as you would find in schizophrenia, but more than the average.

Weinberger's team combined this knowledge of the biological effects of the COMT gene with the knowledge that memory, as well as the amount of activity occurring in the *prefrontal cortex* (PFC) of the brain, often malfunctions in schizophrenia. They reasoned that those with the inefficient version of the COMT gene should therefore have less activity in their PFC compared to those with the efficient version; they should also have poorer memory, just like those with schizophrenia. Using brain scans and cognitive tests, they confirmed this hypothesis. Here was a group of perfectly healthy people with a version of a common gene that resulted in slightly higher levels of brain dopamine showing a pattern of brain activity that was similar to schizophrenia. The study's results raised the possibility that this particular variation of the COMT gene might be a useful early warning sign – a biological marker – for schizophrenia. Weinberger's breakthrough discovery gave a real impetus to the candidate gene approach and started a quest to find specific genes that relate to a variety of mental illnesses.

According to the candidate gene approach, if we want to understand how a gene is affecting our mind, it's better to measure a precise cognitive process or the activity of a particular brain circuit than rely on a clinical diagnosis. This is because conditions like schizophrenia or depression are expressed in so many different ways, and this variety is highly unlikely to be determined by a single gene. Take depression, with its effects on feelings, motivation, sexual desires, and physiology; it's certain that many genes and environmental factors play a role.

The candidate gene approach says that we need to look at what scientists call *intermediate phenotypes*, which are characteristics and mechanisms that are a step closer to the functioning of a gene. As a recent genetics book, *How Genes Influence Behaviour*, has put it, it's a bit like trying to find out about the source of a river when we are a long way downstream. From a distance, it's impossible to see all the way back to where the river begins. The closer we get to the foothills of the mountains, the more likely we are to get a glimpse of the source. A clinical diagnosis is like being miles away, staring back towards the distant hills, where the genes ply their trade. Intermediate phenotypes are like stopping points along the river getting us closer and closer to the original gene.

The central idea here is that there is a long string of events starting with a gene that makes a protein, which then builds a cell that helps to build a brain circuit, which ultimately helps us to see, hear, feel, and remember. All of this eventually results in the development of a particular temperament or personality and, if things go wrong, perhaps even a clinical diagnosis. Thus, the argument goes that knowing how someone's rainy-brain circuit reacts to threat brings us just a little closer to the functioning of a gene than knowing that someone has a diagnosis of depression.

Helle Larsen, a psychologist at the Behavioural Science Institute at Radboud University Nijmegen in the Netherlands, used the candidate gene approach to great effect in a clever experiment to examine the role of a particular gene in the development of alcoholism. She realised that actual behaviours, like smoking or drinking alcohol, are closer to the functioning of genes than a diagnosis such as alcoholism. Most of us will have noticed that we tend to drink more alcohol if we are surrounded by people drinking

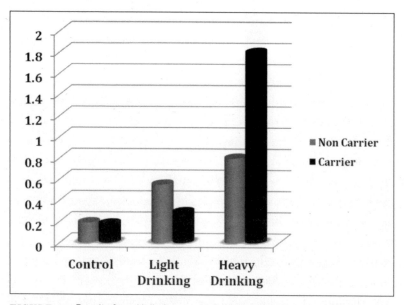

FIGURE 4.3 Results from Helle Larsen et al., 'A Variable-Number-of-Tandem-Repeats Polymorphism in the Dopamine D4 Receptor Gene Affects Social Adaptation of Alcohol Use: Investigation of a Gene by Environment Interaction,' *Psychological Science* 21 (2010): 1064–1068.

heavily. Some people who carry more than seven repeats on the dopamine receptor D4 gene (DRD4) are particularly swayed by the drinking habits of the crowd. Larsen tested one hundred students, some with the long (that is the seven-repeat) version of the gene and some without. She brought everyone into a bar, where they were accompanied by confederates of the experimenter – an old social psychology trick. The confederates either went for soft drinks (control condition), a mixture (light drinking), or only alcoholic drinks (heavy drinking) while they were supposedly waiting for the next part of the study to begin.

The results could not have been clearer. As you can see in Figure 4.3, those with the critical SNP did indeed consume far more alcohol, but *only* when they were with others who were drinking heavily. In a nice demonstration of how genes interact with environments, this variation of the DRD4 gene wires people to adapt their drinking to the pace of their peers, making it especially difficult for them to stop drinking in highly sociable contexts.

In spite of the successes of many candidate gene studies, the other camp of geneticists is not convinced by this approach. One of the most outspoken is Jonathan Flint, who runs a psychiatric genetics unit at the Wellcome Trust Centre for Human Genetics at the University of Oxford. The main problem, as he sees it, is that in large-scale studies that quiz thousands of people, single genes have only a tiny impact on personality traits. In studies of neuroticism, about 2 per cent of the differences between people can be attributed to a specific gene. Take the COMT gene, the one that Danny Weinberger claims might be a risk factor for schizophrenia. In 1996, a geneticist named Michael J. Owen and his colleagues at the Department of Psychological Medicine, University of Wales at Cardiff, measured the COMT gene in people who had schizophrenia. They tested seventy-eight patients who had schizophrenia and seventy-eight healthy people in the same age group. It turned out that 51 per cent of the schizophrenic patients had the inefficient version of the COMT gene, the supposed risky gene, but 53 per cent of the control group also had this version of the gene. As Flint points out, 'The inefficient form of the gene was not any more common in those who had schizophrenia.'

Flint and others simply don't think we know enough about the underlying biology in order to be able to pick the right candidate genes. Steven Hyman, a geneticist at Harvard University, says, 'Candidate genes are like packing your own lunch box and then looking in the box to see what's in it.' The problem is that if you pick the wrong genes, a lot of time and money is wasted. The way forward, according to scientists like Flint and Hyman, are large-scale genome-wide association studies (GWAS), which test every single gene and every single SNP in lots and lots of people. These are large-scale and time-consuming studies that cost millions of dollars to run, but they do have many advantages.

Because GWAS are conducted on very large sample sizes – usually thousands of people – we can have more confidence in the results. This is a simple fact of statistics; the more people you test, the better. Say you wanted to find out whether eating oranges reduced your chances of catching flu, and I told you that I have followed two groups of people for more than a year. Let's imagine that the two groups had the same diet and did the same amount of exercise; the only difference was that one group ate an orange every day, the other group did not. Now, after a year I have discovered that 30 per cent of the group who ate oranges have had the flu, while 50 per cent of those who had no oranges caught the flu during the previous year. You might conclude that you should eat lots of oranges next year. However, if I told you that each group contained only 10 people, so that 3 and 5 people in each caught the flu, you might be less impressed. If there were 1,000 in each group, you will almost certainly be more convinced; if there were 10,000 in each group, you would be out buying oranges. Statistics is all about estimating what is true of the entire population, and since we usually cannot test everyone, the larger the sample size, the better our estimate is likely to be. This is where large-scale GWAS win hands down.

Jonathan Flint was part of a scientific team funded by the Wellcome Trust, which conducted one of the first and the largest GWAS studies on genetics and human disease. They selected seven common illnesses and examined these in great detail. For each illness, they selected 2,000 people with the disease, making a total of 14,000 people in all. They analysed the entire set of gene variations for every person. They then selected another 3,000 control participants who were carefully matched as best as possible with the patients on a range of important factors like age, gender, lifestyle, and so on. This was a mammoth task measuring all the genes of 17,000 people.

When all of the data was analysed, it turned out that there did seem to be some key genetic markers for at least some of the diseases. For coronary artery disease, a single gene did differ between patients and controls, while eight genes differed for Crohn's disease. However, these critical genes did not determine the disease; if you had that particular variant, you did not inevitably have the disease. Instead, possession of the critical variant increased your chances statistically. But here's the rub: the degree of association was very low. Each critical gene increased the chances of having the disease by about 2 to 5 per cent. As Jonathan Flint says, most diseases seem to be influenced by many genes, but each gene on its own contributes to only a small extent. You can see why he's not convinced that studying a single gene is likely to tell us much.

There are also downsides to GWAS. Many scientists point out that these studies take a scattershot approach, throwing the net as wide as possible and seeing what comes up. There's nothing particularly wrong with this technique, especially when we don't really know what we are looking for, but it does mean that we don't have a clear hypothesis about what it is we are looking for, and having a clear hypothesis is an important principle of science. A bigger problem is that because of the sheer scale of the studies it is usually impossible to have detailed measures of brain circuits or cognitive biases. Instead, the typical method is to conduct telephone interviews with people and have them fill out some personality questionnaires. This means that the outcome measures are often not as sensitive as those used in candidate gene studies.

While we don't always know enough to pick the right genes, tremendous progress has been made in uncovering the neurobiology underlying different affective mindsets. The more we uncover about the neurotransmitters underlying mental health, the more appealing the candidate gene approach becomes. If we know that dopamine is involved in schizophrenia, or drinking alcohol, then normal variation (SNPs) on genes that affect dopamine will almost certainly influence the traits we know are associated with schizophrenia or drinking. This was Weinberger and Larsen's approach: you make a prediction, and then you set out to find whether there's any support for it. Thus, Larsen and her team predicted that those with seven repeats on the DRD4 gene would drink more when others were drinking heavily. And they did.

Ultimately, candidate gene and GWAS approaches complement each other. GWAS may well throw up potential candidate genes that can then be investigated in far greater detail by experimentation with a smaller number of people.

My own work has focused on the candidate gene approach, because it is especially useful in the search for genes underlying resilience and emotional vulnerability. I have focused on a gene called the *serotonin transporter gene* for two reasons. First, a fair amount is now known about the neurobiological effects of this gene, and second, a particular variant on this gene has been identified in a number of studies as a likely vulnerability gene for anxiety and depression. It was my work on this gene that was heralded – incorrectly, as it turns out – as the discovery of the optimism gene.

The serotonin transporter gene is one of the most intensively studied genes in neuroscience and psychiatry. Like all neurotransmitters, serotonin has many effects in the brain, but one of its critical functions is to regulate our moods. It's often called the brain's 'happy chemical.' When the functioning of this neurotransmitter goes awry, anxiety and depression can follow.

The serotonin transporter gene moderates the levels of serotonin in the brain and therefore is intimately involved in emotional regulation – controlling our ups as well as our downs. We all have it tucked away in our DNA, but each of us has a different version. Since we inherit either a *long* or a *short* version of the gene from each of our parents, there are three possible genotypes. We can have two short (SS), two long (LL), or one of each (SL). Biologically, the job of this gene is to remove excess serotonin from around brain cells. The short version is not very efficient and takes much longer to remove serotonin following a synapse. Therefore, those with two short versions (SS) have a *low-expression* form of the gene and much higher levels of serotonin hanging around in their brain. Those with two long versions (LL) have a highly efficient, or *high-expression*, genotype, and unwanted serotonin is recycled quickly and efficiently. People with one of each (SL) have an *intermediate-expression* form of the gene.

The serotonin transporter gene was in the spotlight in the very first study of how genes and environments can work together to determine how resilient or vulnerable people are to adversity. A team headed by Terrie Moffitt at the Institute of Psychiatry in London, along with her partner, Avshalom Caspi, conducted a now classic study to see if this particular gene played a role in whether people get depressed in response to life stress. They followed a group of 847 people who were participating in the Dunedin Multidisciplinary Health and Development study based in the South Island of New Zealand for a twenty-three-year period. Everybody who took part was interviewed and tested at regular intervals from the age of three across the entire twenty-three years of the study. Over the last five years of the study – when the participants were ages twenty-one to twenty-six – a particularly careful assessment was made of the number of stressful life events that each person had experienced. Anything like the death of a loved one, a serious illness, or a romantic disaster was duly noted. In the final interview of participants at age twenty-six, a detailed examination of whether anyone had experienced significant depression in the past year was carried out. It turned out that 147 of the volunteers in the study were diagnosed with clinical depression.

The big question that the researchers were interested in was whether genotype played a part. Specifically, was the low-expression (SS) form of the gene more common in those with depression? At first sight, the answer was surprising; for those who reported no major stress, the chances of being depressed was exactly the same whether someone carried two short versions, two long versions, or one of each. Low- or high-expression forms of this gene seemed to make no difference to the chances of developing depression.

A completely different picture emerged when the amount of stress that people experienced in their lives was taken into account. For those who had experienced four or more stressful experiences, the chances of depression rocketed to about 43 per cent if they carried the low-expression form of the gene. If someone had experienced more than four stressful events and had the high-expression (LL) form, their chances of getting depressed were almost halved. This tells us that there is a genuine interaction between our genetic makeup and the environment in which we live in terms of the risk of depression. Genes alone don't have much effect, but in combination with stressful life events a toxic combination emerges. Those with the less-efficient form are far more vulnerable, while those with the high-expression form appear to sail through life's adversities with few negative consequences.

Terrie Moffitt points out that we shouldn't be surprised that genes affect mental health only in combination with what life throws at us. 'We are not likely to find a gene for malaria if we look only in people who live in a malaria-free area,' she says. Likewise, if we want to find genes for depression or anxiety, or even for schizophrenia and other serious problems, we need to turn our searchlight towards people under stress. Vulnerability genes may set up a weakness, but this weakness is only exposed when our life takes a turn for the worse. GWAS typically miss this aspect of vulnerability because they rarely obtain a detailed picture of the kind of life people lead. It's therefore possible that single genes have a much bigger impact than these large-scale studies suggest.

Scientists are now turning their attention towards the study of optimism and good mental health to find out what makes us flourish. In other words, the search is on for 'resilience' or 'optimism' genes, as well as vulnerability genes. This renewed enthusiasm for the positive side of life means that we are gradually learning as much about what makes us hopeful and optimistic as what makes us despair.

Once again, a study by Avshalom Caspi and Terrie Moffitt led the way. Writing in *Science* in 2002, they describe a study in which they spoke to groups of children who either had or had not been exposed to serious child abuse. Not surprisingly, the abused children were much more likely to develop serious mental health problems. They got involved in fights, and many had been arrested for antisocial behaviour. The interesting thing was that many of the abused children did not develop any problems in spite of very serious abuse. How can this be? What was it that made this group of children more resilient?

The researchers discovered that the children's response to the horrors of abuse was strongly influenced by one particular gene called the *Monoamine-Oxidase A* gene, or the MAOA gene. Each of us has either a low-expression form or a high-expression form. For those with a high-expression form, there is better regulation of certain neurotransmitters in the brain. Children who carried this version of the MAOA gene were better able to cope with ill treatment. It was as if the gene buffered them from the adverse effects of child abuse. Children with the low-expression form were more likely to end up in the courts for violent and antisocial behaviour. Once again, it's obvious that both our genetic makeup and the type of situations we find ourselves in work together to influence how our life pans out.

The interleaving of genes and environments is also important for how our pleasure brain functions, especially in terms of how easily we can be lured into taking risks. Psychologists at the Kellogg School of Management at Northwestern University discovered a link between two genes that regulate serotonin and dopamine in the brain with risky financial decision making. Each of the volunteers was given a small amount of money they could invest in either risky or safe options, and they were rewarded with more money based on the performance of their chosen portfolio. Those with the low-expression (SS) form of the serotonin transporter gene took 28 per cent fewer risks than others, consistent with the role of the short version of this gene in risk aversion. Those with the longer (seven-repeat) version of the DRD4 gene – the one associated with higher levels of brain dopamine – took 25 per cent more risks with their money than the other volunteers. These results are remarkable when we consider that these study participants were normal people with normal variation in their genes. Yet real differences were apparent in the degree of risk that someone was willing to take based on very common genetic variations.

Ahmad Hariri, a dynamic advocate of the candidate gene approach, conducted a study to see whether the short or the long versions of the serotonin transporter gene affected how the amygdala – the emergency brain – would respond to threat. His team selected a group of fourteen people who carried at least one short version (SS or SL) and fourteen people who carried only the long version (LL) of the serotonin transporter gene. Each of the volunteers lay in a brain scanner and looked at a series of facial expressions: some fearful, some happy, some without much expression at all. As expected from Ray Dolan's earlier studies, the fearful faces elicited a strong reaction from the amygdala. However, this activation was much more vigorous in those who carried the short version of the gene. To convince themselves of their findings, they tested another two groups and ran exactly the same experiment. Once again, the amygdala reacted more strongly in those with the short version of the gene.

Those with the short form of the serotonin transporter gene have an emergency brain that reacts much more vigorously to danger, which is why they are more vulnerable when things go wrong.

In my own lab, we have probed whether this gene influences the attentional biases that we know are the cornerstones of the rainy brain and the sunny brain. Using our standard attentional probe task to assess people's biases for emotionally positive and negative pictures, we also assessed whether our volunteers had a low-, inter-mediate-, or high-expression form of the serotonin transporter gene.

The results (see Figure 4.4) showed a real difference between the different genotypes. Those with the long version (LL) – the high-

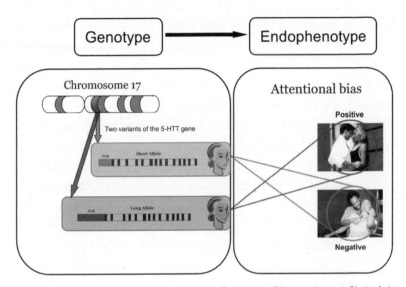

FIGURE 4.4 Image of results from Elaine Fox, Anna Ridgewell, and Chris Ashwin, 'Looking on the Bright Side: Biased Attention and the Human Serotonin Transporter Gene,' *Proceedings of the Royal Society: Biological Sciences* 276 (2009): 1747–1751.

expression form – were drawn towards positive images, while those with a short version (either SS or SL) were automatically pulled towards negative images. Unexpectedly, we also found an additional bias for avoiding certain types of images. People with an LL genotype were also drawn away from negative images. Having the high-expression version of this gene meant that a person's brain automatically tuned in to the positive while simultaneously steering clear of the negative. Those with the shorter – low-expression – version of the gene did not have this protective bias. Instead, they focused on the negative while ignoring the positive.

This study raised the possibility that the high-expression – LL – form of the serotonin transporter gene wired people for optimism. The story was picked up by Michael J. Fox, who invited me to New York to take part in a TV documentary he was making on optimism.

The producer was keen to give Michael our attentional probe task as well as determine his genotype. I duly took a DNA sample from Michael by rubbing a cotton bud inside his mouth and cheek a few times – 'fairly gross,' as he commented – and dispatched it off to the genetics lab. A day later, the results came back: Michael did indeed have the long version (LL) of this gene.

The next day, everything was ready for Michael to take our attentional probe test, and, as we expected, he showed the precise pattern of cognitive biases that we had predicted: a strong predilection to notice positive images while avoiding the negative. Not only did he look on the bright side, but he also actively, albeit unconsciously, avoided the dark.

According to our study of more than a hundred people as well as the results of testing Michael, the pattern of attentional bias associated with optimism was far more common in those who carried the high-expression version of the serotonin transporter gene. The idea that this could be an optimism gene was intriguing, but then came a twist in the tale.

A few days after I returned from New York, the geneticist who had genotyped Michael's DNA phoned me with some news. 'Michael does have the LL version of the gene,' but, he went on to explain, 'there has been a recent discovery that there are two different versions of the LL genotype.' One version, called L_a, is highly efficient in clearing serotonin in the brain, while the other, much rarer form (L_g) is inefficient and works in a similar way to the short version of the gene. In other words, people with an $L_g L_g$ genotype don't differ biologically from those with an SS genotype in terms of their brain serotonin levels, and the highly efficient genotype is $L_a L_a$. Additional analysis had shown that Michael had one copy of the rarer version, meaning that he had a moderately efficient $(L_a L_g)$ genotype, somewhere in the middle, rather than the highly efficient genotype that we had thought.

I was not overly worried, since finding the perfect result with a single person is fairly unlikely, but it did raise the question of whether simply having a long version of the gene was linked to a more optimistic bias. Or was the highly efficient form of the gene, now known to be $L_a L_a$, necessary? This would make more sense biologically.

A couple of papers were published shortly afterwards, which deepened the mystery even further. First, Danny Pine, a psychiatrist at NIMH, finalised a study similar to ours, which found that people with the low-expression form of the serotonin transporter gene (SS or $L_g L_g$) were biased towards angry faces, while those with the high-expression form ($L_a L_a$) were biased towards happy, smiling faces in the attentional probe task. Those with the $L_a L_g$ form, like Michael J. Fox, did not show the positive bias to the same extent.

In another study, Chris Beevers, a psychologist at the University of Texas at Austin, replicated our finding that those with two long versions of the serotonin transporter gene avoided negative items. However, this was only true of those with the high-expression form ($L_a L_a$) and was not found for those with the intermediate expression form, $L_a L_g$. The $L_a L_a$ version, it seemed, might push people towards a more optimistic cognitive style, and we must have been just lucky in Michael's case that he was an optimist.

This idea was compounded when I gave out the LOT-R optimism questionnaire to a bunch of students at my university and found that those with the $L_a L_g$ genotype, like Michael, said they were more optimistic than those with the $L_a L_a$ version. The real surprise was that people with the SS genotype were the most optimistic of the lot. How could this be? How could those with the so-called vulnerability gene be the most optimistic? Getting your head around conundrums like this is one of the great joys as well as one of the great frustrations of science.

Not long after this, the results from a new study we had been running for over a year came in, and it was these results that completely turned the tables on the simple notion that the $L_a L_a$ genotype might predispose people towards optimism. In the new study, we tested people with both low-expression (SS and $L_g L_g$) and high-expression ($L_a L_a$) genotypes on a task designed to change their attentional bias. This is called *cognitive bias modification* and is essentially a learning task that presents pairs of images – positive and negative – followed by a target that people have to respond to, just as in the attentional probe task. The trick is that for some people the target always appears following a nasty picture, whereas for others the target is always linked with happy, positive pictures. It doesn't take long for people to develop strong negative and positive biases depending on the type of contingencies we secretly set up in these experiments. If the target is linked with negative images, people are quick to learn to focus on these pictures rather than on positive images.

Those with the low-expression form of the serotonin transporter were much faster to learn the location of scary objects relative to those with the high-expression form. This made sense; those with the supposed vulnerability gene were more tuned in to threat. The more interesting result emerged when we looked at the groups trained to orient towards positive pictures. Would people with the $L_a L_a$ genotype, if they really are more optimistic, be tuned in to the positive and therefore learn the location of nice pictures more readily than nasty pictures? It emerged that the SS and $L_g L_g$ group were, once again, much quicker at learning the location of positive images compared to the $L_a L_a$ group. Those with the vulnerability gene were also the most responsive to the positive events.

So people with the low-expression form of the serotonin transporter were more sensitive to *both* negative and positive images. How can we explain this? How can those with a risky gene or a vulnerability gene be more tuned in to positive images? Likewise, why are those with a so-called optimism genotype less responsive to positive pictures than those with the risky version of the gene?

I soon realised that these results fit perfectly with a radical new theory that had been put forward by Jay Belsky, a psychologist at

Birkbeck College in London. Belsky had had a closer look at the various gene X environment studies and realised that they shielded a secret that no one had detected. Belsky noticed that the low-expression version of the serotonin transporter gene, as well as several other genes that influence brain neurotransmitters, make people more responsive to both good and bad environments. Most studies looking at how genes and environments interact, like the famous studies by Caspi and Moffitt, look only at negative events and the bad impact they have. When people with a particular version of a gene, like the SS genotype, turn out to be more affected by stress, it then gets labeled as a vulnerability or susceptibility gene. As Belsky points out, we also need to look at how people respond to good events. When he reexamined many studies, he discovered that hidden in the data was the finding that the very same genes that confer greater risk when things go wrong *also* confer greater benefit when things go right.

The classic study by Caspi and Moffitt found that abused children with the less efficient version of the MAOI gene engaged in the most antisocial behaviour when they were adults. What had gone unnoticed was the fact that the children with this genotype who did not suffer any maltreatment went on to engage in much *less* antisocial behaviour. Similarly, in another study conducted by Kathleen Gunthert and colleagues at the American University in Washington, it was found that students with the SS or $L_g L_g$ genotype reported far more anxiety in the evening than the $L_a L_a$ group if they had had a particularly tough day. If they had had a particularly good day, these same people reported significantly *less* stress in the evening. As Belsky suggests, those with the low-expression form of the serotonin transporter are the most susceptible to adversity but at the same time the most likely to benefit from enriching or supportive environments.

My learning experiment converges with this conclusion in showing that those with the low-expression form of the serotonin transporter are much more sensitive to the emotional background, whether it is good or bad, than are those with the high-expression version. So, rather than the serotonin transporter being a vulnerability gene or an optimism gene, if it's a gene for anything, it is likely to be a 'plasticity' gene: those with the low-expression form are simply more open and reactive to their environment and therefore will benefit more from great facilities and support but will also be more severely affected by abuse and lack of support.

These new results made more sense of what we had found with Michael J. Fox. His brain reacted in a highly optimistic way on our attention task, and he had at least one version of the low-expression form, L_g, of the serotonin transporter gene. This meant that he was highly responsive to his environment, both rewards and threats.

About a year after the TV documentary, he agreed to meet me again so that I could explain the new results, and he could tell me a bit more about the roots of his own optimism. It was a damp autumn day, and the leaves were turning brown as I made my way across Central Park to his office on the Upper East Side. Gus, an enormous but thankfully friendly dog, was the first to greet me as the door opened. Michael was looking tanned and fit as he led me down a narrow corridor to a large and comfortable room. Surrounded by pictures and Golden Globe awards, he told me that he had 'pretty much always been an optimist.' His dad had been in the military, and his family were fairly conservative. As a child, they had worried about him constantly. 'I was different,' he explained. 'I wrote stories, drew cartoons, acted, and played in a band' – completely different from his dad.

On one occasion, his father came to a gig. Afterwards, quite impressed, he asked Michael, 'Have you been paid for this?'

'Yes,' replied Michael. 'Two hundred bucks.'

'Great,' said his dad. 'What are you going to spend it on?'

'We paid four hundred bucks for an amp, so we'll have to start by paying that back.'

His dad walked away in despair.

Michael told me that his grandmother was the one who saved him from a family that did not really 'get him.'

'If you really want to know where my worldview comes from,' he said, 'you don't need to look any farther than my grandmother. She was the psychic in the family; if she said it was going to rain, everyone would bring umbrellas and raincoats.'

On one occasion when he was fairly young, spending hours drawing cartoons, Michael remembers his grandmother saying to his parents, 'Don't worry about Mike. One day he'll be famous, and people all around the world will know him.'

From that day on, Michael was given the space to do his own thing. 'It really kept the family off my back,' he said, and 'let me get on with my own thing.'

I told him about the new evidence that the L_g L_g version was more like the SS genotype and that people with this genetic makeup were much more responsive to the environment, good or bad. He agreed that his grandmother had set the tone for a supportive family environment. Even though they were not really understanding of what he was doing, her endorsement gave him the freedom to be himself. This supportive family environment allowed him to maximise his genotype, resulting in a resilient and optimistic outlook on life.

Beyond Nature and Nurture

There's little doubt that variation in our DNA sequence – our genotype – can influence physical traits such as hair colour and height as well as our personality and emotions. However, a tidal wave has surged through genetic science in recent times that overturns the traditional view that DNA is the main player in town. Instead, the fast growing field of *epigenetics* (*epi* coming from the Greek for 'above' or 'beyond') tells us that changes to how our genes operate can arise because of the things that happen to us during our lives. The surprise is that these changes can then be passed on to the next generation *without affecting the DNA sequence itself.*

The setting for this breakthrough is the remote, snow-swept regions of northern Sweden. I went there on a bicycling trip several years ago, little realising that I was travelling through an area that held a secret that would lead to a revolution in genetic science. Norrbotten, in Sweden's isolated northernmost province, is so remote that back in the nineteenth century, if the harvest failed, severe famine and starvation followed. Parish records show that starvation was common in 1800, 1812, 1821, 1836, and 1856. In marked contrast, the years 1801, 1822, 1844, and 1863 were years of abundance, and overeating was common. Lars Olav Bygren, a specialist in preventative medicine now at the Karolinska Institute in Stockholm, capitalised on these feast and famine years to examine the influence that such severe environmental conditions had on the people who lived there.

Using the meticulous Swedish records, Bygren drew a random sample of ninety-nine people who lived in the small town of Overkalix in 1905. When he examined boys who had gone from starvation during one winter to gluttony the next, he found that they produced children, and even grandchildren, whose lifespan was much shorter than the norm. When all other factors known to affect longevity were taken into account, the difference was an incredible thirty-two years. This data revealed an astonishing fact. Living through two successive winters of bust and boom as a child set off a chain of biological events that reverberated down the generations so that one's grandchildren would die years earlier than their peers.

These findings fly in the face of traditional notions of Darwinian evolution that say that genes change very slowly over many generations. Bygren has confirmed these rapid epigenetic inheritance effects in a contemporary population for which much more detailed biological records were available.

The Avon Longitudinal Study of Parents and Children (ALSPAC) is run by Jean Golding, an epidemiologist at the University of Bristol. It was designed to show how a person's genotype combines with environmental conditions to affect health and well-being. The study recruited 14,024 pregnant women in the Bristol area in 1991 and 1992, representing 70 per cent of the women who were pregnant in the region at the time, and has followed these parents and their children ever since. Bygren and Golding, working with Marcus Pembrey, a geneticist at University College London, discovered that 166 of the fathers said that they had started smoking cigarettes before age eleven, just as they were entering puberty, a time when their bodies were ripe for epigenetic changes. When they examined the children of these 166 fathers, they found that sons, but not daughters, had significantly higher body mass indices (BMIs) than other boys by the age of nine. This puts them at a higher risk of obesity and diabetes, and it's very likely that these boys will have a shorter lifespan, as did the children of parents who had two winters of famine and feast in Overkalix.

This shows us that making bad decisions when we are young not only affects our own well-being but also that of our children. Environmental events like famine, or whether we smoke, can leave an imprint on our genes that can then be passed on to the next generation. The things we experience, our diet or lifestyle, can control an array of switches or markers that switch genes on or off in powerful ways.

This goes well beyond what we know about DNA and adds a whole new dimension to genetics. It raises the prospect that people like Michael J. Fox do not have an optimism gene, as such, but rather experience life events that set off a chain of epigenetic effects that, through subtle influences on vital brain circuits, ultimately consolidate a particular worldview.

Could it really be that a good start in life can lead to a cascade of epigenetic changes tipping us towards optimism? The evidence is loud and clear that not only physical traits such as eye colour but also psychological processes like memory can be affected by epigenetics.

Renato Paro is head of the Biosystems Science and Engineering faculty at the Swiss Federal Institute of Technology in Zurich. His laboratory group discovered that by simply increasing the temperature of the fluid around a white-eyed variety of fruit fly embryo from 25 degrees Celsius to 37 degrees Celsius for a brief period, the flies who are genetically programmed to have white eyes later hatch out with red eyes. The more remarkable finding became apparent several generations down the line. When the scientists interbred these red-eyed flies with the more typical white-eyed flies, they still found red-eyed flies for up to six generations later. Remember that the DNA sequences between the white- and red-eyed flies were identical – they had not changed – but a slight increase in temperature as an embryo had led to a biological change that was felt generation after generation.

Discoveries like this are prompting a fundamental rethink of how molecular biology works. Epigenetic inheritance is not restricted to fruit flies: plants do it, animals do it, fungi do it, and even humans do it. Could my great-grandmother's high-fat diet really nudge me towards obesity? The answer, it seems, is a resounding yes.

In research led by the University of Pennsylvania neuroscientist Tracy Bale, pregnant mice were fed a very high-fat diet, and, not surprisingly, their offspring were born longer and heavier than average and were also less sensitive to insulin, both known risk factors for obesity and diabetes. Even with no further exposure to a high-fat diet, these young mice went on to produce offspring that were also larger and less sensitive to insulin. Even two generations down the line, these mice were still larger and ate more than the average mouse. As Bale commented at a Society for Neuroscience conference in 2008, 'You are not just what you eat, but what your grandmother ate.'

Psychological processes, like memory, are also affected by epigenetic changes. Larry Feig, a Tufts University biochemist, exposed mice that had genetically induced memory problems to a rich environment full of toys, exercises, and extra attention. Not surprisingly, these mice showed major improvements in memory as well as changes in a brain process called *long term potentiation* (LTP), which is fundamental for the formation of new memories. These changes also occurred in their offspring, even when they were not treated any differently themselves.

These discoveries resolve many mysteries that traditional genetics struggles to explain. Why one member of a pair of identical twins can develop a severe anxiety disorder even though the other remains well. Or why severe changes in diet in a small Swedish town could lead to dramatic changes in longevity. Geneticists are discovering more and more about these epigenetic effects and how they influence biological and psychological processes. So how does it work?

As Frances Champagne and Rahia Mashoodh of Columbia University in New York explain, we can think of our DNA as books in a library, set out along the shelves in a precise and organised sequence. These books, like DNA sequences, contain a wealth of information and inspiration for anyone who chooses to read them. Left unread, they have little effect on those around them. In the same way, DNA sits in our cells waiting to be read by an enzyme called RNA polymerase, which leads to the production of messenger RNA in a crucial process called 'transcription.' The messenger RNA is a precise copy of the DNA sequence that can be translated into a protein; this transcription is the essential expression of a gene, which can then have limitless consequences.

Without the active process that leads to gene expression, that potential may never be realised. Like a book sitting on a high shelf collecting dust, it is there but has no effect. It is only when a gene is actively expressed that its influence can be felt.

The promotor region of the gene resembles the catalogue in the library: if it's opened, all the books can be read and reordered with

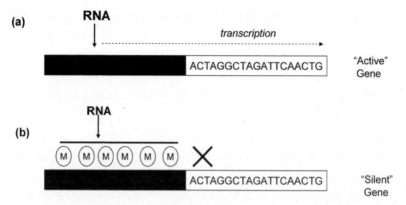

FIGURE 4.5 Illustration of the epigenetic control of gene expression. As shown in the top panel (A), genes consist of a sequence of DNA consisting of C, T, A, and G bases, preceded by a promotor region of DNA (the black bar). In order for transcription to occur, RNA must bind to the promotor region, allowing the gene to become active. As shown in the lower panel (B), when a methyl chemical group (illustrated as circles labeled *M*) attaches to the promotor region, the RNA is blocked, and the gene becomes 'silent.' The genetic code is still there; it just cannot be read.

ease; if the catalogue remains closed, the books remain unseen. A process called *DNA methylation* keeps the genes locked away. These methyl chemical groups lurking near the promotor region of a gene effectively silence the gene, shutting it down. As we can see in Figure 4.5, if RNA can easily read the promotor regions of a gene, this leads to transcription, and the gene then springs into life. If the methyl chemicals block the promotor region, the RNA cannot see the gene, leaving it unexpressed.

It's the environment around the DNA that influences whether a gene will be read or not, and of course it's the environment around the person that influences the environment around the DNA. This is why genes rarely have direct effects on complex behaviours. The journey from a single gene to a change in neurotransmission, to a fine-tuning of neural circuits, to the expression of a sunny disposition is a long and complex road affected by many factors, including other genes, life events, and epigenetic factors. Epigenetics is beginning to uncover how gene–environment interactions unfold over time. In other words, it's not so much the genes you are born with that count, but which of those genes end up being expressed and which remain silent. Your baby may be born with a certain set of genes, but what happens next can influence what particular genes get expressed and which don't.

Can epigenetic changes really make us more or less optimistic? The evidence suggests that this is so. Studies with rats have shown that variations in maternal care have a profound effect on the brain and how it responds to stress. A loving mother rat spends hours licking and cuddling her young, quickly retrieving them if they roll out of the nest. A colder mother spends much less time licking and caring. When gene expression is analysed in baby rats that have experienced these different types of maternal care, there are startling differences in the sets of genes that are expressed.

A fascinating series of studies by Ian Weaver and his colleagues at the McGill Program for the Study of Behaviour, Genes and Environment in Montreal, Canada, has revealed that warm or cold mothering can make a huge difference to the expression of genes that are related to how well we deal with stress. Deep inside the hippocampus, an area of the brain important for learning and memory, we find large amounts of what are called *glucocorticoid receptors* (GR). A bit like stress switches, they can turn the stress response on or off. Lower than normal levels of GR receptors results in an extended response to stress. Instead of getting over things quickly, we tend to dwell on problems.

If we have lots of GR receptors in our hippocampus, it seems we can deal with stress much more easily. Weaver looked at the hippocampal area of young rats and discovered that poor maternal care resulted in elevated levels of DNA methylation in the promotor area of the GR gene. This is a vital process that silences a gene. The implications are profound. A classic environmental effect – maternal care – had a strong effect on how the young deal with stress. What looks like a pure effect of nurture is actually nurture working its magic by changing the expression of genes.

Most epigenetic research has been conducted with rodents, but as Bygren's Swedish data indicated, it's clear that the same mechanisms hold true for humans. Tim Oberlander, from the paediatrics department at the University of British Columbia in Canada, carefully extracted cells from the foetal cord blood in pregnant women. Some of these women were suffering from depression, and some were not. The foetal cells were meticulously examined for the telltale signs of DNA methylation – the process that turns genes off. Sure enough, maternal depression and anxiety during the third trimester resulted in increased levels of DNA methylation. This increased methylation of the GR gene promotor region is the crucial process that silences genes in the hippocampus, making these children more vulnerable to stress.

When, three months later, the scientists followed up with the infants of the women who had experienced antenatal depression, these babies were indeed far more stressed out than the babies of the less depressed mothers. Even when the reduced mother-baby interactions that are typical with maternal depression were taken into account, the link between DNA methylation and the stress response was still there. What happens to us even at a very young age can have long-lasting effects. These influences are the effects of the environment, yes, but they are the effects of the environment working *through our genes*.

Ironically, scientists have known about epigenetic effects for a long time. Cells in the liver and the brain contain the same DNA but do very different jobs. It is only recently that the importance of this malleability has been realised. And the possibilities of epigenetic changes open up a brave new world, where our choices in life not only have profound effects on which of our own genes whisper or shout but also influence the genetic expression of our children and our children's children.

CHAPTER 5

The Malleable Mind

The Remarkable Plasticity
of the Human Brain

The human brain has startling capacity to change. For many years, neuroscientists believed that after a certain age – possibly as young as seven – our brain became inflexible and set in its ways. The burgeoning field of neuroplasticity, however, has completely overturned this notion and shown us that even very old brains are far more flexible than ever imagined. This is not a superficial change at the level of ephemeral thoughts. Instead, this is a real change in physical structure. Neurons, and connections of neurons, respond to the things we do and even the things we think, resulting in real changes in the way that brain circuits operate. The circuits underlying fear and pleasure – our rainy and sunny brains – are especially malleable. This means that our personal experiences with fear and pleasure provide us with a unique brain with our own highly individualised set of circuits and connections. Each of us responds to fear and pleasure in a tailor-made way, and this fundamental difference in how our affective mind responds shapes our interpretation of the world around us. We now know that if we change our cognition, we can also reshape our brains.

There are more than 25,000 streets in London, arranged in a complex maze of junctions and byways that have developed through the years. There is no easy symmetry as you find in New York City, with its easy-to-navigate horizontal and vertical patterns of streets and avenues. Yet, jump in a Black Cab – London's iconic taxis – anywhere in the city, and the driver will get you to where you want to go via the shortest possible route. This feat of spatial navigation does not come easily. Only those who have passed The Knowledge, a test of the ability to memorise and spatially navigate every one of those 25,000 streets, are allowed a license to drive a Black Cab. The Knowledge is so difficult that only half of those who attempt it pass.

In 2000, Professor Eleanor Maguire, a cognitive neuroscientist at University College London, tested sixteen Black Cab drivers in an fMRI brain scanner. She found that the back part of their hippocampuses was substantially larger when compared with other people's. This is the part of the brain that is associated with spatial navigation in birds and animals as well as in humans. Even more remarkable, Maguire found that the size of the hippocampus got correspondingly larger the longer a cabbie had spent in the job.

Following up on this research, Maguire examined the progress of trainee taxi drivers as they were in the process of learning The Knowledge. Again using fMRI, she scanned the drivers' brains as they started the course and then once more, as they were nearing completion of the course. Maguire and her team discovered that those drivers who showed the greatest alteration in the hippocampus were most likely to succeed. This is strong evidence that our unique experience really does lead to real and profound changes in the physical structure of the brain.

Even stronger confirmation comes from studies with professional musicians. Performing music is a complex business. With the requirement to produce hundreds of notes per minute, it is one of the most impressive of all human achievements. Studies using high-resolution MRI brain scans show us that the brains of musicians and nonmusicians differ in significant ways. Several of the brain areas that are involved in hearing complex sounds or in producing detailed motor movements are much larger in musicians than in nonmusicians. You might think that this is a preexisting condition; musicians are musicians precisely because they are born with a brain that gives them a talent for music. This is not the case. Research shows that the size of these brain regions correlates with the amount of practice undertaken: the more practice, the larger these areas of the brain.

The dark side of this plasticity in the brains of musicians is a condition known as *focal dystonia*. This is where a string player might lose the ability to move one finger independently of another. The condition develops because of the way different parts of the body are represented along a thin strip of the brain called the *somatosensory cortex*. In this layer, there is a topographical map of all parts of the body, with lips, arms, hands, fingers, etc., all having a dedicated small amount of cortical tissue set aside to ensure that they are functioning efficiently. Normally, each finger has its own small region of this cortical space, with each region cleanly separated from the next. However, when two fingers are constantly used together, as in guitar playing, the cortical maps gradually grow and enlarge and can become fused together. The somatosensory cortex begins to 'see' the two fingers as a single unit and so represents them in a single cortical map. This leaves the guitarist unable to manipulate each finger separately.

With the discovery of neuroplasticity, we can see that the human brain is capable of far more flexibility than previously thought. Our brains never cease responding to new things, continuing to learn and change from the moment we are born to the day we die. The complex networks of neurons and pathways of nerve fibres inside our heads constantly respond and adapt and rearrange themselves, and this flexibility presents us with fantastic opportunities to change our outlook.

Neuroplasticity is a double-edged sword, however, since, if we do not challenge our brain with new things, beliefs and ways of doing things become entrenched and difficult to shift. If we do not use parts of our brain, these brain areas will gradually be taken over by other functions. But if we do make the effort, even deeply embedded circuits have the potential to change.

Several studies now confirm the central truth of the old wives' tales that tell of superior hearing in those who are blind. Scanning the brains of blind people reveals that the area of cortex right at the back of the brain, the part that normally responds only to visual information (the visual cortex), also responds to auditory input. Sets of neurons that normally spring into action when we *see* something now fire when blind people *hear* something. Cortical real estate, as it's sometimes called, does not lie dormant in the absence of signals coming from the outside world; instead, other senses and activities capitalise on the spare resources. In the case of someone who is blind, what was once reserved for vision is now taken over by hearing.

Alexander Stevens and his colleagues at the Health and Science University in Portland, Oregon, gave blind people cues to listen for faint sounds when they were in a brain scanner. He found that when the alert was given, blood raced to the back of their brain, the area normally reserved for vision. Listening to music or speech not only stimulated the auditory cortex but also activated brain cells that previously only fired to visual signals. Sounds therefore create a double whammy in the brain of the blind.

The opposite is also true. Neuroscientist Helen Neville, also at the University of Oregon, wondered whether deaf people might develop better vision. Would the ability to detect things in the periphery improve in order to compensate for not being able to detect sounds coming from the left or right? Neville flashed lights in the peripheral vision of people who had been deaf since early childhood, as well as of people with typical hearing. When she measured the response of different parts of the cortex to these flashes, parts of the auditory cortex – those areas normally reserved for processing sounds – were now reacting to visual input. Vision in the periphery was indeed enhanced in these deaf people. The tantalising conclusion is that neurons in parts of the brain that are no longer needed are recruited to perform other tasks for people who have lost a major sense.

Ironically, William James, the founder of experimental psychology in the United States, preempted the contemporary notion of brain plasticity back in 1890, when he wrote that the brain is 'endowed with a very extraordinary degree of plasticity.' Because he did not have hard evidence to support his claim, however, it got lost in the mists of time. That is, it was lost until two British neuroscientists conducted some groundbreaking experiments that gave an early clue that the way our brain is wired might be as unique as our fingerprints. Thomas Graham Brown and Charles Scott Sherrington set out in 1912 to see whether the parts of the cortex that deal with movement might be fairly rigid or whether these cortical areas might be shaped by an individual's own particular experiences. Could it be, they wondered, that the way we do things changes the way our brain works?

Imagine that one monkey preferred picking things up with its thumb and forefinger, while another monkey preferred using the thumb and middle finger. Would slightly different areas of the motor cortex take control of the hand's movement? Brown and Sherrington used electrodes to stimulate different areas of the motor cortex in a group of their lab monkeys and recorded which muscle twitched after each zap. If the area of motor cortex dealing with the hand was set in stone, then the same area should move the hand in all monkeys. However, if the individual's own particular experience had changed the way the brain was wired, then each monkey would have a slightly different area of cortex responsible for the hand. Sure enough, they discovered that the area of motor cortex dedicated to movement was unique to each monkey. Here was a vital clue that the brain's organisation was a reflection of each animal's unique history and experience.

Just a few years later, in 1916, the American psychologist Shepherd Ivory Franz found something similar. On the basis of his studies with monkeys, he realised that particular functions were *not* localised in specific areas of the cortex as everyone thought. But he was ignored. The scientific community at the time was just not ready for this message. There was also a genuine scientific concern that the monkeys had simply been born like that, which limited enthusiasm for these findings. Perhaps each monkey's genetic code had produced a slightly different motor cortex, which was then more or less set in stone for that monkey's entire life. (Remember, this was way before the discoveries of modern-day epigenetics.) If that were the case, then the results didn't tell us anything about brain plasticity.

Evidence did emerge seven years later, which demonstrated beyond much doubt that each of us can develop unique brain circuits based on our life experiences. Karl Lashley, one of the most influential of the early American psychologists, had worked with Franz in his early studies at the Government Hospital for the Insane in Washington, DC. He is best known for his obsession to find the *engram*, or physical trace of memory in the brain. Convinced that memories must be laid down in specific areas in the brain, he spent years trying to find this spot. He never did, and this failure led him to consider the possibility that memories, and perhaps other functions, might not be localised in specific parts of the brain after all.

In an important series of studies, he zapped the same monkey's brain on several occasions over a period of several months. He discovered that the same muscles were moved by different parts of the motor cortex at different times in the same monkey. These results dovetailed nicely with the findings of Brown and Sherrington, as well as with Franz's work, which had shown that different areas of the cortex developed in different monkeys. But they were of much greater consequence in that they overturned the possibility that different monkeys had been born with different cortices.

By showing that areas of the motor cortex changed over time in the same individual, Lashley had demonstrated that brain processes were not set in stone. Instead, they were highly malleable and fluid. In a portent of what was to come years later, he developed the principle of 'mass action,' in which he argued that the cortex acts as a whole and that if one part is damaged, another part will take over the role of the damaged portion. This is exactly what we now know occurs in the brains of the deaf and the blind.

A conceptual framework for Lashley's ideas only came years later, when the Canadian psychologist Donald Hebb published his classic book, *The Organisation of Behaviour*, in 1949. Hebb was interested in how learning and memory take place and realised that some structural change had to happen between neurons in order for learning to occur. If we learn a new skill, like riding a bike, some change must take place in our brain. He thought that if a group of neurons were repeatedly stimulated at the same time, then an active circuit, or what he called a 'cell assembly,' might develop. If this circuit gets fired up over and over again, eventually it should become stronger and stable. Imagine a child pressing a particular key on a piano and hearing a specific note. The more the action of pressing that particular note and hearing that particular sound become linked, the stronger the network of neurons involved in hearing the sound and initiating the action will become. When a neuron fires, other neurons associated with that neuron are also more likely to fire. As later commentators have phrased it, 'Cells that fire together wire together.'

In effect, Hebb was proposing that the efficiency of a synaptic connection would increase and become more effective the more often it was used. The converse was also true: if circuits were not regularly used, they would gradually fade away. This seems straightforward to us now, but it was a revolutionary idea for the time and essentially laid the foundations for the contemporary science of neuroplasticity. Somewhat surprisingly, even with all of this mounting evidence, it still took more than thirty years for the plasticity of the brain to become widely accepted in psychology and neuroscience.

When I was studying neuroscience at university in the 1980s, the common wisdom was that brain circuits were only malleable at a very young age. If brain damage occurred after the age of about seven, there was little hope of recovering function. We were taught about the wondrous plasticity of the young brain as shown by the famous Hubel and Wiesel experiments that had been published in the 1960s. Torsten Wiesel had been a Swedish medical scientist working at the Karolinska Institute before he moved in 1958 to a large neurophysiology laboratory at Harvard University, where he began working with David Hubel from Ontario, Canada. It was here they began the series of studies that would culminate in their being awarded the Nobel Prize in 1981. They carefully stitched closed the lids of one eye in a number of kittens at around three to five weeks of age, depriving that eye of any visual stimulation. The eye was reopened when the cats were six months old. They found that activity in the visual cortex usually dedicated to the closed eye was suppressed, leaving the kitten completely blind in that eye. Even though the kittens were born with a perfectly functioning eye and a perfectly functioning visual cortex, it seemed as if they still had to 'learn to see.'

These results were clear proof that if an area of cortex was not used, it soon lost its ability to function. This discovery of a critical period for visual development revolutionised medicine and made doctors realise the importance of intervening in cases of early cataracts or other visual problems in children. The important discovery emerging from these experiments for our purposes was the lesser known fact that the part of the cortex responsible for the closed-up eye did not remain inactive. Instead, it had begun to process signals coming from the open eye. In a classic demonstration of neuroplasticity, the brains of these kittens had rewired themselves so that no cortical space was left idle. The amount of cortex dedicated to the open eye was much larger than normal.

These experiments revealed two important things about how the brain works. First, there is a critical period in development when sensory stimulation is necessary in order for sensory systems to develop normally. Second, the brain is highly flexible and plastic during this critical period. Neurologists for many years assumed that if brain damage occurred during this vital period, the chances of recovery would be fairly good, but that once the brain had wired itself by the end of the critical period, change was impossible. Ironically, Hubel and Wiesel themselves were at the forefront of this notion that brain plasticity in adulthood, or even in late childhood, was well nigh impossible.

We now know that this assumption is wrong. In a much-discussed series of studies at the University of Helsinki, the neuroscientist and psychologist Teija Kujala has shown that major changes do take place in the visual cortex, even in mature brains, in response to sounds. The studies conducted by Helen Neville and Alexander Stevens had shown that cross-modal reorganisation does occur in the cortex. When blind people listen, parts of the visual cortex respond; when deaf people look, areas of their auditory cortex fire into action. However, all of the people tested in these studies were blind or deaf from a very early age, and so the plasticity might have occurred during the critical period. What Kujala and his team at the Cognitive Brain Research Unit in Helsinki set out to do was to find out if the same thing would happen in people who lost a sense well after the critical period.

When they asked people who were blinded in adulthood to discriminate between sounds, they found strong activity in the visual cortex – areas of the brain dedicated to vision were now reacting to sounds. This means that people who became blind even in late adulthood developed more acute hearing. The parts of their brain that normally dealt with vision were now free to help out with hearing. This is still highly controversial work, and many scientists are not convinced that it's really possible.

I have discussed this work with Harvard neurologist Alvaro Pascual-Leone, who is one of the world's leading scientists in the field of neuroplasticity. I invited him to come to England to open our new Centre for Brain Science at the University of Essex in 2009. Alvaro is a bright and youthful scientist who comes to life when talking about brain research, neural plasticity, and Spanish food and wine. Born in Valencia in Spain, he studied medicine and neurophysiology in Germany before moving to the University of Minnesota to train in neurology. His innovative program of work has provided some of the strongest evidence we have that the type of neural plasticity often observed in monkeys can also occur in the human brain.

Following a scintillating talk to a rapt audience, we held a reception in our new centre. 'What about this claim that neuroplasticity can occur even in adulthood?' I asked him.

Not only did he think that Kujala's findings were solid, but he made the even more startling claim that the visual cortex can be activated in response to tactile information in people who have been blindfolded for just a week. He told me about an experiment they had conducted at the Beth Israel Deaconess Medical Center in Boston. A small group of volunteers were persuaded to wear a blindfold – *all the time* – from Monday morning to late on Friday. During this time, these people participated in a variety of experiments, such as learning Braille and other cognitive tasks, as well as eating, drinking, and sleeping and trying to live as normally as possible.

Before the start of the study, the visual cortex of these volunteers did not respond when they thought about a poem, touched something, or listened to music, which is exactly what you would expect. A week later, it was a different story. Now when they tried to distinguish between two tones, or when they touched something, their visual cortex sprung into action. Just one week of 'blindness' had an impact on the wiring of their brain. Even Alvaro was surprised by the results.

'It's unlikely that new connections really formed in just a week,' he told me. It was more likely that little used connections were brought back to life and reengaged. This work remains unpublished, and Alvaro himself says that further research needs to be conducted to look at the mechanisms in more detail. If verified, these results are truly remarkable, suggesting that changes in cortical plasticity can occur extremely rapidly.

The evidence for neural plasticity, even in adults, is growing. This science raises the possibility that major new treatments might be developed for a range of degenerative brain disorders, such as Parkinson's and Alzheimer's disease. My own hunch is that mental health problems like anxiety and depression might also be helped by the power of plasticity.

As if this is not dramatic enough, it has also been discovered that brand-new brain cells can be produced even when we are old. It's one thing to modify entrenched neural pathways, but can new brain cells really be made? While my neuroscience teachers in the 1980s were clear that the brain was fixed once the critical period was over, they were even more adamant in their assertion that brain cells could never be regenerated. 'Once a brain cell dies, it's not replaced,' we were told repeatedly. This is why the impact of brain damage is so devastating and long lasting. All of this is now being questioned, as rapid developments in neuroscience open up controversial but exciting new areas of exploration. Could *neurogenesis* – the development of *new* neurons – be possible?

According to Fred Gage, who heads a large neuroscience laboratory at the Salk Institute in La Jolla, California, 'we are not limited to the neurons we are born with.' Instead, 'even the adult brain can generate new brain cells.' Gage came to these conclusions on the basis of experiments he conduced with young mice. For mice, there's nothing better than discovering a world full of tunnels, toys, and spinning wheels that they can run on as often as they like. It was already known that mice reared in these enriched environments had larger cortices, mainly as a result of an increased density of synaptic connections in their brains. Just as neuroplasticity research predicts, learning and having fun led to increased connections in the brain.

Gage then divided mice into two groups: one lived for forty-five days in the interesting fun environment, while the other spent forty-five days in comfortable, but rather barren, cages. The results were startling: the mice placed in the enriched environment grew about three time more cells in their hippocampus than did mice left in their normal environment. It is not yet fully understood whether this neurogenesis is due to increased activity and fitness, or increased social interaction, or even to less stress. Whatever the reason, the really intriguing question is: Could the same thing happen in the far more complex human brain?

Realising that this was the big question, Fred Gage spent a lot of time thinking about how they could possibly find the answer. The breakthrough came at one of the coffee breaks at the lab, when Gage was chatting with a Swedish neurologist, Peter Eriksson, who was visiting the Salk Institute for a sabbatical year. It dawned on Eriksson that cancer specialists often injected the brains of seriously ill patients with a substance that would light up any new malignant cells being produced in their brains. But this substance did not differentiate whether the new cells it was highlighting were cancerous or not. Eriksson realised that any new brain cell that was formed would be lit up in fluorescent green. The problem was that the cancer specialists only took biopsies of the cancer cells, so the only way to check whether new healthy cells had also been produced would be to examine slices of brain tissue after the patient had died.

This is what Eriksson did when he returned to the University of Gothenburg in Sweden after his sabbatical. At the Sahlgrenska University Hospital, he explained the study to a number of terminally ill patients with brain cancer, and some agreed to donate their brains to science after their death. In total, five of these people who had had the appropriate treatment died. The brain tissue of these patients, in their late fifties to over seventy, now held the answer to whether new neurons could be produced in humans.

Eriksson and his team removed thin slices of brain tissue from the hippocampus area of each of these individuals during an autopsy. These slices were then flown across the Atlantic to Gage's lab in California. The tension and excitement in the lab must have been palpable when the brain tissue was placed under the microscope for the first time. Sure enough, the telltale signs of brand-new cells glowing green under the microscope were apparent as slide after slide was examined. As Gage told a small conference in 2004, 'All of the brains had evidence of new cells exactly in the area where we'd found neurogenesis in other species.'

Even though some of these people were over seventy years old – and dying from cancer – parts of their brain were still busily producing new brain cells. The message is that the brain never ceases to change and respond. We can, it seems, teach old dogs new tricks after all.

While much of the work on neuroplasticity has concentrated on such cognitive skills as improving memory and attention span, as well as motor skills, it does raise the exciting possibility that the neural pathways underlying pessimism and optimism could also be modified.

The functioning and reactions of our sunny brain and rainy brain networks tell us that we all share a natural tendency to seek out pleasure and to avoid danger. Even the humble earthworm moves towards good (warmth) and moves away from bad (cold). What we also know is that each of us lies along a spectrum of reactivity, with people differing markedly in how strongly they respond to both fear and fun. Some will do almost anything for a reward, oblivious to danger, while others are highly adverse to risk. These differences lie at the root of our affective mindset, and ultimately they are what nudge us onto the different journeys and trajectories our lives may take. If these affective brain circuits are also malleable and open to change, we have the possibility of profoundly changing our outlook on life.

There are several subtle clues, as well as solid evidence, that the circuits underlying the sunny brain and rainy brain are indeed open to change. It is abundantly clear that each of us has a brain that is unique. Even as a scientist interested in individual differences, I was surprised by this discovery. When you look at raw brain scans, the first thing that strikes you is that some brains are bigger than others, they all have slightly different shapes, and none look like the pristine symmetrical images you see in the scientific journals. By averaging several different brain scans – maybe images from twenty different people all overlaid one on top of the other – the typical view you see in the science journals and books airbrush out all the messy details of individuality.

Individual brain scans tell a different story. As well as overall shape and size, the location and number of important chemical receptors also differ dramatically from person to person, from brain to brain. Some people have a greater preponderance of dopamine receptors in their pleasure brain, some have an amygdala that reacts to the faintest hint of danger, and others need a serious and imminent threat to get their amygdala going.

The brain circuits that regulate our emotional response develop in an individualised way for each of us. All of our joys, fears, thoughts, and dreams merge together over time to shape our affective mind, producing a unique set of brain circuits that makes us who we are. While these circuits sit in roughly the same place for all of us and involve the same structures – the PFC, the amygdala, the NAcc – the degree to which they react to events, good or bad, varies dramatically from person to person. It is these highly reactive and flexible circuits that form the wellsprings of our personalities and our outlook on life.

The circuits that make up our rainy brain and our sunny brain highlight what's important, tuning us in to the motivational landscape of our environment. The amygdala, working in tandem with the nucleus accumbens – our panic button and our pleasure button – help us figure out what's bad and what's good in our environment. In an ever-changing world, even the slightest imbalance, the tiniest shift of focus towards the positive or the negative aspects of the motivational landscape, can tilt a myriad of brain circuits, strengthening or weakening connections and circuits within our rainy brain or our sunny brain. It is this tilting of these circuits that underlies the development of the 'glass half-empty' or the 'glass half-full' mindset that can have such a profound impact on our lives.

During our evolutionary history, our cortex grew at an exponential rate while simultaneously developing numerous connections with ancient subcortical brain regions. As the cortex increased in size, a myriad of connections developed that linked our enlarged cortex with the more ancient structures that drive our emotions and our responses to pleasure and threat. This means that the amygdala and the NAcc have not remained unchanged since they first evolved millions of years ago; they are no longer 'Stone Age,' as is often assumed. Enhanced connections and neurotransmitters cascade from the higher cortical regions to the emergency and pleasure-seeking brains, allowing for some degree of regulation of these areas. This means that we can learn to regulate our fears and excitements to a much greater extent than other animals can. While a cat finds it virtually impossible not to chase a mouse, we generally can suppress our primal urges when the context dictates.

Nevertheless, our fear and pleasure circuits are fiercely dominant forces in our brain. Our rainy brain in particular reveals its plasticity with its unrivalled capacity to instil fear in superquick time. Scary things are learned and remembered easily. Nature could have orchestrated a system in which all dangers are hardwired into our brain so that response is instant, with no need for detailed analysis.

That system works well for some creatures, but the downside is that it's highly inflexible. If the world changes, even slightly, you're in big trouble.

Instead, the learning power of our fear brain, when combined with the phenomenal flexibility that our large cortex allows, gives us humans a real edge in adapting to changing circumstances. If the world changes, it doesn't take us long to figure out what we need to do to cope. This is why we are the only species on earth that can live in virtually any climate. The fusion of newer cortical areas with ancient fear circuits – our rainy brain – makes for superfast learning.

Even with the brain's significant capacity for learning, evolution still pulls the strings. Thus, our brain is prepared to learn some things more than others; it is not a blank slate that learns everything equally. The fear system stacks the cards in favour of ancient dangers. This predisposition plays a significant role in shaping our cognitions and beliefs about the world. Our pleasure brain also has a powerful effect on shaping our cognitions and behaviours. However, because fear has an edge over pleasure, and because science knows much more about the brain circuits underlying fear relative to any other emotion, we shall concentrate on the fear system to illustrate how our affective mind controls our life.

Fear orchestrates and shapes a wide range of our behaviours. These include social learning – what we learn to fear or not to fear most easily – our beliefs about the world, our memories of what has happened, our prejudices, and even our health and well-being. Psychologists have learned a tremendous amount about how fears can be learned and unlearned, and much of this knowledge has come from a surprisingly simple experimental procedure. Known as *fear conditioning*, this task shows us how responsive and flexible fear learning can be, and why it plays such a dominant role in shaping our lives.

In the famous 'Little Albert' experiment, the behavioural psychologist John B. Watson and his graduate student Rosalie Raynor exposed a young infant, Albert, to a number of objects like a burning newspaper, a monkey, a rabbit, and a rat. Little Albert did not appear to be particularly afraid of any of them. The psychologists then made a loud noise every time the white rat was shown, and this clearly frightened Albert. Before too long, a deep fear of the rat was instilled. As Watson and Raynor write: 'The instant the rat was shown, the baby began to cry.'

Nowadays, psychologists are reluctant to frighten babies, instead scaring the life out of laboratory rats and mice in the quest to understand the nature of fear. Figure 5.1 shows the typical scenario in fear conditioning. A rat is first habituated to the testing chamber, and no signals are given. Once the rat is relaxed and used to its surroundings, a nonscary thing like a specific tone is presented. The animal usually does not react much. This is called the 'conditioned stimulus' (CS).

The next stage is when the CS is sounded at the same time as something that is naturally scary, like a mild shock to the feet. An electric shock will typically elicit a freezing reaction, the classic fear response in rats, and hence is called an *unconditioned stimulus* (US). Once the US and the CS – the tone and the shock – occur together a couple of times, the rat gradually becomes conditioned to freeze in response to the tone alone. Just as Little Albert developed a fear of the white rat, rats in these conditioning studies quickly develop a fear of the sound itself – a conditioned fear.

Once a conditioned fear has developed, it does not last forever. If the tone is presented again and again without any electric shock, the fear response gradually diminishes and disappears. In a process known as extinction, the more the tone occurs without the shock, the more likely the fear is to disappear. If this did not happen, we would end up with many more fears than we need.

Imagine that you get a sting from a bee lying unseen in your bath towel. For several days, you are likely to remain wary of the towel, carefully examining it for hidden bees. Over time, your fear of the

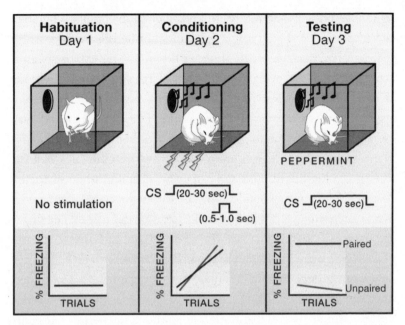

FIGURE 5.1 Illustration of an auditory fear-conditioning procedure. Rats are habituated to the chamber on day 1 (no stimulation). On day 2, the rat receives a small number of training trials (typically 1–5) in which a tone CS is paired with a foot-shock US. Control animals receive unpaired presentations of the CS and the US. On day 3, the CS is presented in a novel chamber with a unique odour (peppermint), and fear response (freezing) to the CS is assessed. Animals that received a shock with the tone (paired) on day 2 show high levels of freezing, but animals receiving unpaired training show little freezing. *Source:* J. Johansen, Christopher Cain, Linnea Ostroff, and Joseph E. LeDoux, 'Molecular Mechanisms of Fear Learning and Memory,' *Cell* 147 (2011): 509–524.

towel will diminish, and eventually you will start drying yourself immediately on coming out of the shower without a second thought. This ability to unlearn fears is an essential feature of our fear system.

Interestingly, fear memories do not seem to be completely forgotten. Rather, extinction itself is an active learning process in which the new, safe memory supplants the old, fear memory. University of Vermont psychologist Mark Bouton conditioned rats to a tone in one chamber and then extinguished their fear responses in another.

When the critical tone was presented again in the original chamber, the fear came rushing back. Even though it had been successfully extinguished elsewhere, the link with the original context was so strong that the fear was easily reinstated. The fear memory had not been erased; it was instead overlaid with a new memory.

Results like these explain how human fear can return suddenly in the most inappropriate situations. Remember my Northern Irish friend Sandra all those years ago? In spite of all the cues that she was safe, a fear association was instantly reinstated when she heard a car backfire. Even though she was in Dublin, not Belfast, and it was many years later, that primordial fear signal still had her diving for cover.

Neuroscience is starting to uncover the brain mechanisms that support this kind of fear learning and why it is so deeply embedded. It comes as no surprise that the amygdala, which is highly involved in the rainy brain, is also involved in how we learn to fear. Damage to even one tiny part of the amygdala – known as the *basolateral nuclei* – can severely disrupt fear learning. Should this region be surgically impaired in rats, the animals will no longer acquire a conditioned fear response. Their reaction to the electric shock itself remains perfectly normal, but no fear response to the associated tone develops. This shows us that in order to learn to be afraid, we need this tiny section of the amygdala.

Things get more complex when we examine research with fear conditioning in more detail. It turns out, for example, that the wider context in which fear learning takes place is also important. This is why a friend of mine can still remember the smell of the perfume her doctor was wearing when she was given the news that she had cancer. Even many years later, the scent of that perfume elicits unhappy, frightening memories.

Such contextual fear associations depend on a separate, also ancient, area of the brain called the *hippocampus*, which lies fairly close to the amygdala and, as we saw with London taxi drivers, is crucial for memory. People who damage this area of the brain following a stroke generally develop severe short-term memory problems. If the hippocampus is surgically removed in rats, fear conditioning to the tone occurs quite normally, but no fear response develops to the context. The hippocampus allows us to learn about the wider context in which fear takes place, while the amygdala is the brain area that's essential for learning to be afraid of specific things.

Similar conditioning procedures are used in human research when a mild electric shock or a loud noise is presented when something such as a photograph (CS) is being viewed. A typical outcome measure used in human research is the sweatiness of the hands, called the galvanic skin response (GSR), which is a classic indicator of stress and fear in humans. When an innocuous photograph is consistently presented with an electric shock, people quickly develop a fear response, as measured by their GSR, to the pictures alone. As with rats, these fear responses diminish gradually if the pictures are continually presented without the natural stressor.

In one study conducted in my lab, people were shown pictures of knives, guns, snakes, and spiders to try to work out whether they would learn to fear contemporary threats as quickly as they learned to fear ancient threats. Every time particular pictures – a specific gun or a specific snake – came up on the screen, a loud aversive noise would also be presented. The fear response, as measured by the GSR, was picked up quickly for pictures of snakes as well as pictures of guns. As the experiment progressed, a difference emerged between the ancient and contemporary threats. When we looked at the typical pattern of extinction – how long it took for the fear to disappear – it became obvious that the fear of snakes was much harder to switch off than the fear of guns. Many more trials presenting the pictures without the aversive tone were necessary in order to eliminate the fear response to snakes relative to guns. Here is proof, yet again, that our fear system is not democratic: ancient threats exert a stronger hold on the mechanisms of learning.

Nowhere is this more obvious than in a classic experiment conducted by Susan Mineka, a psychologist who is now at Northwestern University, with Michael Cook when they were both at the University of Wisconsin–Madison. In an elegant experiment, they studied young rhesus monkeys that had been born and raised in the laboratory and had had no prior experience of snakes. Convinced that monkeys had an instinctive fear of snakes, Mineka was intrigued that the young monkeys with no experience of snakes generally showed no fear at all and would even reach over very realistic toy snakes to get a treat. Mineka suspected that the instinctive fear needed to be socially triggered; it must occur by means of observational learning.

Cook and Mineka set up an experiment to test out the theory. They first gave young monkeys realistic toy snakes and crocodiles as well as a bunch of flowers and a toy rabbit to play with. Having never seen any of these things before, the monkeys were curious and played happily with all of the objects. Then came the clever part: a video of an adult monkey demonstrating a classic fear response to a boa constrictor in the wild was spliced, so that one version showed the genuine response in front of the snake, while the other showed the identical response but with the snake replaced by one of the other objects (a crocodile, a bunch of flowers, or a rabbit). To the young monkeys, it now looked as if the adult monkey was alarmed and afraid of all the items.

Each version of the video was shown to new groups of young monkeys, none of which had ever seen snakes or bunches of flowers or crocodiles or rabbits before. Sure enough, a strong fear reaction occurred. Crucially, the fear reaction occurred only to the toy snake or crocodile, not to the flowers or rabbit. Thus a single exposure to an adult exhibiting fear towards a snake or a crocodile was enough to induce a strong fear in young monkeys. This was clearly a *selective* learning process, for the identical fear display to other items, like a bunch of flowers, did not elicit a fear reaction. Mineka and Cook had discovered an instinctual form of learning. Their fear brain had *pre-pared* these monkeys to rapidly learn to be scared of some things more than others.

The same thing happens to us. Just like monkeys, we also learn to link certain things with adverse outcomes far more readily than others, and this tendency can lead to various biases and quirks of mind that in turn can ramp up our level of fear and anxiety. The best demonstration of how this works comes from an experimental task showing what has been called the *covariation bias*. Sue Mineka and Michael Cook now teamed up with psychologist Andrew Tomarken to run a study at Vanderbilt University in Nashville. They brought volunteers into the lab, and each person was asked to simply observe a series of slides presented on a projector screen. Some of the slides showed scary pictures of snakes and spiders, while others were more mundane pictures of flowers and mushrooms. Immediately after each slide was shown, one of three things could happen: you could receive a mild electric shock, you could hear a tone, or nothing would happen at all. Each of these outcomes was equally probable following each type of slide. Thus, whether a snake, spider, mushroom, or flower was presented, the chances of getting a shock was one in three. Equal chances.

But this is not what people reported. When asked whether there was any link between particular pictures and getting a shock, almost all the volunteers said yes. When a snake or spider was shown, they thought they were much more likely to get a shock compared to when a flower or mushroom was shown. The shocks seemed to be more frequent following the scary pictures. In a classic example of what psychologists call an *illusory correlation*, a frightening item was associated with a bad outcome even though it really wasn't.

The same type of thing happens for more general anxieties, like worrying about our weight. Richard Viken and his colleagues at the psychology department in Indiana University showed 186 women a series of photographs of women who varied on a range of attributes. Two of the key attributes they were interested in were how happy or sad the women looked and whether they seemed to be overweight or underweight. The psychologists were careful to make sure that there was no *actual* association between people's weight and how happy they looked. Overweight, underweight, and normal-weight women were equally likely to be smiling. What the volunteers 'saw' was something very different. They were convinced that the thinner women were much happier and that the fatter women looked sadder. And this illusory correlation was even stronger among those women with higher levels of eating disorder. This shows how easily our fear brain can colour our perceptions of the world, tricking us into making misinterpretations and false assumptions about how things really are.

Studies like these tell us that certain things, especially ancient threats, act like prepared stimuli so that we don't need much experience of them to learn to be afraid. Like Mineka's young monkeys, a single bad experience is all we need to make us wary for life. If we fall off our bike when we are five, we probably won't be afraid of bikes as we grow up. A single sting from a bee, on the other hand, is more likely to leave us with a deep-seated fear of bees and wasps. When such a fear develops, whether it's of snakes and spiders or of putting on weight, our mind starts to play tricks on us, forming illusory associations between the feared thing and bad outcomes.

The fluidity and power of the fear system is generally of great benefit in keeping us safe from things that might harm us. But the tendency of the fear brain to elicit illusory correlations has a real downside and can even make us ill. A few years ago, a friend of mine I'll call Niamh took a train from the English seaside town of Brighton to London. Niamh was excited about travelling to London but also a bit nervous, as she was going for an interview for a job that she really wanted. Dreaming of a fancy apartment in the city, she imagined the fun life she could have in the capital. She knew that she had all the qualifications and experience and had a great chance of getting the job, but she hoped that she would not blow it in the interview.

Rehearsing endless questions and answers in her head during the ride, she was becoming increasingly irritated by the man beside her who was constantly talking on his mobile phone. As soon as one conversation was finished, he would make a new phone call and start again. Niamh tried to calm down by breathing deeply and looking out the window as the train edged its way towards London.

As her mind was beginning to drift, an abrupt and severe bolt of pain suddenly struck her. She described it to me later as being like an arrow shooting through her left eye, down through her neck, with slivers of pain arching above her head. The man next to her stopped his conversation, turned off his phone, and asked whether she was okay. The pain subsided, and, in great British style, he got her a cup of tea. Within about ten minutes, she felt better.

Niamh made it to the interview and the next day was offered the job in a swish accountancy firm. A month or so later, she moved to the longed-for apartment in a smart area of London and began her new job and a new life. However, her first couple of months were marred by several repeat episodes of the stabbing pain through her eye, which was now usually followed by a light tingling rash on the left side of her face that lasted for a couple of hours after each incident. Numerous X-rays, medical examinations, and CT scans could find nothing amiss, but the excruciating bouts of pain continued to occur at regular but fairly random moments. The doctors were mystified.

Then one day, Niamh was sitting in a café when she made a startling discovery. While trying to read a report that was overdue, she was vaguely aware of someone speaking loudly on a mobile phone at the next table. Just as she started to become annoyed, she suddenly experienced the piercing pain again, accompanied by a kind of fizzing on her skin. She immediately made the connection – the pain was due to the mobile phone!

Convinced she had found the cause of her strange affliction, she wondered whether the electromagnetic radiation from the mobile phone was causing all her other problems. Doing a little research on the Internet, she found a flood of alarmist websites warning of the dangers of mobile phones and identifying a syndrome scarily called *electrosensitivity*, an allergy to electromagnetic fields.

It sounded very much like what she was experiencing. From then on, Niamh tried to keep away from mobile phones as much as possible. Weeks went by without incident. But living in the centre of London, it was virtually impossible to keep completely away from people using mobile phones, and she continued to have some painful incidents – what she now referred to as her 'moments' – when she was near someone talking on a cell. As time went on, she became more and more convinced of the connection. She stopped using a cell, trying as best she could to shield herself from what she believed was the dangerous radiation emanating from mobile phones.

Coincidentally, a few years later I found myself leading one of the world's largest studies on whether mobile phones affect our health. After testing hundreds of volunteers over an eight-year period, we concluded that it is not the electromagnetic fields from mobile phones that cause the problems; rather, it's the *belief* that they are causing harm that's dangerous. It turned out that what I knew about the fear system held the answer all along.

Talking to my friend Niamh, I realised what I should have appreciated much earlier: the fear system persuades our brain to make connections, and these connections can work against us. Niamh's first episode occurred when she was feeling very excited, but also very stressed, on her way to an important interview. The irritation from the guy talking on his mobile phone was caught up in her memory of the event. Deep in her subconscious, her fear system had linked feeling stressed and unwell with the mobile phone. Later on, when she had another one of her 'moments' in the café, this memory and the critical association were reactivated. Niamh's fear brain associated mobile phones with danger.

The problem from then on was that Niamh fell into the classic trap of the confirmation bias; she always noticed mobile phones when she had her painful episodes but *failed to notice them when she felt okay.*

The characteristics of the fear system we see in simple conditioning experiments even explain why prejudice and racial hatred have been so common throughout history. Liz Phelps, a leading psychologist at New York University, along with Andreas Olsson, a Swedish PhD student who travelled to New York to study with her, investigated whether the type of prepared learning that Sue Mineka had found with monkeys could be extended to fear associated with members of another racial group. Prejudice is almost always associated with fear and ignorance, leading Phelps and Olsson to wonder whether this fear played a part in encouraging intolerance in the first place. When we meet people from a different culture or social group, we are often apprehensive because we are not familiar with their habits and customs. This leads us to be far harsher in judging members of a racial or social out-group than we are of members of our own group – a phenomenon that social psychologists call the *in-group bias.*

Given what we know about illusory correlations, Phelps and her team thought that perhaps racial prejudice itself stems from the very same mechanisms that underlie fear learning. The unfamiliar scares us a little, so people of another race might be more readily associated with fear. They tested both black and white volunteers in a typical fear-conditioning experiment. For the aversive stimulus a mild electric shock was used, which was described as 'very unpleasant and annoying' by the volunteers; GSR – sweatiness of the hands – was used as the measure of stress. Photographs of two black and two white faces were flashed up on a computer screen, one after the other, and one black and one white face was always accompanied by an electric shock. This was the conditioned stimulus, or CS+. Every time the other black or white face was presented, no shock would be delivered. This was the unconditioned stimulus, or CS-. Not surprisingly, it did not take the volunteers long to develop a fear response to the conditioned faces: every time the CS+ was presented, their GSR increased. They had learned to fear the CS+, even when later in the experiment it was no longer accompanied by shock.

Interestingly, black volunteers did not learn to fear white faces any more quickly than black faces, or vice versa. In other words, the acquisition of fear was not any quicker for the out-group versus the in-group.

A very different story emerged during the extinction phase. When the CS+ was presented without any electric shocks, the fear response diminished, but a clear racial difference was apparent. For the white volunteers, their enhanced GSR declined rapidly when they saw the white face, but not when they saw the black face; fear of their own-race face was extinguished quickly. Exactly the same happened for the black volunteers: the fear response to the black face diminished quickly, while fear of the white CS+ face lingered. Unfamiliar members of a racial out-group did indeed act like a prepared stimulus so that fear was much harder to forget.

Brain scanning experiments have shown that when we are asked to evaluate others, the fear system gets more involved when the faces are from another racial group. In one study, Phelps and her colleagues showed white volunteers a series of black and white faces as they lay in the brain scanner. Amygdala activity was stronger in response to the black, or out-group, faces, raising the possibility that humans have evolved a mechanism to fear those who are unlike us, the traditional fear of the stranger.

An intriguing finding from Phelps's studies was that those who showed a bigger fear response, as measured by the amount of amygdala activation to out-group faces, also had a more racist attitude. This link completely disappeared when the black faces were of familiar individuals or of people who were highly regarded. Thus, while our fear brain does fire into action when faced with a stranger from a different ethnic group, it's clear that familiarity can reduce the fomenting within our ancient fear system. These results also suggest that dampening down the fear brain is likely to reduce prejudice and stereotyping.

Andreia Santos and colleagues from the University of Heidelberg in Germany have direct evidence for the theory that the fear brain plays a role in the development of racial prejudice. They tested a group of girls with Williams syndrome, a genetic disorder characterised by a complete lack of social fear. Children with this disorder, which only occurs in females, show no fear of strangers, giving the researchers a unique opportunity. In a series of tests, these girls were as quick as other girls to pick up gender stereotypes from adults, but when adults discussed negative racial stereotypes, the girls with Williams syndrome did not pick up on them, unlike the girls without the syndrome, who acquired these stereotypes very easily. An absence of social fear, it seems, had prevented the development of racial stereotypes.

Our fear brain pays little heed to logic, so fears about things like strangers or new technologies are easy to generate but extremely difficult to erase. Once a connection with danger is made, it's almost impossible to shake. This is a central characteristic of our emergency brain, which, while crucial for survival, can be lethal when combined with our enlarged thinking brain.

The bigger point here is that our automatic, unconscious biases have a direct effect on our perspective on life. People with an overactive rainy brain, who cannot cast off an overwhelming pessimism, are drawn to things that are negative, and they invariably interpret ambiguous social signals in a negative way. Those who have an optimistic outlook are drawn to the positive side of life; they have an automatic tendency to see the potential benefits of any given situation.

If our cognitive biases have such a profound influence on our outlook, then perhaps changing them may be a powerful way to change our outlook. People who are chronically depressed or anxious are especially adept at seeing things in the bleakest terms. With the good things in life leaving little impression, disappointments and failures loom large in the depressed mind. Could changing biases provide a type of psychological immunity by actively modifying a negative and potentially damaging slant of mind?

The possibility of changing entrenched and potentially toxic mind-sets has captured the imagination of a number of cognitive and clinical psychologists who are now engaged in a progressive research program. Simple computerised techniques known as cognitive bias modification (CBM), like those I used in my plasticity gene study, have proved that changing our automatic biases is, in fact, surprisingly easy. CBM represents a new approach in cognitive psychology that attempts to change how we construe the events going on around us.

CBM involves sitting in front of a computer for about fifteen to twenty minutes per day a couple of times a week. These techniques have been experimented with on a diverse range of people from children and soldiers to those with clinical disorders of anxiety and depression. When used as a therapy, the goal of CBM is to modify the potentially dangerous biases that draw the anxious person towards the very things that frightens him or her.

The typical way to undo dangerous biases is to present someone with two pictures or words – one negative and one benign – on a computer screen. In the case of a soldier with post-traumatic stress disorder (PTSD), these might be a gun pointing directly towards him and a pencil lying on a desk. The soldier with PTSD will instinctively be pulled towards the pointing gun, filling his mind even further with notions of the world being a dangerous place. The CBM program pushes his affective mind to avoid this picture, orienting instead towards the innocuous image. This is achieved by requiring the soldier to detect small probes that appear in the location of the benign image. Over hundreds and hundreds of trials, the soldier's mind is retrained to divert its attention away from threatening, scary images and towards more benign images.

The assumption is that with the mind retrained, the new way of thinking becomes a habit that takes over automatically in flashpoint situations. As Emily Holmes, a psychologist at the University of Oxford, describes it, it's rather like administering a 'cognitive vaccine' that inoculates a person against dangerous ways of thinking. Many addictions are associated with strong impulses that are difficult to control. An alcoholic who opens a fridge to be confronted unexpectedly with bottles of cold beer will find it difficult to suppress the urge to take a bottle of beer rather than the carton of milk she was looking for. CBM aims to intervene in precisely these treacherous moments, leading the mind to seamlessly override the dangerous thought.

Reinout Wiers, a psychologist at the University of Amsterdam, developed a CBM intervention designed to turn around the impulsive responses that are typical of heavy drinkers. His team designed a video game that involved pushing or pulling a joystick in response to images on a computer screen. When an image is pulled towards the person, it gets bigger and bigger; when the joystick is pushed away, the image recedes into the distance. Heavy drinkers are much quicker to pull images of alcoholic drinks towards them than soft drinks, a pattern that does not occur with lighter drinkers. Moreover, light drinkers trained to pull alcoholic beverages towards them also consume more alcohol in a subsequent taste test.

This tendency to respond impulsively to temptation is a reflection of the pleasure brain pushing a person towards a reward; the bias directly influences behaviour. Wiers and his colleagues wondered whether such impulses could be reversed by CBM. They recruited 214 alcoholic patients from a clinic in Germany and assigned half to an experimental condition and half to a sham condition. All volunteers were instructed to 'push' away a picture presented in portrait format and to 'pull' a picture in landscape format towards them. Images of alcoholic drinks were always in portrait format, so that they were always pushed away while landscape soft drinks were pulled closer. Those in the control group pushed and pulled the alcoholic and soft drinks equally often. The initial tendency to approach images of alcohol was reversed to an avoidance response

The Malleable Mind

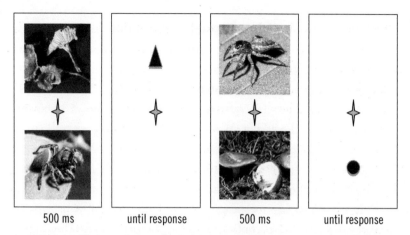

| 500 ms | until response | 500 ms | until response |

FIGURE 5.2 Diagram of a couple of trials in a cognitive bias modification procedure designed to retrain people with spider phobia to redirect their attention away from the spider. A pair of images is presented for five hundred milliseconds, and these are followed by a single target (a triangle or circle) that people have to respond to (e.g., press the left-hand button if the target is a circle). On training trials, the target always appears in the opposite location from that of the spider image. For control participants, the target appears equally often in the locations of the spider-related and nonspider images.

for those in the experimental CBM group. All patients then underwent a normal three months of talking therapy to help them tackle their problems with alcohol. A year later, less than half (46 per cent) of the patients in the experimental group had relapsed, while 59 per cent of those who had received the sham CBM had relapsed.

The historical development of CBM came from the hope of counteracting the potentially toxic biases driven by the fear brain. In the late 1990s, Colin MacLeod, a psychologist from Scotland who is now at the University of Western Australia, began to wonder whether it was possible to alter the unhealthy attentional biases that were typical of people with anxiety disorders. He realised that modifying biases in attention would not only provide an effective therapy for people with a tendency to notice the negative aspects of life, like those with anxiety disorders, but also give psychologists an effective way to work out whether biases in attention can cause mental health problems to develop in the first place.

Untangling whether it is our biases that lead to an optimistic or pessimistic outlook or whether our perspective and outlook lead to our own unique biases is a chicken-and-egg task that is notoriously difficult to resolve. An association between a negative bias and anxiety is just that: no matter how strong the bias we can never know the *direction* of the association. If we can change people's biases, only then can we really know the direction of the relationship.

MacLeod's plan was to induce a bias that was not there before and then see how people respond to a stressful event. The Australian team used the standard attentional probe task with pairs of negative and neutral words, but with a twist. Instead of the probe appearing in the location of a threat-related word (e.g., *assault*) half the time and in the location of a neutral word (e.g., *table*) half the time, as is typical, they played around with these contingencies. For the avoid threat group, the probe always appeared in the location of the neutral word and never followed the threat words. When pairs of negative and neutral words were presented side by side (e.g., *failure-factory; attack-account*), regardless of whether the neutral word was on the right or on the left, the probe that volunteers had to react to always followed the neutral word, never the threat word. For the attend threat group, the contingency was reversed; the same pairs of words were used, but the probe always appeared in the location of the threat-related word.

In a major breakthrough, both groups did develop the appropriate bias. For the first time, it had been shown that selective processing could be instilled in people by a simple computer test that lasted for about an hour.

This ability to induce a bias where none had existed before – to switch on and off a preference for negativity – gave the team a unique opportunity to investigate if a particular bias would determine how someone responds in a demanding situation. Finally, they could work out if a negative bias was as toxic as had always been suspected and, just as important, if a benign bias could provide a buffer for people against the effects of stress.

The volunteers were subjected to a mildly stressful test shortly after the CBM procedure. We cannot subject people to the types of severe stress that might be encountered in real-life trauma situations, like car accidents and so on, but even relatively minor stressors can be highly effective in helping us uncover the underlying mechanisms.

MacLeod's team decided to stress people by having them solve a series of difficult anagrams under time pressure. When university students are told that the ability to resolve anagrams quickly is related to IQ, you would be surprised at how competitive and tense they can become. Each participant was presented with a card with 'GNAAMRA' printed on it and told that they had just twenty seconds to solve the anagram.

To get a taste of how this works, have a go at the three anagrams presented below. Get a stopwatch, set it for sixty seconds, and see whether you can resolve all of the anagrams in the time allowed.

SIAAVEBR
OSLURDEH
VETIIFUG

MacLeod and his team gave each of their participants long lists of these anagrams and, for good measure, threw in some that were impossible to solve. The students found this task fairly stressful, but those who had been in the avoid threat group reported far less stress than those who had been in the attend threat group. This confirmed the causal link: a toxic bias, induced in the lab, led to increased stress, and a benign bias, also induced in the lab, resulted in a reduced stress response. At long last, what scientists had long suspected – that attentional biases could lead to increased vulnerability to anxiety – could now be manipulated and tested in the lab.

Unbeknownst to MacLeod and his team, former colleagues of his in the United Kingdom were conducting similar experiments using a different task but exactly the same logic. Andrew Mathews is one of the world's leading clinical scientists and is an inspirational figure for many psychologists interested in the relationship between our emotions and our mindset. MacLeod himself was first introduced to this field of research when he was undertaking clinical studies with Mathews in London in the 1980s. Now at the University of California, Davis, Mathews spent many years at the Cognition and Brain Sciences Unit in Cambridge, England, and it was here that he teamed up with Bundy Mackintosh, a dynamic and enthusiastic researcher who was intrigued by the links being discovered between how we think and how we feel.

Mathews and Mackintosh in Cambridge also realised the potential benefit of being able to modify and induce cognitive biases under the controlled conditions of the laboratory. But instead of attention, they focused on quirks and tendencies in how we *interpret* ambiguous situations. They gave people simple scenarios like, 'You stand up to speak at a friend's wedding, and the crowd begins to laugh. So how do you feel? Do they like you and are looking forward to a humorous talk? Alternatively, perhaps they don't take you very seriously and are laughing at how silly you look.' The way we interpret ambiguous situations like this affects how anxious or otherwise we feel.

The Cambridge team was aware that clinical conditions like anxiety and depression are associated with the tendency to interpret ambiguous social situations in a negative way. A smile is interpreted as a smirk rather than interest; being kept waiting for a meeting is taken as a sign that you are not considered important, rather than your colleague simply missing his train. Given the constant interpreting and reinterpreting of events that go on around us, everyday life is ripe for interpretative biases.

To find out which comes first – the bias or the mood state – the Cambridge team set about developing hundreds of ambiguous scenarios that could be resolved in either a negative or a positive way. A sentence like, 'The doctor examined little Emily's growth,' would be presented on a computer screen, and then followed by a sentence with a critical word missing, something like, 'Her _____ had increased by 2 centimetres.' Then two words are rapidly flashed up on the screen. If a word makes sense in the sentence, it should be chosen as fast as possible. The trick is that both words make a sensible sentence, but one resolves it in a negative way, whereas the other resolves the sentence in a positive way. In this instance, the choice is 'height' or 'tumor.'

You can guess the result – the pessimists can't help going for the negative option. Because they routinely make negative interpretations, 'her *tumor* had increased by 2 centimetres' made more sense. Those who take a more upbeat view of things are quicker to recognise that 'her *height* had increased by 2 centimetres.' In a sneaky way, this technique gives us a glimpse into the subconscious interpretations people are making at lightning speed.

As with MacLeod's studies, the Cambridge psychologists presented hundreds of examples, but the twist was that one group was always given positive resolutions by the computer, and the other group was always given negative solutions. This constant training to make either positive or negative interpretations eventually overrides the person's natural tendencies. This was an important breakthrough.

Changing how people interpreted ambiguity also made a real difference to how they reacted to stress. When the volunteers had to watch a series of unpleasant video clips, the type you might see on police action TV shows, those who had been trained to interpret situations in a positive way were much less affected by the upsetting images than those who had developed a negative bias.

In psychology laboratories in Australia and England, the evidence was growing that what we notice and how we interpret things has a profound effect on the way we are. In the decade or so since these first forays into the changing of cognitive biases, we have learned that these results stand up outside the lab. In one clinical trial,

Florida State University psychologist Norman Schmidt tested CBM with patients who had a particularly severe form of social anxiety. Following eight sessions of attentional training (like MacLeod's task) twice a week, he found that 72 per cent of the patients in the avoid threat group no longer met the diagnostic criteria for severe social anxiety. While 11 per cent of the patients in the control CBM group recovered, 72 per cent of patients with an anxiety disorder were no longer ill following this simple intervention.

Depression is also helped by these procedures. Chris Beevers, a psychologist from the University of Texas at Austin, persuaded a large group of depressed students to take several sessions of CBM over a two-week period. Those in the avoid threat group were far less depressed up to four weeks after the intervention, whereas those in the control group didn't change.

Great excitement surrounds the development of these new CBM techniques in the scientific community not least because they are cheap and easy to implement and they can even be presented to people in their own homes by means of the Internet. While such techniques will never replace more established therapies, the hope is that they can be used alongside more conventional talking therapies or drug therapies.

And here is the kernel of an idea: just as practice with spatial memory leads to changes in the hippocampus, or musical practice expands the brain areas involved in fine motor movement, perhaps practice in seeing or interpreting things in a particular way can lead to fundamental changes in the brain circuits underlying our affective mind.

CHAPTER 6

New Techniques to Reshape Our Brains

From Fear to Flourishing

We need our fear brain. Without it our lives would be accident prone and probably very short. When the fear system becomes hyperactive, however, people can become overwhelmed by feelings of anxiety and despair. Such pathological levels of fear can all too easily turn into anxiety disorders and depression, with devastating consequences. Psychology and neuroscience have spent decades developing a variety of methods – from drugs to talking therapies – to help people keep these insidious problems under control.

Eliminating abnormal levels of fear and despair from our lives is one thing; boosting well-being and a flourishing way of life is another. An encouraging finding emerging from recent research is that most of us are surprisingly resilient. When the worst happens – a terrorist attack, a serious illness, the death of a loved one – most of us recover from the profound shock quickly. Some even find that they have become better people, experiencing post-traumatic growth, as opposed to post-traumatic stress. Advances in psychological science tell us that, with some effort, we can resculpt our brain not only to reduce abnormal fear but also to set us on the way to truly flourishing.

The American aviator, engineer, and industrialist Howard Hughes experienced a severe disorder of the fear system, obsessive-compulsive disorder (OCD), which consumed much of his energy right up until his death in 1975. OCD affects millions of people around the world. Interestingly, people with OCD know that all is fine – they know that they turned off the stove or locked the door – but they still have a compulsive need to check and check and check again. OCD begins when a basic fear – *I am going to die from germs* – becomes an obsession that, in the mind of the sufferer, can only be countered by repetitive behaviours such as incessant hand washing. Like most anxiety disorders, OCD wreaks havoc in people's lives, as it becomes an all-consuming preoccupation.

Thirty years after the death of Hughes, the actor Leonardo DiCaprio played him in the movie *The Aviator*. To fully engage with the role, DiCaprio spent several days with psychiatrist Jeffrey Schwartz to learn more about OCD. DiCaprio also spent time with some of Schwartz's patients so that he could see up close what it is like living with the illness. So immersed in the role did he become that DiCaprio developed many of the thoughts, feelings, and symptoms of OCD. A transient case of OCD had been induced in his own brain. It took almost three months of intensive therapy and practice to rid himself of OCD after filming had stopped.

The National Institute of Mental Health estimates that more than 20 million Americans are affected by fear disorders, most commonly by phobias, generalised anxiety disorders, post-traumatic stress disorder, panic attacks, and obsessive-compulsive disorder. Sometimes the overwhelming fear and worries seem to emerge from out of the blue; sometimes they are linked to a specific event. Either way, anxiety disorders are invasive and often become the defining feature of a person's life.

To get a better understanding of fear system disorders, let's have a look at the following accounts of two women who were treated for anxiety problems at a UK clinic in which I conduct some of my research.

One woman – let's call her Angela – survived a vicious attempted rape. Out jogging one day, Angela was grabbed on an isolated woodland trail. She remembers clearly that a man standing by the side of the path looked a bit self-conscious as she ran towards him. When she passed, he grabbed her and tried to drag her into the bushes. Angela struggled, but she was overcome with terror and anger, kicking and screaming for what seemed like an age. 'I eventually managed to get away and just ran and ran back towards town,' she told me.

Angela managed to bang on the door of a house but doesn't remember much else. The next thing she knew, she was waking up in the hospital with her parents at her bedside. She had multiple injuries, including a broken nose, a black eye, and a fractured rib. These injuries healed in time, but as is often the case, it was the trauma that took longer to get over. 'I was always nervous in my flat,' she explained, 'constantly checking that windows and doors were locked.' For months she was too terrified to go out alone. She eventually moved to a new house with some friends, but even here she was nervous and became more and more socially isolated.

During a visit to her local supermarket, Angela experienced her first panic attack: 'I was overwhelmed by panic and intense fear. I felt sick to the core of my stomach and could not wait to get home to the safety of my room.'

Even at home, there was little respite, for soon she started having flashbacks of the attack. 'I would see his face, smell his sweat,' she said, and she would wake up regularly in the night in a state of terror. 'I kept imagining a knife,' even though she was not sure that he had had a knife. Angela stopped eating and stayed in her room almost all the time.

Eventually, she sought help, and after much time, her symptoms, typical of post-traumatic stress disorder, began to subside. She still has some problems and is still too nervous to go out running or walking alone, but her life almost four years after the attack is more or less back to normal.

Jayne's anxiety is more pervasive and difficult to explain. 'It just came out of nothing,' she told me. At the age of thirty, she began to worry about all sorts of things, constantly feeling apprehensive and nervous. 'I was overwhelmed with the feeling that something bad was going to happen,' she said. Jayne could not think of anything specific that had sparked off these fears, but they became more and more entrenched as time went on. Just like Angela, she began to retreat into her room, becoming nervous about going out.

She experienced a couple of terrifying panic attacks, but it was the feelings of dread and worry that bothered her most. Jayne was experiencing the typical symptoms of generalised anxiety disorder, which is one of the most common problems that clinical psychologists are faced with. Jayne also had problems with depression, fearing that things would never get better. She was often overcome by negative thoughts and beliefs. 'I really think I'm a useless person,' she said. 'I feel like I'm a waste of space.'

When fear takes over, it's virtually impossible to live a normal life, let alone nurture an optimistic mindset. Finding ways to get rid of fear is one way to stem the rising tide of these distressing emotional disorders. As DiCaprio's experience shows, the brain circuits underlying our rainy brain are highly plastic, allowing us to form difficult-to-shake habits and ways of thinking very quickly. The good news is that these dysfunctional circuits can also be reversed and set on a more positive direction.

Psychology and neuroscience have now developed several techniques that are capable of making real changes to the dysfunctional brain circuits that underlie many of the disorders of the affective mind. These are not, I'd emphasise, the superficial sort of 'positivity' or 'just think happy thoughts and everything will be fine' kind of thing that you find in many self-help books. What I am talking about is the possibility of a real change, reflected at the level of neurons and their connections deep within our brains. Everything that makes us ourselves – our memories, our beliefs, our values and feelings, even our habits and character – are all linked with patterns and connections of neural networks within our brain. If we can change these connections, we can also change ourselves. These techniques can help not only rid us of fear disorders, like OCD or PTSD, but also move us from just getting by to leading a life of genuine flourishing and well-being.

Overcoming Fear and Anxiety

As many veterans coming back from Afghanistan and Iraq can testify, experiencing a severe trauma can lead to the formation of seemingly indelible memories that constantly reignite the trauma. Reliving the bad memories prevents people from moving on with their lives. Angela's flashbacks of the face of her attacker are an example of how these memories play a crucial role in maintaining conditions like PTSD. The science of fear has established a number of ways to help rid ourselves of these types of fears. The phenomenon of extinction that occurs in fear-conditioning procedures provides one obvious way in which fear can be reduced. As we know, if a feared object, such as a tone in a laboratory study, is presented many times in the absence of electric shock, then the fear gradually diminishes. Just like getting back on the horse after a fall, repeated exposure to a scary thing will eventually result in new learning that this is now safe.

These insights from fear-conditioning studies with animals have led to the development of exposure therapy, which is a highly effective treatment for specific fears, like spider phobia. Exposure therapy works by teaching people how to confront and suppress scary memories. People with phobias go to great lengths to avoid what they are afraid of, so they never put themselves in a position to realise that nothing too bad is going to happen. But forcing people to confront the terrifying object over and over is a highly effective way of eliminating the fear. The phobic's racing heart, sweaty palms, and panicky feelings, which they have when first exposed to the feared thing, begin to subside. After a few sessions, most people with spider phobia get to the point where they can pick up the spider.

This type of exposure seems to work along the same lines as the extinction of conditioned fears we see in laboratory studies. In recent developments, an antibiotic called d-cycloserine, originally used as a treatment for tuberculosis, has been found to speed up this process; people administered the drug require far fewer sessions of exposure therapy to overcome their fears. D-cycloserine by itself has no effect at all on fear reactions, but in combination with exposure therapy the drug escalates the new learning that the feared thing is now safe.

To understand how this works, we need to revisit what happens when neurons talk to each other at the crucial point of synaptic transmission. During a synapse, brain cells communicate with each other by squirting neurotransmitters out from one neuron to another. If this chemical comes into contact with an appropriately shaped receptor, then any neuron with that shape receptor will also become activated, creating waves and ripples of activity in the brain. A class of receptors known as glutamate receptors have been discovered to play a particularly important role in laying down fear memories. These receptors can be divided into two types: AMPA, which control rapid excitatory synapses, and NMDA, which play a critical role in the longer-term plasticity and development of neural circuits.

When NMDA receptors are activated, a sequence of changes is initiated throughout the brain that creates a semipermanent trace. Much as a river carves out a channel, regular thoughts create new pathways through the neural networks that make it easier for messages to slide around the brain. This is the mechanism that many neuroscientists now believe underlies the development of PTSD. The idea is that PTSD is caused by the formation of an indelible pathway from the senses to the amygdala by means of NMDA receptors. This is why the flashbacks and fearful memories of PTSD are so hard to shake. While D-cycloserine has many effects in the brain, we know that it directly influences the NMDA receptors in the amygdala, the heart of our fear brain, which is why it boosts the unlearning of embedded fears. In this way, the NMDA receptors loosen and become more malleable, allowing the psychological therapy to have a greater impact.

Research is ongoing, but there is little doubt that combining psychological therapies with drugs like D-cycloserine will provide powerful new ways to combat the devastation caused by disorders of the brain's fear system.

We know from fear-conditioning studies that extinction does not erase the original fear, however, but seems only to suppress the fear, which means that it can be easily reinstated. My friend Sandra discovered this when a backfiring car made her dive for cover. This is why the hunt is on for more permanent ways of erasing fear.

Liz Phelps and Joseph LeDoux, the New York University fear researchers, exploited the dynamic nature of human memory to find a way to permanently erase our fears. Psychologists used to think that memories were laid down in a fairly inflexible and rigid way in our brain. Now, it has been discovered that memories, especially emotional memories, are reactivated when they are recalled, leaving them in a temporarily vulnerable state in which new information can be added to the original memory. This means that every time we bring a memory to mind, it gets slightly changed and laid down again as a newer member, subtly different from the original. Technically called *reconsolidation*, this reactivation period, which lasts for about six hours, opens a window of opportunity in which the memory can be altered.

The New York team discovered that reactivating a fear memory did indeed allow them to update the memory trace with new non-fearful information. By attaching small electrodes to the wrists of sixty-five volunteers, a fear memory was created by associating a mild electric shock with the appearance of a blue square: this was the CS+ stimulus. A yellow square, in contrast, was never accompanied by a shock: the CS- stimulus. All the volunteers developed a fear response to the CS+, the blue square, as measured by their galvanic skin response.

The next day, during the extinction period, volunteers were divided into three groups. Two groups were reminded of the feared item by being shown a single presentation of the CS+; this was intended to get the reconsolidation process going. For one group, the extinction trials began ten minutes later, during the critical reconsolidation period. For the second group, the trials began six hours later, when this window of opportunity should be closed. A third group was given no reminder and went straight into the extinction trials, which consisted of a series of presentations of blue and yellow squares with no further electric shocks.

Twenty-four hours later, all volunteers were tested again to see whether the fear memory remained. When the CS+ item was presented, there was a spontaneous recovery of the fear memory in the group that had received no reminder as well as in the group that had received extinction training outside the reconsolidation window. But for the group that had extinction training when the memory was unstable, during the reconsolidation window, fear responses did not return. In other words, when a feared item was brought to mind and then presented over and over again without anything bad happening, the original fear memory was erased.

A small number of the volunteers were tested again a year later, and the fear memory was still not present in the group who had had their extinction training during the critical reconsolidation window. This suggests that the old fear memory had been permanently changed.

Richard Huganir, along with his postdoctoral assistant Roger Clem at Johns Hopkins University, have followed up on this work with mice and found startling evidence that the complicated molecular machinery that consolidates fear memories in the first place may also be the key to how they can be undone. They discovered that neurons in the amygdala are replete with glutamate receptors – the AMPA variety – and that during the critical period when fear memories are being laid down, these receptors undergo a major overhaul, with a constant reshuffling of receptors among different neurons. During this reshuffling, the glutamate receptors slip on and off neurons easily. This is what Huganir and Clem speculate makes the fear memories so fragile. Support for this notion came when they injected mice with a drug that prevented this reshuffling of receptors and found that fear memories became impossible to erase.

The finding that reminding people of their traumatic memory prior to extinction training can permanently erase memories of fear presents an exciting opportunity for the development of new treatments for anxiety. The new technique gives a noninvasive way to remove the traumatic memories for good.

Our knowledge of the anatomy of the fear system suggests another way to tackle the development of pathological fear. Rather than focusing on the amygdala and the fear itself, perhaps we can target the higher cortical centres that dampen down the amygdala. By strengthening the emotional control centres of the brain, fear can be suppressed and perhaps diminished for good. With this in mind, many pharmacological and cognitive therapies have been designed to improve people's ability to regulate their emotions.

We know that standard fear extinction effectively establishes a new memory in the brain, and that this inhibition of fear is achieved by activation of a brain area towards the middle, or what's called the *medial prefrontal cortex*. Nerves from this area are linked directly with the amygdala, an anatomical arrangement that provides a means by which the fear response can be suppressed. Directly stimulating cells in this region of the PFC leads to a strong reduction in the activity of the amygdala. Once activated, the cortical control centre can quiet the emergency brain, which in turn suppresses fearful and traumatic memories. Conversely, rats with damage to this area of their PFC are unable to unlearn fear.

It seems that people with post-traumatic stress disorder may have an underdeveloped control centre. When people who experienced a severe trauma, like Angela, were asked to look at trauma-related pictures in the brain scanner, it was discovered that the medial PFC was smaller and less active in those who had PTSD compared to those who did not. Those who had more active control centres also had less severe PTSD symptoms like flashbacks and hot sweats. If we can figure out ways to activate this middle part of the PFC and other human brain control centres, we would have a vital weapon in the battle again anxiety disorders.

The evidence is growing that we can learn to regulate our emotions effectively by simply reevaluating how we interpret things. If overwhelmed by distressing thoughts, we can attempt to modulate them by using strategies to tell ourselves that maybe they aren't that bad after all. Not only can this reduce our fears, but it also can change the brain circuits that make up our rainy brain.

In the 1960s Richard Lazarus was among the first to show that reappraising how we interpret a distressing scene can quell the fear response. He presented people with distressing video clips – of aboriginal circumcision rites, for instance – telling some, 'This was real: the boy is in great pain,' and others, 'This is an educational video: the boys are actors and are not really in pain.' Those told the boys were acting showed less fear as measured by their galvanic skin response, and they also said they were far less upset than those who thought it was for real. How people interpreted the scenes made a difference.

Sophisticated brain-imaging technologies are now revealing that these attempts to control our fears cognitively are implemented within our brains. A network of brain areas – our rainy brain – sends inhibitory messages from cortical areas to lower, more reactive areas that help us regulate our emotions. Thoughts alone, it seems, can influence the control centres of our prefrontal cortex.

By merely giving a label to an emotional thought or picture, the brain's control centre – the PFC – can be activated, which in turn dampens down responses in the amygdala. Ahmad Hariri, the Duke University neuroscientist, scanned the brains of eleven healthy volunteers while they looked at lots of pairs of images – say, a snake and a pointing gun – and then matched the picture to another target picture. This forced them to concentrate on the perceptual aspects of the scenes, and because the images were fearful, the assumption was that their emergency brain would sit up and take notice.

In the more interesting set of trials, the same pictures were presented, but instead of matching the pictures, the volunteers had to select one of two simultaneously presented words to indicate whether the negative scene was 'natural' (e.g., sharks, snakes, spiders, etc.) or 'artificial' (e.g., guns, knives, explosions, etc.). This forced the volunteers to interpret the scenes linguistically rather than emotionally.

The pattern of activation in the brain turned out to be very different for these two situations. As Hariri's team expected, the 'match' condition led to a strong and intense response of the amygdala. The 'label' condition's response was fascinating, showing that the natural reactivity of the amygdala was subdued in tandem with a strong increase in parts of the prefrontal cortex. When people had to label a picture, the strong response in the PFC led to a weaker response in the amygdala.

This linked pattern shows us that the dynamic interactions between the PFC and the amygdala provide a system that allows us to regulate and direct our emotional responses through consciously evaluating our experiences. When faced with a threat – a growling dog, for instance – we do not just react in line with what our amygdala, the panic button, is telling us; instead, areas of the PFC allow us to evaluate the degree of threat, such as whether we can easily escape. In this way, activity in the Stone Age part of our brain – the amygdala – can be subdued. These circuits underlying our rainy brain are critical in helping us to regulate our emotional responses to fear, and it is these same circuits that become dysfunctional in a wide range of disorders, such as anxiety, panic, phobias, PTSD and depression.

To investigate how well we can implement control, volunteers are shown upsetting images when they are in the brain scanner – severely injured people following a bomb blast or a blood-stained, severed hand are typical examples. If the word 'Attend' appears, people are told that they should let themselves become aware of the emotional elements of the scene. If the word 'Reappraise' appears, the volunteers have to do their best to regulate their emotions and try to find ways of feeling less negative about the scene. You might tell yourself, for instance, that the severed hand is just a plastic dummy; it just looks realistic. When we take a peek inside the brain when people are doing this, the results are remarkable. When concentrating on the emotional aspects of a scene, the 'attend' condition, the amygdala becomes active, but when people are 'reappraising,' areas of the PFC become active, and the amygdala activity is reduced.

The truth is that we regulate our emotions all the time, but we are often not aware of what we are doing. Maria, a friend of mine, once explained how she dealt with observing surgery in her early days as a medical student. Concentrating totally on the anatomy, naming each internal organ as she could see it, helped her to suppress the queasiness and revulsion that she experienced. She had learned a powerful way to control the distress that her emergency brain was telling her was appropriate. When in danger of being overcome by revulsion, for instance, Maria might have thought about how the patient would have no more pain after her surgery, how her quality of life would dramatically improve. All of us develop techniques like this to control our emotions in difficult situations, and brain science is now showing that these mental techniques make real differences to how our brain responds.

This ability differs markedly among people. Some panic in the face of mild danger, while others remain calm and focused in the most trying of times. Neuroscience research is now beginning to tell us why.

Justin Kim and Paul Whalen, working at Dartmouth College, used fMRI and a newer technique called *diffusion tensor imaging* (DTI) to map the connections between different areas of the brain. DTI is similar to fMRI, but instead of telling us which areas of the brain are in current use, this technique allows us to see the actual connections between different brain areas by observing how water molecules diffuse around brain tissue. By observing these patterns of dispersion, a map begins to emerge of networks throughout the brain, revealing which area is linked to which.

The Dartmouth team asked twenty volunteers to look at various facial expressions while lying in the brain scanner and found that activity increased in a general way when people were looking at fearful expressions, as opposed to any other kind of facial expression. They traced this increased activity back to a thick bundle of nerve fibres called the *uncinate fasciculus* (UF), which connects the area of the brain containing the amygdala – the temporal lobe – to the PFC. An intriguing finding was that the thickness of the connecting fibres was inversely related to individual differences in the level of self-reported trait anxiety. The more anxious people were, the thinner or weaker the connection. The low anxious had a strong connection.

Structural differences in how the amygdala connects to the PFC means that a low-anxious person can quiet their amygdala quickly and effectively by activating the control centres in his PFC. Inhibitory messages are fired down the strong interconnecting fibres – the UF – to quell the panic reaction. In a highly anxious person, things become more difficult. Not only is there a more reactive panic centre to start with, there is also a weaker PFC, which makes it more difficult to implement control. To make matters worse, the connection, or relay station, between the emergency brain and the control centre is also weaker, making it even harder to quell one's fears.

It is possible that low-anxious people are born with a stronger UF, so that they have a head start in learning how to control their emotions. But given what we know about neuroplasticity, this seems unlikely. Chances are, experience and learning over the years bolster and shape the connections between emotional and control centres. Just as we can strengthen muscles and increase our physical flexibility by working out in the gym, practice can strengthen the connections between different areas of our brain. These shifts of cognition can lead to real changes in how our brain reacts when confronted with fears and with pleasures.

The evidence now indicates that all therapies for emotional disorders target these same fundamental brain circuits underpinning our rainy brain. Once these begin to move and become malleable, the principles of neuroplasticity can take over, strengthening the 'good' circuits and weakening the 'bad.' The classic talking therapy – cognitive behavioural therapy, or CBT – causes a reduction in the activity of the emergency brain alongside an increase in activity in the areas of the PFC. These treatments improve people's ability to control their emotions and are often the treatment of choice for anxiety and depression. CBT is a highly complex psychological intervention that operates on a conscious level, providing people with guidelines and strategies to change dysfunctional patterns of thinking and ways of behaving. While highly effective in the treatment of anxiety and depression, the complexity of CBT makes it difficult to pinpoint the precise mechanism of change. The assumption is that CBT works, at least in part, by changing the low-level biases in cognition that divert the minds of the anxious and depressed towards the negative aspects of life.

This notion is supported by the correlation between changing these biases and the symptoms of anxiety and depression. If a negative bias is shifted in a more positive direction – by CBM, say – the symptoms decrease, and mood stabilises. CBM techniques operate at a preconscious level, the idea being that by retraining our basic tendencies to interpret or attend to the negative, this technique can glide in under the radar of conscious control to change our brain without us even knowing it. What this means is that, as our brain forms a habit of noticing the positive rather than the negative, the underlying brain circuits will gradually begin to change.

While much more research is needed here, there is growing evidence that CBM procedures do change brain circuits, and, like CBT, it seems to be the control centres in the PFC that are changed rather than the amygdala itself. Thus, psychological interventions like CBT and CBM may alter dangerous biases by actively strengthening the ability to regulate and control the spilling over of our fear brain.

In one study in my laboratory, we wanted to see whether CBM could boost the brain mechanisms that lead us to avoid danger as well as boost the brain mechanisms that lead us to approach reward. A large number of electrodes were strapped onto people's heads so that we could measure the pattern of electrical activity that occurs in the brain when they observed positive and negative images. Would the degree of electrical activity shift in a more leftwards or rightward direction depending on the type of CBM training? More activity in the left half of the brain, relative to the right, is related to the tendency to approach good things, while more relative activity in the right half is associated with the avoidance of bad things. If we train people to notice positive images, and this changes the brain circuits underlying the sunny brain, then brain activity should shift leftwards following the procedure. Alternatively, if we train people to notice negative images, and this changes the rainy brain networks, then the pattern of brain activity should shift towards the right.

Using highly emotive pictures of positive and negative scenes, we gave different CBM training interventions to two groups of people. One group was trained to orient towards the positive images and

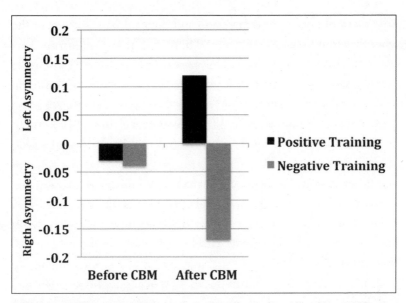

FIGURE 6.1 The results of our study on the effects of cognitive bias modification training on cerebral asymmetry. Positive CBM training induced an increased leftwards asymmetry, whereas negative CBM training resulted in a higher degree of cortical activity in the right side of the brain.

avoid neutral scenes, while the other group saw highly negative as well as neutral scenes and was trained to orient towards the negative images and away from the benign. EEG measures were taken both before and immediately after the CBM.

The results (see Figure 6.1) suggested that we had succeeded in changing not only people's biases but also their brain circuits. Those who were encouraged to notice the pleasant pictures showed more activity in the left half of their brain after training. The direct opposite was found for those who had been through the negative training. CBM training, it seems, can modify our brain's reaction to both fear and fun.

Psychological interventions, like CBT and more recently CBM, are likely to play increasingly important roles in the treatment of severe emotional disorders, but psychoactive drugs are still often the treatment of choice for depression and many other disorders of the affective mind, such as anxiety. There is a real conundrum surrounding how these drugs actually work. At a molecular level, most antidepressants lead to a sharp increase in the amount of serotonin and other neurotransmitters at synaptic junctions. This effect can be detected almost immediately, although clinical changes like improving mood and other symptoms do not occur until several weeks later. Also, antidepressant drugs do not enhance mood in people who are not depressed, while drugs that do enhance our mood, like cocaine for instance, typically are not effective in treating depression. This suggests that antidepressant drugs do not work by improving a person's mood state.

An intriguing explanation of how they do work has come from Oxford University psychologist Catherine Harmer and her colleagues. Realising that antidepressant drugs reduce the negative cognitive biases that are typical of anxiety and depression, they put forward the idea that this shift in processing to a more positive direction leads to a gradual change in social reinforcement and mood over time. In other words, once a bias is shifted in a more positive direction, the depressed person responds more positively in social situations; this, in turn, is reinforced by more positive and friendly social interactions, which eventually lead to an upward spiral of positivity. Findings from animal studies showing that antidepressant drugs promote synaptic plasticity fits nicely with this idea that changing a toxic bias is the first step on a path of relearning and retraining the brain to respond in a more healthy and positive way.

Even the slightest tendency to avoid negativity and approach pleasure and positivity becomes second nature over time, which leads to fundamental changes in how we react to the world. At a cognitive level, then, it seems that drug treatment and psychological therapies all work by changing negative biases. While the psychological therapies affect our ability to regulate and control our emotions, drugs like antidepressants seem to have a more direct impact on the amygdala. These drugs, via changing cognitive biases, directly subdue the overactivity of the fear brain that is a common feature of emotional disorders.

Many psychologists are energised by the findings that we can change these deep-rooted distortions. Neither our genetic makeup nor our experiences should set the course of our life in stone. The world is full of stories of people overcoming adversity to lead happy and fulfilled lives, just as many have thrown away advantage and squandered their opportunities and talent. While our nature and our nurture certainly make it more likely that we will react in one way or another, the science suggests that there is nothing inevitable about this. By shifting our mindscape – the patterns of biases and distortions unique to us – we are able to shift the way we see the world.

A particularly impressive demonstration of this comes from the brain scans of a group of Buddhist monks who agreed to meditate while their brains were being analysed. The practice of meditation is at least 5,000 years old and forms an essential part of many spiritual traditions, including Tibetan Buddhism. People who regularly practice meditation speak of how they can train their minds to be still, thereby dissolving the negative influence of destructive emotions such as anger and jealously. Once these 'mental irritants' have been quelled, the mind can then be set free to pursue a pure form of concentration and insight, ultimately leading to a more fulfilled and happier life.

Focused attention, or FA, is a form of meditation that requires the practitioner to concentrate on a single object – it might be one's own breathing, a candle, or a single word – so that one can block out the clatter of thoughts and images that usually occupy one's mind. Richard Davidson at the University of Wisconsin wanted to find out whether this type of meditation could improve our brain's ability to resist distraction. As many a parent will testify, it is extremely difficult to concentrate when children are screaming and arguing among themselves, but for those who master the FA form of meditation, ignoring the distracting noise and screams seems to become easier.

With his colleague Julie Brefczynski-Lewis, Davidson found that people who practice FA meditation do indeed strengthen the brain circuits that allow them to concentrate and avoid distraction. They studied a group of expert meditators, who had an average of 19,000 hours of practice, and compared them with novices who were just starting meditation. As expected, the brain circuits in the PFC that help ignore distraction were much stronger in the experts, whose brains were able to switch into focus mode in an instant. The more intriguing finding was that for experts with even more practice – an average of 44,000 hours of meditation – there was less activation of these same circuits, even though their powers of concentration and resistance to distraction were much better. It seems that the extensive mental training that these meditators had undergone had strengthened their brain circuits to such an extent that now they needed less effort to concentrate.

Another common form of meditation is known as *open monitoring*, or *mindfulness* meditation. The aim here is to monitor the ordinary experiences of the present moment, allowing all of the sounds, smells, feelings, and thoughts to pass through your mind without judging or reacting to them, which allows the mind to be sufficiently open and free to fully experience the nature of self-awareness. A common strategy used in this form of meditation is labelling of some aspects of your experience. By labelling your feelings, it is thought you can create a sense of detachment that allows you to regulate your emotions more effectively.

In essence, mindfulness meditation requires a person to take the stance of the detached witness. Imagine that you are meditating and trying to keep your mind open to everything, but a distressing thought comes into your mind. Instead of engaging with the content of the thought, the meditator learns to label the thought *this is upsetting* and lets it pass by. This is not easy to achieve, but people who become expert at this form of meditation can gain great control in regulating their emotional experiences. And this form of mindfulness meditation strengthens the neural networks within the prefrontal cortex that regulate how we respond to emotional events.

Much of the distress and worry we experience in everyday life does not come from external events but from our *interpretation* of those events. It is what goes on in our head that really affects us. Letting it float away as a nonmaterial thought is a potent antidote to the disruptive effect of anger. This fits with the substantial evidence that any therapy – whether drug or talk – that strengthens the inhibitory powers of the PFC can decrease the activation of the amygdala and thus greatly improve how we regulate our response to stress. This is why trying to normalise these disrupted circuits is the aim of most interventions to treat mood and anxiety disorders. Given the plasticity of brain circuits, even entrenched 'toxic' circuits can be normalised by mental practice.

In a pioneering study, this principle was illustrated in one of the most difficult mental disorders to treat, OCD. The constant feeling that something is wrong, which is what really bothers people with OCD, is reflected in hyperactivity in an area of the brain called the *orbitofrontal cortex* (OFC), the brain's error detector system, which sits on the underside of the front of the brain just below the PFC. The OFC forms a circuit with the amygdala, and in OCD increased activity in both these areas results in a dysfunctional circuit that is difficult to shift.

UCLA psychiatrist Jeffrey Schwartz, who advised Leonardo DiCaprio, has spent a lifetime trying to rid people of distressing OCD symptoms. He made a real breakthrough when he started wondering whether mindfulness meditation might be helpful for these patients. As a practicing Buddhist himself, he knew the personal benefits that meditation could bring. Instead of teaching his patients the details of meditation per se, he decided to develop a form of cognitive behavioural therapy that included aspects of meditation. This has become known as *mindfulness-based CBT*. Schwartz trains people not to give in to the urge to check the stove but instead to relabel their symptoms as a sign of a disordered brain circuit and not something worth worrying about.

In a pioneering study, Schwartz scanned people's brains both before and after ten weeks of mindfulness-based CBT. He found that, following the treatment, activity in the crucial OFC area had decreased significantly. Not only did people feel less inclined to act out their compulsions, but the error-detecting system in their brain was subdued, allowing them to get on with their lives. This was a major breakthrough, since standard CBT is generally fairly ineffective for OCD. Adding in the mindfulness component made all the difference.

Mindfulness-based CBT has also been successful in undoing the dysfunctional circuits underlying severe depression. Mark Williams, a psychologist at Oxford University, realised that a difficult problem in depression is not so much dealing with the immediate despair and sadness but preventing relapse. Talking therapies like CBT, as well as drug therapies, are often effective to start with in treating the symptoms of depression, but the vast majority of people plunge into despair and depression again and again. In fact, well over 60 per cent of people who benefit from treatment in the short term cannot maintain this benefit over time.

Williams, along with his colleague John Teasdale from the Cognition and Brain Sciences Unit in Cambridge, have conducted a number of important studies with Zindel Segal, who runs a cognitive behaviour therapy clinic at the University of Toronto. All three have battled with the difficulties of helping people who suffer from chronic depression and were often disheartened by their inability to keep people away from the clinic. Teasdale had begun learning and practicing a mindfulness-based stress reduction technique (MBSR) that was being developed by Jon Kabat-Zinn at the University of Massachusetts. The MBSR technique is an eight-week program involving weekly meetings of around two to three hours, along with a home-based practice that people are encouraged to do every day. People are trained to focus their attention on one part of their body after another. 'Focus on your left hand,' they might be told; then, 'move your attention to your left knee.' The aim is to focus their entire concentration on their own breathing without letting any other thoughts enter their head. This is easier said than done, but if your mind does wander, the instruction is to let it go and not to let yourself get dragged down by the thought.

The three psychologists realised that a mindfulness approach like this might be exactly what was needed to prevent people with depression from triggering the network of depressive thoughts that is a key to relapse. Someone who has suffered depression learns through CBT to challenge and negate their negative thoughts: just because someone did not want to go on a date with you does not mean that you are a worthless person. This is effective for a while, but eventually old habits return, and networks of negativity become activated again. One or two stray thoughts like, 'She doesn't like me,' can spiral into hopeless beliefs like, 'I am totally unattractive,' or 'Nobody is ever going to love me.' Before you know it, full-blown depression is back.

Teasdale, Williams, and Segal recruited 145 people between eighteen and sixty-five, all with a history of recurring depression. The volunteers came from all walks of life: the rural environs of the small town of Bangor in North Wales; the mixed rural/city environment of Cambridge, England; and the metropolitan area of Toronto, Canada. About half of the patients received mindfulness-based therapy as well as their usual treatment, while the other half received treatment as normal.

The MBSR intervention cut the rate of relapse in half compared to controls, and this was especially the case for those who had had more than three serious episodes of depression. For these severely depressed individuals who could not shake recurring episodes of depression, a mindfulness-based approach had made a real difference. These are incredibly exciting results, suggesting that we might finally have a treatment to crack the most difficult nut of all – preventing relapse in serious depression.

Not long after this landmark study, Jon Kabat-Zinn turned to Richard Davidson to see whether the MBSR technique was changing actual brain circuits. The clinical results were looking positive, but to ensure an enduring change it is necessary to change brain circuits. Was mindfulness training modifying the way the brain worked?

Davidson recruited forty-eight employees of a Madison biotechnology company, assigning half of them to the intervention while the other half remained on a waiting list. The team measured the electrical activity of the brain to see whether the telltale increased activity in the *right* relative to the *left* PFC that is typical in those who are withdrawn or depressed could be reversed.

The Madison workers had electrodes attached to their scalp on three occasions: at the beginning of the study; immediately after the eight-week MBSR intervention, which was conducted by Kabat-Zinn himself; and once again four months later. As an added twist, the team also injected all of their volunteers with an influenza vaccine to see whether the mindfulness training made any difference to the number of flu antibodies produced. This was done because Davidson had long suspected that meditation might have a beneficial effect on immune system functioning, too.

With the standard eight-week package, people who had practiced mindfulness meditation showed changes in brain activity as well as an improvement in immunity. Even though a change in asymmetry was not observed on all electrodes across the front of the scalp, the telltale shift to more left-sided activation was present on at least some of the electrodes for the mindfulness group. A pattern of brain activity that is typical of happy, optimistic people was strengthened by meditation. It was also discovered that those who had practiced mindfulness meditation for eight weeks produced far more flu antibodies than those on the waiting list.

The next question to ask is whether this type of intense mental training is affecting the amygdala directly, as psychiatric drugs seem to do, or affecting the ability to control emotions, as both CBT and CBM almost certainly do. The answer comes from a study conducted by David Creswell and Mathew Liberman, two psychologists at UCLA. They selected twenty-seven students and gave them a questionnaire to measure their degree of mindfulness. Even without any meditation training, people differ in the degree to which they are mindful, and the UCLA team capitalised on this naturally occurring variation.

While lying in an fMRI brain scanner, each of the volunteers was asked to label photographs of intense facial expressions with either emotional labels (*Angry* or *Scared*?) or gender labels (*Andrea* or *Tom*?). The gender labelling had little effect, but the emotional labelling created waves of activity all over the brain. The more mindful people showed the classic regulatory response: intense ripples of activity across their PFC with a corresponding reduction in the amygdala. In marked contrast, the students who had scored low on the mindfulness questionnaire showed lots of amygdala activity but almost no increase in the PFC to dampen this primitive fear response. Their emergency brain just kept ringing the alarm bells. Neuroscience had confirmed what the Buddha himself had proposed: that labelling our feelings and treating them as nothing more than objects of attention can encourage a sense of detachment from negative experiences.

Subsequent studies have gone even further and shown that structural changes in the parts of our brain that help us to regulate our emotions, especially fear, underlie the improvements in mood that people report following a course of mindfulness-based meditation. In one study, sixteen volunteers were given brain scans before and after eight weeks of the MBSR program developed by Kabat-Zinn. When compared with control volunteers, who did not meditate over the same time period, the MRI scans of the volunteers who had meditated showed an increased density – more neurons – in several key areas of the brain that help regulate our emotions. Those who said that they experienced the greatest reductions in stress over the period also showed a decreased density in the amygdala. The MBSR program had reduced the physical size of their emergency brain and increased the size of the control centres of the brain.

Given that there are individual differences in how well we can regulate our emotions, it is important to ask whether these differences relate to differences in well-being and happiness. Psychologist Stéphane Côté from the University of Toronto asked precisely this question along with his colleagues Anett Gyurak and Bob Levenson from the University of California, Berkeley. They realised that lots of people know about different mental strategies to keep their emotions under control, but being able to implement these strategies, especially when under pressure, is a different story. They conducted a laboratory study in which volunteers were bombarded by a series of loud, unpleasant bursts of noise, which causes a natural startle reflex, but the volunteers had to try to suppress any expression of fright.

What they found was that some people are much better at hiding their startle than others; in the team's terms, they were better 'emotion regulators.' The more novel finding was that these variations were related to real-life differences in subjective well-being; the best regulators were the happiest.

In a second study, the researchers turned the tables and presented their volunteers with various video clips of graphic scenes like the treatment of a badly burned person or an arm amputation. While watching these clips, people now had to *amplify* their emotions;

rather than trying to hide what they were feeling, they now had to let their feelings show.

As before, there were clear individual differences in how well people could up-regulate their emotional reaction. Those who were better able to amplify their emotions also reported higher levels of well-being and happiness. What was even more startling was that when average incomes were compared, it turned out that the good emotion regulators earned substantially more money than those less able to control their emotions. As the former world snooker champion Steve Davies once commented, 'The secret of success is being able to play like it means nothing, when it actually means everything.'

In the heat of the moment, being able to regulate our emotional responses is associated with greater levels of success and feelings of satisfaction with life. And most of us are expert emotional regulators. From the screams and tantrums of our earliest years, over time we learn to gain more control over how we are feeling. The better we can do this, the better we can cope with most of life's ups and downs. This is why anxiety disorders, while on the increase, afflict only a minority of people. Most people are highly resilient and bounce back from problems quickly.

Following the 9/11 attacks, there was great concern that there would be a pandemic of anxiety and PTSD in New York and beyond. It never happened. While most were anxious and frightened at the time, these fears gradually faded, and people began after a while to return to their normal lives. Some people do experience long-lasting problems after disasters, but for all the hype, and all the anxieties generated by politicians and the media, the fact is that most people are highly resistant to the negative long-term effects of fear. A small number did develop severe anxiety disorders, but a small percentage experienced what has been called post-traumatic growth. These resilient characters claim that they have grown and flourished because of their traumatic experience.

George Bonanno, a psychologist at Columbia University in New York, has spent most of his career documenting how people respond to major trauma, and has found, again and again, that people regain their emotional equilibrium after even the most severe trauma and distress. With his colleague Dachner Keltner, he examined the emotions expressed by people who had recently lost a loved one. While sorrow was common, these bereaved people expressed many different emotions – some positive, some negative. Although grief-stricken, most were also capable of laughter and enjoyment from time to time. This ability to bounce back is a key characteristic of our sunny brain. If we can boost our sunny brain mindset, we can also boost our resilience and ability to deal with stress.

Neuroscience and psychology are now trying to understand the mechanisms underlying the resilience and optimism of our sunny brain as much as our rainy brain. One factor that has emerged repeatedly from lots of different areas of research is that feelings of being in control are crucial. If we have a real sense that we control our destiny, this not only helps us bounce back from setbacks but also maximises our enjoyment of life.

The initial hint that a sense of control is important for resilience came from work with animals. When dogs were given repeated electrical shocks that they could not escape, they developed what Martin Seligman, a psychologist at the University of Pennsylvania, called 'learned helplessness.' In his original experiments, Seligman and his colleague Steven Maier placed dogs in a test chamber containing two compartments divided by a low barrier. The floor of the test chamber emitted harmless electric shocks from time to time, which the dog could escape by jumping over the low barrier.

But some dogs were presented with a series of inescapable shocks *before* being placed in the testing chamber. Dogs were paired together and given a series of mild electric shocks. One of the dogs could cut the shock short by pressing a lever with his nose, while the other dog could not. When this second dog pressed the lever, nothing happened. The key was that both dogs received exactly the same number of shocks, but only one dog had any control over the situation.

When subsequently placed in the testing chamber, it was the dogs that previously had control that did not hesitate to escape the shock by hopping over the low barrier. Those who had had no control didn't even try to escape; the majority (about two-thirds) just lay there taking the shock, even though the escape route was easily available. The dogs that had had control never developed this depressive style of coping and did not seem to be particularly stressed. These dogs developed resilience, or psychological immunity, to future stress.

The development of this psychological immunity is heavily dependent on the functioning of the areas of the PFC that are involved with implementing emotion regulation. Steven Maier, Seligman's former colleague, teamed up with Jose Amat at the University of Colorado's Center for Neuroscience and discovered that the immunity to stress that comes by being able to control shock is completely eliminated if certain areas of the PFC are inactivated. This tells us that increasing the regulation of subcortical areas by the PFC is an important neural mechanism underlying the development of resilience to adversity. Take this ability to control away and immunity seems to disappear.

So control, or even perceived control, of a situation is crucial for well-being. If we believe we have even a small degree of control over a difficult situation, it becomes far easier to deal with. Imagine the terror you might feel on the back of a speeding motorcycle or as a passenger in a skidding car. If you are driving, the fear seems somehow muted: your perceived control of the situation confers confidence. Studies with rats have even shown that a lack of control leads to the development of stress-related illnesses like stomach ulcers.

In a now classic study conducted with the elderly residents of a New England nursing home called Arden House in the 1970s, psychologists Judith Rodin and Ellen Langer from the City University of New York wondered whether the inability to make decisions – common among nursing home residents – was caused by their lack of control over their environment. Mindful of Seligman's findings of learned helplessness with rats, these researchers thought that the same process might be occurring in nursing home residents.

To find out, they designed a clever experiment. Two floors of Arden House (floors 2 and 4) were randomly selected, and all residents on these floors were given a plant as well as the opportunity to watch a movie once a week. Everything was kept as identical as possible between the floors, except for the degree of control that the study participants were given. Those on the fourth floor chose their own plant, and they could decide when to water it. They were also allowed to choose which night of the week to watch their movie. In contrast, those living two floors down were given a plant that was watered by a member of the staff. The nursing staff also informed these elderly residents which night of the week was their movie night.

When Rodin and Langer returned to the nursing home eighteen months later, they were astounded by the results. Not only were the fourth-floor residents happier and healthier, twice as many residents on the second floor had died. Taking control had increased people's longevity. No one had expected to find such a difference in life span.

Subsequent research confirms that a sense of control is crucial for health and happiness. Intriguingly, the results of several studies show that you don't have to have any control – the benefits are just as great if the control is illusory. When I spoke to Michael J. Fox, he was keen to point out that he is not unaware of risk, but he has an unshakeable confidence that he can deal with whatever happens. 'I have the armoury to cope with any crisis,' he said. This confidence is a critical aspect of a sunny-brain style, and the science backs this up.

A classic study by psychologists Lauren Alloy and Lyn Abramson published in 1979 shows how this works. Lightbulbs were flashed on and off randomly, and study volunteers could press buttons that had no effect on whether the bulb lit up or not. Mildly optimistic people were convinced that they had some degree of control over lightbulbs – an illusion of control. But those who were mildly depressed were more accurate in realising that they had no control – a phenomenon called 'depressive realism,' or, as the authors put it, the more pessimistic folk were 'sadder but wiser.'

Are pessimists really more accurate at estimating control while optimists have an overly rosy view of things? The answer turns out to be a bit more complicated. In subsequent studies, the researchers asked people to estimate the amount of control both they and other people had over events. The pessimists were, once again, accurate in judging their own lack of control, but they overestimated the amount of control that other people had. They were sure that while they had no control, others did. The optimists inaccurately thought that they themselves had some control, especially when the outcome was good. If an optimist throws a pair of dice and wins £10, he assumes he has had something to do with it.

Psychological research now shows us that, in fact, most of us think we have control over many everyday events. This goes some way towards explaining why most of us are mildly optimistic. It also explains why we think we have a better chance of winning the lottery if we choose the numbers ourselves rather than letting a computer choose the numbers. Likewise, most people think they have a better chance of winning if they throw dice themselves, rather than allowing someone else to throw them. The allure of control is a powerful and integral part of optimism.

Psychological research has identified a number of other factors that are also important elements in the quest for happiness. Our rainy-brain and sunny-brain circuits are the critical radars honing in on the motivational landscape that fill our heads with bad stuff or good stuff. The reactivity of these brain areas determine what we tune into and what we respond to. When our rainy brain becomes overly active, it can lead to devastating conditions such as anxiety and depression. Just as our emergency brain evolved in response to what threatened our ancestors, our pleasure brain evolved in response to what was good for them – access to food and shelter, the protection of togetherness, love, forgiveness, compassion, and so on.

In the modern world, our basic needs – food, shelter, warmth – are usually met, but it is the connectedness with others and a sense of meaning in our lives that are often missing. This is the root of what George Easterbrook calls the 'Paradox of Progress.' He found that in the United States and Europe, while the level of wealth grew substantially over a fifty-year period from the 1950s onward, happiness levels did not budge, and rates of anxiety and depression soared. Survey after survey reported that people did not feel any happier and were often deeply pessimistic about the future. There is a genuine disconnect between the level of material wealth in a society and the subjective feelings of happiness and well-being of its citizens.

So how do we go about creating happier and more flourishing societies? One way is to tackle the rising tide of depression and anxiety disorders head-on, because these problems cause misery to millions of people across the globe. For every person suffering from one of these disorders, you can be sure there are at least five members of their family also affected by the illness, in addition to work colleagues and others in the wider community.

But it is not enough to focus on how we can rid ourselves of un-happiness; it is also important to identify those factors that help us flourish. There are general things, like being physically fit and active and eating a good diet, that support our well-being. Positive psycho-logical features, like certain patterns of cognitive bias or the feeling of personal control, are also critical to developing a more flourishing lifestyle.

More important, science has found that genuine changes in hap-piness only come about when three things come together: lots of positive emotions and laughter, being fully engaged in our lives, and finding a sense of meaning that is broader than our day-to-day life.

Of these three components, engagement in what we are doing, whether it is work or leisure, seems to be especially important. One of the most consistent, if surprising, messages to come from happiness research is that things like a better job, a bigger house, a nicer car don't lead to a lasting increase in happiness. In spite of what the marketers might tell you, that shiny new watch or mobile phone doesn't make you any happier in the long term. Survey after survey shows that once a basic level of wealth has been achieved (having a place to live and having enough food to eat), extra money makes very little difference to people's sense of well-being. What does make you happier is getting involved in something that is meaningful for you. This is a real hallmark of optimists. They're able to throw themselves into a cause and strive to obtain a meaningful goal.

The Hungarian psychologist Mihaly Csikszentmihalyi (pronounced cheek-sent-muh-hy-ee), at Claremont Graduate University in California, calls this type of engagement 'optimal experience' or 'flow.' In this moment there is no sense of past, no sense of future, just an intense present, an overwhelming feeling of being 'in the moment,' or what sports people call 'in the zone.' This is the magical moment when the mental and physical merge in an effortless way. When you play tennis, your stance, your grip of the racket, your release of the ball in a gentle arc above your head, a glance at your opponent across the net, your body swaying gently forward, the perfect strike of the ball with the racket, and the perfect follow-through all come together to make the perfect serve. Everything just seems to click in that enchanted moment.

According to Csikszentmihalyi's research, most of us experience this type of flow about once every couple of months. About 12 per cent of people say they never experience flow, while 10 per cent say that they experience flow daily. The trick is to find the right balance between your level of skill and the degree of challenge. If the task is too easy, boredom is the most likely outcome. Too hard, it becomes stressful. But when the difficulty level presents you with a genuine but realistic challenge, then a trancelike state where nothing else matters can be entered.

Happiness and optimism research are often linked, but it's important to remember that they are not the same thing. Happiness is largely about how we feel here and now: the joy we experience when watching our loved ones play in the sea on a sunny day or the contentment we feel about how our life is going. Optimism and hope relate to how we think and feel about the future. If we really do believe that things will work out for the best, all the setbacks become easier to deal with.

Not all optimists flourish, but a sunny-brain take on the world, especially when linked with realism, does seem to be a great starting point. I have interviewed many of these optimistic realists during the course of writing this book, and it was obvious that most of them do get the best out of life. Many were highly successful, some were wealthy, some were not, but all seemed to enjoy what they did and looked forward to the future.

So what does psychology tell us about flourishing, and what does it take to flourish ourselves?

Psychologist Barbara Fredrickson is an expert on flourishing and has been an advocate of finding ways to bring more positive emotions into our lives. In her research she discovered a critical 3 to 1 ratio, indicating that we need to have three positive emotions for every negative one in order to thrive. Positive emotional experiences include things like a sense of wonder, compassion, contentment, gratitude, hope, joy, love, and sexual desire, while negative feelings are those like anger, contempt, disgust, embarrassment, fear, sadness, and shame, to name just a few.

Fredrickson has found out that if we really want to prosper, we shouldn't try to eliminate negative emotions; rather, we should work on keeping the ratio at three positive for every one negative. Most of us, she has found, have two positive experiences for every negative. This gets us by, but it is effectively languishing. Once we can get this ratio up to three positive for every bad experience, we can begin to truly flourish.

In an important study with Brazilian mathematician Marcial Losada from the Universidade Catholica de Brasilia, Fredrickson discovered not only that the 3 to 1 ratio was critical but that the experience of positive emotions and human flourishing are linked by a precise mathematical formula. To *flourish* means living at the top of your range, enjoying a life filled with goodness, growth, and creativity, and, when things go wrong, a strong resilience to get over the hump. Fredrickson and Losada pinpointed such 'flourishing' mental health in 45 people from a survey of 188 university students. Forty-five out of 188 (23 per cent) may seem very few, but several surveys have shown that only about 20 per cent of Americans are flourishing in this sense.

Once they had identified their 'flourishers' and 'nonflourishers,' Fredrickson and Losada asked everybody to log on to a secure website every evening for an entire month. Each evening all the volunteers filled out a form indicating the number of different emotions they had experienced over the previous twenty-four hours. At the end of the month, the number of positive and negative emotions people had experienced was tallied, and a 'positivity ratio' was computed by dividing the total number of positive emotions by the total number of negative emotions experienced. If I had felt 'angry' 15 times, 'afraid' twice, 'sad' 7 times, 'happy' 10 times, 'content' 14 times, 'grateful' 6 times, and 'filled with love' 10 times, my positivity ratio would be: 40 (total positive emotions) / 24 (total negative emotions) = 1.66. For every negative emotion I experienced, I would have had almost two positive emotions (1.66 to be precise) to compensate.

When the researchers compared the positivity ratios for their flourishers and nonflourishers, they found a large difference: those who were flourishing had a positivity ratio of 3.3, whereas the average for the rest was 2.2. As found in other studies, the 3 to 1 ratio was the critical dividing line between those who were getting the most out of life and those who were not.

Positivity ratios are also important for a happy marriage. Dr John Gottman from the Gottman Institute in Seattle has applied strict scientific principles to how couples relate to each other. Through his extensive research on happiness within marriage, he learned that a key predictor of who stays together and who doesn't is the ratio of positive to negative experiences that couples have with each other. The magic ratio seems to be five positive interactions for every negative. As the number of negative episodes creeps up relative to positive experiences, divorce becomes more and more likely.

Positivity ratios seep out into every aspect of our lives, affecting how we deal with other people, how effective we are at work, and even how healthy we are. Perhaps this line of research answers the paradox of why most of us say we are happy even though pessimism has a more powerful draw. We know that fear wins over joy, that danger cues are stronger than pleasure cues, making optimism relatively more difficult than pessimism to take hold. In spite of this, most people report that they are optimistic about the future and happy and contented with their lives.

The critical ratio of good to bad things might be the answer to this paradox. The truth is that we do pay more attention to negative events, but this is trumped by the greater frequency of the positive in our lives. To overcome the potential toxicity of negative emotions, we need to ensure that for every negative we have at least two, preferably more, positive experiences. In order for happiness and optimism to stay with us, we need to aim higher and have at least three positive experiences for every bad.

Having a healthy and responsive rainy brain as well as a healthy and responsive sunny brain is crucial. Research conducted by psychologist Tali Sharot with her colleague Liz Phelps shows that elements of both the emergency brain *and* the pleasure-seeking brain are essential for a happy outlook on life. They asked people to recall past negative events when their brains were being scanned. Someone might recall how she had felt when her mother died or how she felt when she split up with a partner. As people brought these bad experiences to mind, their amygdala responded strongly. Then people were asked to imagine how they might feel if these same negative experiences were to occur in the *future*. This time the response of the amygdala was much weaker, especially for those who reported that they were optimists. The optimists simply found it harder to imagine bad things happening in the future. Sharot and Phelps speculated that this weakened consideration of a dark future might be a neural mechanism underlying the optimism bias.

The work of developmental psychologist Anthony Ong and his colleagues at Cornell University fits nicely with this account. They find that resilient and optimistic people experience more positive and negative emotions than less resilient folk when they are going through a difficult patch. When people are dealing with the death of a spouse, the most resilient will pass through a range of emotional highs and lows. Lots of researchers are beginning to believe that being able to experience positive emotions is an important way of coping that helps us to regulate our negative emotions. Good times, in other words, can neutralise the effects of the bad. As Barbara Fredrickson found in the aftermath of September 11 in New York, it's not the ability to suppress negativity that's critical; rather, it's getting the balance right.

Creating Healthy Minds

Positive thoughts that are not connected to real changes in brain circuits are unlikely to support us when the winds of adversity sweep through our lives. 'Into every life, a little rain must fall' is surely true. None of us can escape disappointments and sadness completely. Therefore, having the capacity to experience lots of emotions, alongside the ability to apply the brakes to these emotions if need be, is one of the keys to a well-balanced life. We need a responsive sunny brain that happily cohabits our mind-space with a healthy rainy brain.

Both aspects of our affective mind are influenced by what life throws at us, our genetic makeup, and which genes are turned on and off by the experiences we have. Most importantly, the crucial biases or quirks of mind that set our affective mind into solid foundations can be sculpted by mental training, whether it is through mindfulness-based techniques, cognitive bias modification techniques, drug treatments, or traditional talking therapies. Our mind is highly plastic, and the affective mind is no exception. While it's not necessarily easy to change, the possibility of shifting our fundamental affective mindset is always there.

As I was coming to the end of writing this book, I visited Richie Davidson at the Waisman Center for Neuroscience at the University of Wisconsin to see his new Center for Investigating Healthy Minds for myself. Like many psychologists, Davidson started his career trying to understand and change the type of emotional styles that lead people into anxiety and depression; now, like many of us, Davidson concentrates much of his research efforts on what allows people to flourish. 'We know a lot about unhealthy minds,' Davidson said, 'but almost nothing about healthy minds.'

'So what is a healthy mind?' I asked.

'I couldn't tell you,' he said. 'But you know it when you see it.'

The day I was due to leave, Davidson showed me around his new centre, which had just been built and was still being decorated. The centrepiece is a large atrium made of soft-coloured wood flooded with natural light.

'This is the meditation centre,' he said, 'and here are the rooms that will house the state-of-the-art fMRI machines.'

The centre was an intoxicating mix of an ancient contemplative tradition with cutting-edge contemporary neuroscience. As I walked away, I realised how far we have come in recent years in learning ways to overcome anxiety and fear as well as discovering ways to boost flourishing and optimism. By capitalising on new approaches emerging from psychology, neuroscience, and genetics, and integrating them with ancient wisdoms from Eastern traditions, we are well on the way towards creating people and societies that will allow healthy minds to truly flourish.

ACKNOWLEDGEMENTS

It has been a real privilege to contemplate the vagaries of our rainy brains and sunny brains with a host of innovative and inspiring scientists from across the disciplines of psychology, neuroscience, and genetics during the writing of this book. How our ways of thinking influence our emotions is at the core of my own research, and many of those at the forefront of this field have become close friends and colleagues over the years. I am especially grateful to Yair Bar-Haim, Phil Barnard, Eni Becker, Brendan Bradley, Tim Dalgleish, Naz Derakshan, Paula Hertel, Colette Hirsh, Emily Holmes, Ernst Koster, Jennifer Lau, Bundy Mackintosh, Colin MacLeod, Andrew Mathews, Sue Mineka, Karen Mogg, Mike Rinck, Mark Williams, and Jenny Yiend for numerous discussions on the power of cognitive biases and the possibilities opened up by the capacity to change them.

Scientific work on the science of fear and the science of pleasure forms much of the bedrock of this book and was spearheaded by Kent Berridge, Andy Calder, Richie Davidson, Ray Dolan, Joseph LeDoux, Arne Öhman, and Liz Phelps. I am grateful to all of them for answering my questions on the nature of fear and pleasure and how these fundamental drives are implemented in the human brain. Equally generous with their time has been a group of scientists who have changed the way we think about genes and how they influence our behaviour. They don't always agree with each other, but collectively their work has helped me to develop a deeper understanding of how genes and environments work together to produce rainy brains and sunny brains. It's been fun, too! I'm particularly grateful to Avshalom Caspi, Thalia Eley, Jonathon Flint, Ahmad Hariri, Ken Kendler, Terrie Moffitt, and Essi Viding.

Acknowledgements

I could never have written this book without the understanding of a succession of PhD students and research workers in my lab at the University of Essex. Most recently Pavlina Charalambous and Rachael Martin have been great. Over a longer period Stacy Eltiti, Kelly Garner, Anna Ridgewell, Helen Standage, Denise Wallace, Alan Yates, and Konstantina Zougkou have kept things ticking over when I was away writing. I also thank the Wellcome Trust, which provided generous support for my research program on rainy brains over a fifteen-year period.

My good friends Michael Brooks, Cathy Grossman, Alexa Geiser, Stephen Joseph, Peter Tallack, and Christine Temple have spent many hours encouraging me to present this material for a general audience. Along with Hugh Jones, Deborah Kent, Nick Kent, Pippa Newman, and Richard Newman, they have provided vital support and encouragement at crucial moments. Late nights and fine wines in Wivenhoe with Nigel Stratton and Lisa Tuffin were also a great help along the way. As always, my wonderful husband, Kevin Dutton, makes everything worthwhile. Thanks for everything – including the title!

The enthusiasm and sound advice of my agent, Patrick Walsh, has been an inspiration. The help of all at Conville and Walsh, especially Jake Smith-Bosanquet and Alex Christofi, ensured that the book got written and published. I am grateful to Lara Heimert at Basic Books and Drummond Moir at William Heinemann for helping me to bring some structure to a first chaotic draft. The book also benefited from the editorial guidance of Liz Stein at Basic and Tom Avery and Jason Arthur of Heinemann. I am also grateful to Pete Wilkins for developing a great website. This book was completed while I was a Visiting Fellow at Magdalen College, Oxford. I am grateful to the fellows and staff of Magdalen who provided such a supportive and uplifting environment in which to finish *Rainy Brain, Sunny Brain*.

Finally, I have questioned, probed, and tested hundreds of people suffering with depression and anxiety over the years. My strong belief is that science will gradually develop more effective ways to calm afflicted minds. This book is dedicated to all of those who volunteer to take part in research studies around the world, to those who conduct the studies, and to those who provide the funding. My hope is that the various research strands discussed in these pages will eventually help to create happier, healthier minds and flourishing societies.

NOTES

Chapter 1: Rainy Brains and Sunny Brains

1 **I later found out:** Paul Castle's suicide was reported in the *Daily Mail* (London), 20 November 2010: www.dailymail.co.uk/news/article -1331308/Prince-Charless-friend-Paul-Castle-commits-suicide -business-hit-recession.html.

2 **'I realised it was nowhere':** The story of Adan Abobaker's brave rescue was reported in the *Evening Standard* (London), 19 November 2010: www.thisislondon.co.uk/standard/article-23899334-homeless-man-plunges-into-icy-thames-to-save-woman-from-drowning.do.

3 **The influence that our personalities:** The study described here can be read in B. W. Headey and A. J. Wearing, 'Personality, Life Events and Subjective Well-Being: Towards a Dynamic Equilibrium Model,' *Journal of Personality and Social Psychology* 57 (1989): 731–739.

5 **documentary with the unlikely title:** The documentary was made by ABC and aired on 7 May 2009, in the United States. Michael's book *Always Looking Up: The Adventures of an Incurable Optimist* (New York: Hyperion Books, 2009) presents a number of interesting stories and descriptions of very optimistic people.

6 **Levi chronicles the horrific story:** Primo Levi's first book describing everyday life in Auschwitz was recounted in *If This Is a Man* and was first published by the Italian publisher Einaudi in 1956 and subsequently reprinted many times all around the world. His subsequent book, *The Truce*, describes his gradual recovery from the impact of his year in Auschwitz. Levi died at the age of sixty-seven, when he fell down a narrow stairwell. Mystery surrounds his death, with some believing it was suicide as a result of increasing depression, while others claim that there is no evidence for this theory.

7 **The original meaning of *optimism*:** A good and accessible introduction to Leibniz's thoughts on optimism can be found in Lloyd Strickland, *Leibniz Reinterpreted* (New York: Continuum, 2006).

8 **A revised version called the LOT-R:** The LOT-R was developed by Michael Scheier and Charles Carver, and further details can be found in Michael F. Scheier, Charles S. Carver, and Michael W. Bridges, 'Distinguishing Optimism from Neuroticism (and Trait Anxiety, Self-Mastery, and Self-Esteem): A Re-Evaluation of the Life Orientation Test,' *Journal of Personality and Social Psychology* 67 (1994): 1063–1078. In order to find your score, fill out the questions on page 9, and then follow the scoring instructions below. First, ignore your scores on questions 2, 5, 6, and 8, as these are just filler questions. For questions 1, 4, and 10, score your answers as follows: A = 4, B = 3, C = 2, D = 1, and E = 0. Then for questions 3, 7, and 9, score your answers as follows: A = 0, B = 1, C = 2, D = 3, and E = 4. Now, add all six of your scores together, and you should obtain a number between 0 and 24. Most people score around 15, which is 'mildly optimistic,' while 0 indicates 'extreme pessimism,' and 24 indicates 'extreme optimism.'

13 **'blooming, buzzing confusion':** This explanation of an infant's view appears in William James, *The Principles of Psychology* (New York: Henry Holt, 1890), 488. William James studied medicine but never practiced and was subsequently appointed to teach anatomy and physiology at Harvard University. He soon turned his attention to understanding the human mind, however, and established the first US laboratory in experimental psychology at Harvard in 1875. He is acknowledged as the first American psychologist and was the brother of the noted novelist Henry James. While James speculated that infants had poor perceptual acuity, hence the reference to 'blooming, buzzing confusion,' subsequent work has shown that young infants do actually have much sharper perceptual abilities than was originally thought. For a good overview of this topic, see R. N. Aslin and L. B. Smith, 'Perceptual Development,' *Annual Review of Psychology* 39 (1988): 435–473.

16 **Schneirla spent a lifetime:** Much of the original work was conducted by T. C. Schneirla at New York University from the 1920s to the 1960s. A good summary of his views can be found in T. C. Schneirla, 'An Evolutionary and Developmental Theory of Biphasic Processes Underlying Approach and Withdrawal,' in *Nebraska Symposium on Motivation*, ed. M. R. Jones (Lincoln: University of Nebraska Press,

1959). An interesting description of Schneirla's life and work can be found in Ethel Tobach, 'T. C. Schneirla: Pioneer in Field and Laboratory Research,' in *Portraits of Pioneers in Psychology*, vol. 4, ed. Gregory A. Kimble and Michael Wertheimer (Washington, DC: American Psychological Association, 2000). Good overviews of more recent neuroscientific and psychological research on approach and withdrawal mechanisms can be found in Richard J. Davidson and W. Irwin, 'The Functional Neuroanatomy of Emotion and Affective Style,' *Trends in Cognitive Sciences* 3 (1999): 11–21, and in S. Whittle et al., 'The Neuroanatomical Basis of Affective Temperament: Towards a Better Understanding of Psychopathology,' *Neuroscience and Biobehavioural Reviews* 30 (2006): 511–525.

18 **a 'visual cliff' apparatus:** This apparatus was designed by Eleanor Gibson and Richard Walk, who conducted a variety of experiments with both human infants and a variety of other animal species. Human infants would not venture out over the 'cliff' even when they could feel the solid surface with their hands. This was also true for a variety of other species, showing the dominance of vision over touch. However, rats, with their reliance on their sense of smell rather than on vision, were quite happy to run across the deep part of the cliff with little apparent fear. A good description of the apparatus and the experiments is available in E. J. Gibson and R. D. Walk, 'The "Visual Cliff,"' *Scientific American* 202, no. 4 (1960): 64–71.

19 **'Cocktail Party Effect':** Cherry's work was inspired by the problems faced by air-traffic controllers in the 1950s. The voices of many different pilots would be broadcast in the control tower over loudspeakers, and the resulting chaos of intermixed voices made the task very difficult for the controllers. To try to understand how this might be improved, Cherry conducted a series of experiments at Imperial College in London. His big breakthrough came when he played different messages to each ear of a listener in what he called a *dichotic listening task*. The results from these experiments are reported in E. C. Cherry, 'Some Experiments on the Recognition of Speech with One and Two Ears,' *Journal of the Acoustical Society of America* 25 (1953): 975–979. Some experiments in other laboratories extended and refined these initial studies, such as N. L. Wood and N. Cowan, 'The Cocktail Party Phenomenon Revisited: How Frequent Are Attention Shifts to One's Own Name in an Irrelevant Auditory Channel?' *Journal of Experimental Psychology: Learning, Memory and Cognition* 21 (1995): 255–260; and N. L. Wood and N. Cowan, 'The Cocktail Party Phenomenon

Revisited: Attention and Memory in the Classic Selective Listening Procedure of Cherry (1953),' *Journal of Experimental Psychology: General* 124 (1995): 243–262. An overview of more contemporary work on selective processing biases can be found in Elaine Fox, *Emotion Science: Cognitive and Neuroscientific Approaches to Understanding Human Emotions* (New York: Palgrave Macmillan, 2008).

20 **A technique called the *attentional probe task*:** There are many variants on the attentional probe task, and I have given a brief history in the following book chapter: Elaine Fox and George Georgiou, 'The Nature of Attentional Biases in Human Anxiety,' in *Cognitive Limitations in Aging and Psychopathology*, ed. Randall W. Engle, Grzegorz Sedek, Ulrich von Hecker, and Daniel N. McIntosh (Cambridge, UK: Cambridge University Press, 2004), 249–274. One of the earliest studies to use this paradigm presented pairs of negative and neutral words on a screen; when the words disappeared, the task was simply to detect the presence of a target probe as quickly as possible by pressing a button. In this study, Colin MacLeod and his colleagues found that very anxious people were faster to detect the probe when it followed a negative word compared to when it followed a neutral word. People who were not anxious did not show this difference. The paper is C. MacLeod, A. Mathews, and P. Tata, 'Attentional Bias in Emotional Disorders,' *Journal of Abnormal Psychology* 95 (1986): 15–20. Several later studies have replicated these effects, and an excellent review is available in Y. Bar-Haim et al., 'Threat-Related Attentional Bias in Anxious and Non-Anxious Individuals: A Meta-Analytic Study,' *Psychological Bulletin* 133 (2007): 1–24.

22 **Study after study told us:** While early studies, such as MacLeod et al., 'Attentional Bias,' found that anxious people were drawn to negative information, some studies found that nonanxious people tended to show the opposite bias; in other words, they *avoided* negative information. See Elaine Fox, 'Allocation of Visual Attention and Anxiety,' *Cognition and Emotion* 7 (1993): 207–215, and Colin MacLeod and Andrew Mathews, 'Anxiety and the Allocation of Attention to Threat,' *Quarterly Journal of Experimental Psychology* 40A (1988): 653–670.

23 **In his experiments, Bower:** An overview of this work can be found in G. H. Bower, 'Mood and Memory,' *American Psychologist* 36 (1981): 129–148; G. H. Bower and P. R. Cohen, 'Emotion Influences in Memory and Thinking: Data and Theory,' in *Affect and Cognition*, ed. M. S. Clark and S. T. Fiske (Hillsdale, NJ: Erlbaum, 1982), 291–331; G. H. Bower and J. P. Forgas, 'Mood and Social

Memory,' in *Handbook of Affect and Social Cognition*, ed. J. P. Forgas (Mahwah, NJ: Erlbaum, 2001), 95–120; G. H. Bower, K. P. Monteiro, and S. G. Gilligan, 'Emotional Mood as a Context of Learning and Recall,' *Journal of Verbal Learning and Verbal Behaviour* 17 (1978): 573–585.

23   **Bower again used hypnosis:** In memory experiments with words like these, great care has to be taken to make sure that the positive and negative words are closely matched for things like how frequently they occur in the language and how familiar they are. Each word has a specific frequency of how often it occurs in both spoken and written language, and the more frequent a word is, the easier it will be to remember. Because of this, it is very important that the positive and negative words are as similar as possible, so that any difference in ease of remembering can be put down to the emotionality of the word and not to its frequency.

25   **What psychologists call the *confirmation bias*:** Much has been written about the confirmation bias – our tendency to seek out only confirming evidence for what we believe. The study on extroverts and introverts by Mark Snyder is reported in M. Snyder and W. B. Swann, 'Hypothesis Testing Processes in Social Interaction,' *Journal of Personality and Social Psychology* 36 (1978): 1202–1212. An excellent overview of how our beliefs determine our social reality can be found in Mark Snyder, 'When Belief Creates Reality,' in *Advances in Experimental Social Psychology*, vol. 18, ed. L. Berkowitz (New York: Academic Press, 1984), 247–305.

26   **dramatic story of Vance Vanders:** The story of Vance Vanders along with many other intriguing tales of how strong beliefs can lead to medical symptoms is told in Clifton K. Meador, *Symptoms of Unknown Origin: A Medical Odyssey* (Nashville: Vanderbilt University Press, 2005). This story is also recounted in an article: Helen Pilcher, 'The Science and Art of Voodoo: When Mind Attacks Body,' *New Scientist* 2708 (13 May 2009).

28   **the *nocebo* effect:** An excellent review of scientific studies on the nocebo effect – findings that beliefs can cause illness – can be found in Arthur Barsky et al., 'Nonspecific Medication Side Effects and the Nocebo Phenomenon,' *Journal of the Medical Association of America* 287, no. 5 (2002), and nocebo effects are also discussed in Pilcher, 'The Science and Art of Voodoo.' The University of California study showing that beliefs can cause headaches is reported in A. Schweiger and A. Parducci, 'Nocebo: The Psychologic Induction of Pain,' *Pavlov-*

ian Journal of Biological Science 16, no. 3 (July–September 1981): 140–143.

28 **Jon-Kar Zubieta and his colleagues:** A description of Zubieta's studies demonstrating that beliefs can have a direct effect on brain physiology can be found in David J. Scott et al., 'Placebo and Nocebo Effects Are Defined by Opposite Opioid and Dopaminergic Responses,' *Archives of General Psychiatry* 65, no. 2 (2008): 220–231.

29 **Evidence from the large-scale Framingham Heart Study:** The finding that women who believe they are prone to heart disease are more likely to die is reported in Rebecca Voelker, 'Nocebos Contribute to a Host of Ills,' *Journal of the Medical Association of America* 275, no. 5 (1996): 345–347.

Chapter 2: Sunny-Side Up

33 **Psychologists and neuroscientists are now:** Detailed academic descriptions of the neural mechanisms underlying the pleasure system can be found in Kent C. Berridge, 'Measuring Hedonic Impact in Animals and Infants: Microstructure of Affective Taste Reactivity Patterns,' *Neuroscience and Biobehavioural Reviews* 24 (2000): 173–198; Kent C. Berridge, 'Comparing the Emotional Brains of Humans and Other Animals,' in *Handbook of Affective Sciences*, ed. R. J. Davidson, K. R. Scherer, and H. H. Goldsmith (New York: Oxford University Press, 2003), 25–51; and K. C. Berridge and T. E. Robinson, 'Parsing Rewards,' *Trends in Neurosciences* 26 (2003): 507. A more accessible introduction can be found in Morten L. Kringelbach, *The Pleasure Center* (New York: Oxford University Press, 2009).

34 **James Olds and Peter Milner:** The now famous electrode studies, in which rats choose to stimulate their own nucleus accumbens rather than indulging in other pleasures like sex or food, was published in J. Olds and P. Milner, 'Positive Reinforcement Produced by Electrical Stimulation of the Septal Area and Other Regions of Rat Brain,' *Journal of Comparative and Physiological Psychology* 47 (1954): 419–427.

35 **one of the most controversial research programs:** A book by Robert Heath called *The Role of Pleasure in Behaviour: A Symposium by 22 Authors* (New York: Harper & Row, 1964) makes for interesting reading. Some of the case histories of patients with deep brain electrodes are reported in R. G. Heath, 'Pleasure and Brain Activity in Man: Deep and Surface Electroencephalograms During Orgasm,' *Journal of Nervous and Mental Diseases* 154 (1972): 3–18. Many of the earliest

studies on deep brain stimulation are also described in a book by Jose Delgado, *Physical Control of the Mind: Towards a Psychocivilised Society* (New York: Harper & Row, 1969). Delgado and Heath have both been accused of working for the CIA on a 'mind control' project, although there does not seem to be any hard evidence for this. Heath's work on deep brain stimulation was particularly controversial. For instance, the twenty-four-year-old B-19 described by Heath was gay, and Heath went on to try to 'cure' his homosexuality by trying to train him to experience pleasure when shown erotic images of women, even going so far as to encourage him to have sex with a prostitute – or 'lady of the night' as she was described – in the clinic while his electrodes were being activated. Try getting that through a modern-day ethics committee!

38   **Otto Loewi:** 'The Nobel Chronicles 1936: Henry Hallett Dale (1875–1968) and Otto Loewi (1873–1961),' *Lancet* 353 (January 30, 1999): 416; *Nobel Lectures in Physiology or Medicine 1922–1941* (Amsterdam: Elsevier, 1965). Unfortunately, just two years after he won the Nobel Prize, Loewi was arrested (for the 'crime' of being Jewish) and forced to hand his Nobel Prize money over to a Nazi-controlled bank. After fleeing to England without a penny to his name, he was a visiting professor at Oxford for a short time before eventually moving to the College of Medicine at New York University in 1940.

40   **an intriguing study using student volunteers:** This study was the first demonstration of how behaviours like playing a video game could lead to the release of dopamine in the human brain. This was achieved by persuading people to play a video game while their brain was being scanned by positron emission tomography (PET), which allows us to see the release of neurotransmitters in different areas of the brain. It is published in M. J. Koepp et al., 'Evidence for Striatal Dopamine Release During a Video Game,' *Nature* 393, no. 6682 (1998): 266–268.

40   **the story of pleasure is much:** An excellent overview of the science of pleasure can be found in Morten L. Kringelbach and Kent C. Berridge, eds., *Pleasures of the Brain* (New York: Oxford University Press, 2009). This book features leading experts discussing all aspects of the science behind our pleasure system. For a more accessible introduction to this material, see Morten L. Kringelbach, *The Pleasure Center: Trust Your Animal Instincts* (New York: Oxford University Press, 2009). An entertaining read on the science of pleasure can also be found in Paul Martin, *Sex, Drugs and Chocolate: The Science of Pleasure* (London: Fourth Estate, 2008).

40   **Kent Berridge, a psychologist:** Several good reviews of Berridge's research are available. For example, the following article provides a concise overview of this fascinating research program: M. L. Kringelbach and K. C. Berridge, 'Towards a Functional Neuroanatomy of Pleasure and Happiness,' *Trends in Cognitive Science* 13, no. 11 (2009): 479–487. There is also an interesting chapter by K. S. Smith et al., 'Hedonic Hotspots: Generating Sensory Pleasure in the Brain,' in Kringelbach and Berridge, eds., *Pleasures of the Brain*, 27–49. For more details, see Berridge's web pages at the University of Michigan: www.personal.umich.edu/~berridge/.

43   **tested this theory with twenty-seven people:** This study is reported in A. S. Heller et al., 'Reduced Capacity to Sustain Positive Emotion in Major Depression Reflects Diminished Maintenance of Fronto-Striatal Brain Activation,' *Proceedings of the National Academy of Sciences* 106 (2009): 22445–22450.

44   **Using such electroencephalography (EEG) techniques:** A good overview of this research can be found in Richard J. Davidson and William Irwin, 'The Functional Neuroanatomy of Emotion and Affective Style,' *Trends in Cognitive Sciences* 3 (1999): 11–21.

45   **Ruut Veenhoven, a sociologist:** R. Veenhoven, 'Hedonism and Happiness,' *Journal of Happiness Studies* 4 (2003): 437–457.

46   **sensation seeking lies on a spectrum:** An excellent overview of the psychology of sensation seeking and the willingness to take risks for the sake of intense experiences can be found in Marvin Zuckerman, *Sensation Seeking and Risky Behaviour* (New York: American Psychological Association, 2007).

46   **the Brief Sensation Seeking Scale:** This scale was developed by Rick Hoyle and colleagues at Duke University. Further details can be found in R. H. Hoyle et al., 'Reliability and Validity of a Brief Measure of Sensation Seeking,' *Personality and Individual Differences* 32, no. 3 (2002): 401–414. In order to find your score, answer each question on page 47 and then follow the scoring instructions below. First, you will see that each question is scored from 1 to 5. Simply add up all of your questions and then divide by 8 to get your total sensation-seeking score. Thus, if you scored 5 for everything, your total would be 40; dividing by 8 would give you a mean sensation-seeking score of 5. You can obtain your score for each of the four components of sensation seeking: simply add the total score for each of the two questions and then divide by 2 to get the mean for that component. *Experience Seeking* is question 1 and 5, *Boredom Susceptibility* is 2 and 6, *Thrill and*

Adventure Seeking is 3 and 7, while *Disinhibition* is 4 and 8. Studies have shown that on average adolescent males score from 3.07 to 3.14 in terms of their total score (mean = 3.1), while females score a bit lower, from about 2.95 to 3.02 (mean = 2.98). Mean sensation-seeking scores also tend to differ across ethnic groups and generally decline as we get older. For further information, see D. Vallone et al., 'How Reliable and Valid Is the Brief Sensation Seeking Scale for Youth of Various Racial Ethnic Groups?' *Addiction* 102, supp. 2 (2007): 71–78.

47 **psychologists at the University of Kentucky:** The work of Jane Joseph and her colleagues showing that the brains of high sensation seekers differ from those of us who avoid risk is published in J. E. Joseph et al., 'Neural Correlates of Emotional Reactivity in Sensation Seeking,' *Psychological Science* 20, no. 2 (2009): 215–223.

48 **psychologist Suzanne Segerstrom:** Suzanne Segerstrom, *Breaking Murphy's Law: How Optimists Get What They Want – and Pessimists Can Too* (New York: Guilford Press, 2006), 33.

49 **Barbara Ehrenreich in her book:** For an entertaining overview of how unthinking optimism can be bad for us, see Barbara Ehrenreich, *Smile or Die: How Positive Thinking Fooled America and the World* (London: Granta Books, 2009).

50 **a survey conducted by the United Kingdom's National Lottery:** Full details of this survey can be found online at www.lottery.co.uk/news/lotto-optimism-report.asp.

51 **A survey of 17,356 people:** Full details on this poll, conducted by the BBC World Service, can be found online at news.bbc.co.uk/1/hi/world/americas/obama_inauguration/7838475.stm.

52 **Why are our brains biased:** For some of the first studies demonstrating the optimism bias or what has often been called the 'positivity illusion,' see Neil D. Weinstein, 'Unrealistic Optimism about Future Life Events,' *Journal of Personality and Social Psychology* 39 (1980): 806–820. Stuart Sutherland's *Irrationality: Why We Don't Think Straight!* (New Brunswick, NJ: Rutgers University Press, 1994) is a classic overview of how humans are characterised by irrational thinking. Lots of more recent examples of the optimism bias, especially as they relate to behavioural economics, can be found in Dan Ariely, *Predictably Irrational: The Hidden Forces That Shape Our Decisions* (New York: HarperCollins, 2008), and Tali Sharot, *The Optimism Bias: A Tour of the Irrationally Positive Brain* (New York: Pantheon Books, 2011).

52 **Science gives us several clues:** The tendency of many men to interpret friendliness as sexual interest has been reported in many studies,

including the experiment discussed here by F. E. Saal, C. B. Johnson, and N. Weber, 'Friendly or Sexy? It May Depend on Whom You Ask,' *Psychology of Women Quarterly* 13 (1989): 262–276. Several other examples are discussed by Martie Heselton and his colleague David Buss in 'Error Management Theory: A New Perspective on Biases and Cross-Sex Mind Reading,' *Journal of Personality and Social Psychology* 78 (2000): 81–91.

53   **the simple Satisfaction with Life Scale:** The SWLS was developed by Ed Diener, the Josseph R. Smiley Distinguished Professor of Psychology at the University of Illinois, and his colleagues. The original paper is E. Diener et al., 'The Satisfaction with Life Scale,' *Journal of Personality Assessment* 49 (1985): 71–75. Extensive discussion about the SWLS and the meaning of the various scores can be found at internal.psychology.illinois.edu/~ediener/. Adding together your scores on all the questions gives you an overall score between 5 and 35. Diener explains the meaning of the different categories as follows: 30–35 is 'Highly Satisfied.' If you score in this range, you clearly love your life and feel things are going well. Life is enjoyable, and all the major domains (e.g., work, leisure, family) are all going well. A score in the 25–29 range is also a high score indicating that most domains of life are going well. A score from 20 to 24 is the average in economically developed countries. A score within this range indicates that you are mostly satisfied with life, but see some areas for improvement. Scoring between 15 and 19 is slightly below average. If you score in this range, the chances are that you will have small but significant problems in several areas of your life. A score in the range 10–14 is 'Dissatisfied.' A score in this range suggests that there are a number of domains of life that are not going well. A score between 5 and 9 is 'extremely dissatisfied.' Dissatisfaction at this level is usually due to problems in multiple areas of life according to Diener, and the help of other people is almost certainly required. For further information and explanations of these categories of scores see internal.psychology.illinois.edu /~ediener/.

55   **In a now famous study:** The study described here is D. D. Danner, D. A. Snowdon, and W. V. Friesen, 'Positive Emotions in Early Life and Longevity: Findings from the Nun Study,' *Journal of Personality and Social Psychology* 80 (2001): 804–813.

56   **her 'broaden and build' theory:** This theory is accessibly presented in Fredrickson's excellent book *Positivity: Groundbreaking Research Reveals How to Embrace the Hidden Strength of Positive Emotions,*

Overcome Negativity, and Thrive (New York: Crown, 2009). The study on the role of positive emotions in building resilience after the September 11 attacks in New York is B. L. Fredrickson et al., 'What Good Are Positive Emotions in Crises? A Prospective Study of Resilience and Emotions Following the Terrorist Attacks on the United States on September 11, 2001,' *Journal of Personality and Social Psychology* 84 (2003): 365–376.

58 **A study led by Mika Kivimaki:** M. Kivimaki et al., 'Optimism and Pessimism as Predictors of Change in Health After Death or Onset of Severe Illness in Family,' *Health Psychology* 24 (2005): 413–421.

59 **Madam C. J. Walker:** Walker lived a remarkable life. In spite of being born into a poor family of former slaves in the deep South in the late 1800s, she managed to found and run a major company and become one of the wealthiest women in America. Her story is beautifully recounted by her great-great-granddaughter: A'Lelia Bundles, *On Her Own Ground: The Life and Times of Madam C. J. Walker* (New York: Scribner, 2001).

59 **It's difficult to measure:** The lab study of persistence described here is L. Solberg Nes, S. Segerstrom, and S. E. Sephten, 'Engagement and Arousal: Optimism's Effect During a Brief Stressor,' *Personality and Social Psychology Bulletin* 31 (2005): 111–120.

60 **Testing large numbers of law students:** S. Segerstrom, 'Optimism, Goal Conflict, and Stressor-Related Immune Change,' *Journal of Behavioural Medicine* 24 (2001): 441–467.

60 **the results of a meta-analysis:** H. N. Rasmussen et al., 'Optimism and Physical Health: A Meta-Analytic Review,' *Annals of Behavioural Medicine* 37 (2009): 239–256.

62 **'Optimism is an essential ingredient:** Bezos's comments on the importance of optimism for business are quoted in Jack Roseman, 'Entrepreneurship: Optimism Vital to Entrepreneurs, As Is Ability to Calculate Risks, Costs,' *Post-Gazette* (Pittsburgh), June 6, 2004, and in Alan Deutschman, 'Inside the Mind of Jeff Bezos,' *Fast Company*, December 19, 2007, www.fastcompany.com/magazine/85/beos1.html. Jeff Bezos was declared *Time*'s Man of the Year in 1999; a detailed history of his life story and the founding of Amazon.com can be found in *Time*, 27 December 1999.

62 **Nelson Mandela:** The remarkable story of Nelson Mandela's incredible and inspiring life can be read in his wonderful book *Long Walk to Freedom: The Autobiography of Nelson Mandela* (Boston: Little, Brown, 1994).

62 'the almost willful ignorance: The quotations here are taken from Barack Obama's speech to the National Democratic Convention on July 27, 2004 (see www.dems2004.org). A more extensive description of these views are available in Barack Obama, *The Audacity of Hope: Thoughts on Reclaiming the American Dream* (New York: Crown, 2006).

63 **Shirin Ebadi is a case in point:** Dr Shirin Ebadi was born in 1947 in Hamedan, a city in the northwest of Iran. She is a leading human rights campaigner, and details of her life can be found at nobelprize.org /nobel_prizes/peace/laureates/2003/ebadi-autobio.html. Further details of her views can be found in an interview with Voice of America on November 12, 2009 (http://www.voanews.com/english/news/middle -east/a-13-2009-11-12-voa1-69822647.html). In June 2009, Ebadi described how the government closed down her office and confiscated her apartment as well as her bank account. Several members of her family are continually harassed and threatened by the authorities. Yet Ebadi continues to fight for justice, imploring women in particular to assume a wider role in society through education and active participation in politics. Social justice is only achieved because of people like her.

Chapter 3: The Rainy Brain

67 **intriguing experiments on this subject:** The experiments showing that people are faster to notice snakes and spiders in visual search tasks compared to non–fear-related pictures is reported in A. Öhman, A. Flykt, and F. Esteves, 'Emotion Drives Attention: Detecting the Snake in the Grass,' *Journal of Experimental Psychology: General* 130 (2001): 466–478. An accessible overview of the hypothesis that the brain has an evolved fear module that is especially reactive to ancient threats can be found in A. Öhman and S. Mineka, 'The Malicious Serpent: Snakes as a Prototypical Stimulus for an Evolved Module of Fear,' *Current Directions in Psychological Science* 12 (2003): 5–9. For a wonderful and entertaining account of how the presence of snakes in our ancient environment was a primary driver of human evolution, see Lynne Isbell, *The Fruit, the Tree, and the Serpent: Why We See So Well* (Cambridge, MA: Harvard University Press, 2009).

69 **We now know more about fear:** A highly accessible and entertaining account of how the fear system operates can be found online in an exhibit called Goose Bumps: The Science of Fear, developed by the California Science Center (see www.fearexhibit.org). A lively account of

how our mind works when in extreme danger can also be read in Jeff Wise, *Extreme Fear: The Science of Your Mind in Danger* (New York: Palgrave Macmillan, 2009). One of the best books on fear written by a leading scientist in the neurobiology of fear is still Joseph E. LeDoux, *The Emotional Brain: The Mysterious Underpinnings of Emotional Life* (New York: Simon & Schuster, 1996). For more academic overviews, see E. A. Phelps, 'Emotion and Cognition: Insights from Studies of the Human Amygdala,' *Annual Review of Psychology* 57 (2006): 27–53; J. E. LeDoux, 'Emotion Circuits in the Brain,' *Annual Review of Neuroscience* 23 (2000): 155–218; and A. J. Calder, A. D. Lawrence, and A. W. Young, 'Neuropsychology of Fear and Loathing,' *Nature Reviews Neuroscience* 2 (2001): 352–363.

70 **A friend of mine who worked:** My friend's experience is an example of a well-known phenomenon in psychology called the 'weapon focus effect,' which is the finding that the presence of a weapon tends to draw attention and therefore reduces the validity of eyewitness testimony. A good overview of studies examining this effect can be found in a paper by Nancy Mehrkens Steblay, 'A Meta-Analytic Review of the Weapon Focus Effect,' *Law and Human Behaviour* 16, no. 4 (1992): 413–424.

70 **Convincing evidence that the amygdala:** An early study showing differential activation of the human amygdala to fearful and happy expressions is J. Morris et al., 'A Differential Response in the Human Amygdala to Fearful and Happy Facial Expressions,' *Letter to Nature* 383 (1996): 812–815.

71 **the amygdala would react to *unconscious* threat:** The study showing that the human amygdala responds to unconscious threat is published in J. S. Morris, A. Öhman, and R. J. Dolan, 'A Sub-Cortical Pathway to the Right Amygdala Mediating "Unseen" Fear,' *Proceedings of the National Academy of Sciences* 96 (1998): 1680–1685.

72 **I conducted a series of tests:** The experiment with JB was published in E. Fox, 'Processing Emotional Expressions: The Role of Anxiety and Awareness,' *Cognitive, Affective, and Behavioural Neuroscience* 2 (2002): 52–63.

73 **Marco Tamietto and Beatrice de Gelder:** The team led by Beatrice de Gelder in Tilburg has conducted some remarkable studies with brain-damaged patients suffering from blindsight and visual neglect. This work is explained in an excellent article by Beatrice de Gelder, 'Uncanny Sight in the Blind,' *Scientific American* (May 2010): 43–47. The paper demonstrating that patients with spatial neglect can still

notice fearful body language is M. Tamietto et al., 'Seeing Fearful Body Language Overcomes Attentional Deficits in Patients with Neglect,' *Journal of Cognitive Neuroscience* 19 (2007): 445–454.

74 **de Gelder and her team conducted:** The study reporting that unseen fearful expressions can trigger emotional contagion in blindsight is M. Tamietto et al., 'Unseen Facial and Bodily Expressions Trigger Fast Emotional Reactions,' *Proceedings of the National Academy of Sciences* 106 (2009): 17661–17666. It is of course possible that the demonstrations reported by de Gelder and colleagues are not blindsight after all because of the neuroplasticity that can take place following brain damage. We now know that the brain has a remarkable capacity to rewire itself very quickly following damage, and therefore blindsight patients might have learned to see via other routes. Even if this is the case – and research is now looking into it – the finding that fear signals are especially salient confirms that our emergency brain is one of the most powerful and pervasive brain circuits in our head.

75 **Adam Anderson, a psychologist:** The study showing that pulling a fearful face leads to better vision is published in J. M. Susskind et al., 'Expressing Fear Enhances Sensory Acquisition,' *Nature Neuroscience* 11 (2008): 843–850.

75 **NYU psychologist Liz Phelps:** The study by Liz Phelps and her team demonstrating how briefly seeing a frightened face can improve our vision is published in E. Phelps, S. Ling, and M. Carrasco, 'Emotion Facilitates Perception and Potentiates the Perceptual Benefits of Attention,' *Psychological Science* 17 (2006): 292–299.

76 **Fear's capacity to hijack the system:** Colin Stafford Johnson's account of his encounter with a tiger in India was reported in an interview with Michael Kelly in '21st Century Fox,' *Irish Times Magazine*, March 29, 2008.

78 **the *heartbeat detection task*:** The study reported here can be found in H. D. Critchley et al., 'Neural Systems Supporting Interoceptive Awareness,' *Nature Neuroscience* 7 (2004): 189–195. The following two short articles also provide good accounts of the science behind how our brain supports conscious feelings of emotions: A. D. (Bud) Craig, 'Human Feelings: Why Are Some More Aware Than Others?' *Trends in Cognitive Sciences* 8, no. 6 (2004): 239–241; John S. Morris, 'How Do You Feel?' *Trends in Cognitive Sciences* 6, no. 8 (2002): 317–319.

78 **Supporting James's original theory:** Dolan and Critchley assume that being able to detect our heartbeat might help in translating these bodily states into feelings. However, another possibility is that people who

are more anxious and fearful might have better perception, as we have seen from the work of Liz Phelps and Adam Anderson, and therefore the relationship goes in the opposite direction. In other words, perhaps feeling mildly fearful leads to better perception of heartbeat, and not the other way around.

80 **the notorious 'daisy ad':** The story of the campaign ad is recounted in Drew Westen's excellent book *The Political Brain: The Role of Emotion in Deciding the Fate of the Nation* (New York: PublicAffairs, 2007). Westen discusses the role of emotions in influencing voting patterns and political persuasion.

81 **the ad unconsciously persuaded people:** Drew Westen's book provides many examples of political persuasion. For a broader and highly accessible account of how hijacking our mind can leave us more open to being persuaded, see Kevin Dutton, *Flipnosis: The Art of Split-Second Persuasion* (London: William Heinemann, 2010), also published as *Split-Second Persuasion: The Ancient Art and New Science of Changing Minds* (Boston: Houghton Mifflin Harcourt, 2011).

81 **people who have sustained damage:** A description of two patients (DR and SE) with amygdala damage can be found in A. J. Calder, 'Facial Emotion Recognition After Bilateral Amygdala Damage: Differentially Severe Impairment of Fear,' *Cognitive Neuropsychology* 13 (1996): 699–745, while the results from another five patients, including RS, are reported in P. Broks et al., 'Face Processing Impairments After Encephalitis: Amygdala Damage and Recognition of Fear,' *Neuropsychologia* 36 (1998): 59–70. A good general reference is R. Adolphs et al., 'Fear and the Human Amygdala,' *Journal of Neuroscience* 15 (1995): 5879–5891.

83 **Andy and his team have also found:** The paper showing that DR cannot recognise fearful and anger-related sounds as well as facial expressions is S. K. Scott et al., 'Impaired Auditory Recognition of Fear and Anger Following Bilateral Amygdala Lesions,' *Nature* 385 (1997): 254–257.

84 **amygdala damage leads to real problems:** The finding that the amygdala is important for the evaluation of trustworthiness and other personality traits is reported in R. Adolphs, S. Baron-Cohen, and D. Tranel, 'Impaired Recognition of Social Emotions Following Amygdala Damage,' *Journal of Cognitive Neuroscience* 14 (2002): 1264–1274.

84 **the characteristics that lead us to make:** Interesting demonstrations of the features of trustworthy and untrustworthy faces can be

seen on Alexander Todorov's website: webscript.princeton.edu/~tlab /demonstrations/. Several publications can be found on this website; one that reports interesting results on the features of trustworthy and untrustworthy faces is A. N. Oosterhof and A. Todorov, 'Shared Perceptual Basis of Emotional Expressions and Trustworthiness Impressions from Faces,' *Emotion* 9 (2009): 128–133.

85   **Ray Dolan and his colleagues:** An experiment showing that the amygdala and the insula react to untrustworthy faces is published in J. S. Winston et al., 'Automatic and Intentional Brain Responses During Evaluation of Trustworthiness of Faces,' *Nature Neuroscience* 5 (2002): 277–283.

85   **Adolphs's team tested SM:** The study showing that amygdala damage leads to risky gambles is B. De Martino, C. F. Camerer, and R. Adolphs, 'Amygdala Damage Eliminates Monetary Loss Aversion,' *Journal of Neuroscience* 107 (2010): 3788–3792.

86   **the amygdala is important in orchestrating:** The paper showing that SM has a smaller personal space than normal is D. P. Kennedy et al., 'Personal Space Regulation by the Human Amygdala,' *Nature Neuroscience* 12 (2009): 1226–1227.

87   **Richard Davidson, the University of Wisconsin psychologist:** A good overview of work showing that a right-sided cerebral asymmetry is related to higher anxiety levels is provided in R. J. Davidson, 'Affective Style and Affective Disorders: Perspectives from Affective Neuroscience,' *Cognition & Emotion* 12 (1998): 307–330. The experiment showing that this pattern of brain activity was related to increased levels of cortisol in the bloodstream is published in N. H. Kalin et al., 'Asymmetric Frontal Brain Activity, Cortisol, and Behaviour Associated with Fearful Temperament in Rhesus Monkeys,' *Behavioural Neuroscience* 112 (1998): 286–292.

88   **the State-Trait Anxiety Inventory (STAI):** The Spielberger STAI is widely used around the world to measure the two components of state and trait anxiety. Further details can be found at www.mindgarden .com/products/staisad.htm.

88   **a short questionnaire to students:** My colleagues and I developed the Essex Neuroticism Scale to allow us to quickly identify potentially high and low trait-anxious people to take part in our studies. It has not been validated, but on tests with 146 students who filled out this questionnaire as well as the Spielberger Trait Anxiety questionnaire, the correlation was found to be .82, a high positive correlation. That is, if someone scores high on the Essex scale, they are very likely to score

high on the Spielberger scale; if they score low on this scale, they will almost certainly report low trait anxiety on the Spielberger. To score the scale you simply need to add up all the numbers you circled, reversing items 5, 7, 9, and 10. Thus, if you circled 5 for any of these items you would score it 1, while a 4 becomes 2, a 3 stays at a 3, a 2 becomes 4, and a 1 become 5. The average score we have found is usually around 24, with low scores being around 18 and below. A score over about 40 is considered fairly high.

89 **Karin Mogg and Brendan Bradley:** The study described here was published in K. Mogg et al., 'Selective Attention to Threat: A Test of Two Cognitive Models of Anxiety,' *Cognition & Emotion* 14 (2000): 375–399.

90 **I have used a task called the *attentional blink test*:** The study demonstrating that people who report high levels of trait anxiety are more likely to notice fearful, relative to happy, facial expressions in an attentional blink test is reported in E. Fox, R. Russo, and G. Georgiou, 'Anxiety Modulates the Degree of Attentive Resources Required to Process Emotional Faces,' *Cognitive, Affective, & Behavioural Neuroscience* 5 (2005): 396–404.

92 **Just as Ray Dolan and others:** Several studies have now been published showing that the amygdala reaction to danger is stronger as anxiety increases. Our paper showing that anxiety influences the amygdala response to threat, especially for angry faces looking right at you, is published in M. P. Ewbank, E. Fox, and A. J. Calder, 'The Interaction Between Gaze and Facial Expression in the Amygdala and Extended Amygdala Is Modulated by Anxiety,' *Frontiers in Human Neuroscience* 4 (July 2010): Article 56.

93 **Sonia Bishop and her colleagues:** The study showing that high trait-anxious people have a harder time activating their inhibitory centres when faced with threat is published in S. J. Bishop et al., 'Prefrontal Cortical Function and Anxiety: Controlling Attention to Threat Related Stimuli,' *Nature Neuroscience* 7 (2004): 184–187.

Chapter 4: Optimism and Pessimism Genes

95 **the discovery of the 'optimism gene.':** My study that generated media reports of the discovery of an optimism gene can be found in Elaine Fox, Anna Ridgewell, and Chris Ashwin, 'Looking on the Bright Side: Biased Attention and the Human Serotonin Transporter Gene,' *Proceedings of the Royal Society: Biological Sciences* 276 (2009): 1747–1751. The experiment reported in this paper shows that

variation in the serotonin transporter gene underlies biases in attention for negative or positive material, which are of course linked with
pessimistic and optimistic mindsets, respectively.

96   **almost 46,000 twins and their relatives:** The study referred to here is
published in Robert I. E. Lamb et al., 'Further Evidence Against the
Environmental Transmission of Individual Differences in Neuroticism
from a Collaborative Study of 45,850 Twins and Relatives on Two
Continents,' *Behaviour Genetics* 30 (2000): 223–233. Our study on
the heritability of optimism as measured by the LOT-R is currently
being prepared for publication. Another study with 3,053 twins over
the age of fifty also used the LOT-R and found a heritability of 36 per
cent. This study is reported in Miriam A. Mosing et al., 'Genetic and
Environmental Influences on Optimism and Its Relationship to Mental and Self-Rated Health: A Study of Aging Twins,' *Behaviour Genetics* 39 (2009): 597–604.

100   **the two camps of genetic science:** As I became more familiar with
these divergent perspectives I was aware that their views were given
a sharper edge by the eye-watering amounts of money required to
answer a deceptively simple question: What genes predispose us to
mental illness or happiness? In 2007 the Stanley Medical Research
Institute in Chevy Chase, Maryland, donated £100 million to the
Broad Institute in Cambridge, Massachusetts, to fund GWAS to
find risky genes for psychiatric illness. A year later, the Essel Foundation, founded by the Liber family, donated about the same
amount to Daniel Weinberger and his team to pursue candidate
gene studies in psychiatry. The funds are pouring in to both sides,
and as new data comes in from all around the world, chances are
that scientists from both sides of the great divide will eventually
start working together.

100   **Danny Weinberger, an experimental psychiatrist:** The study discussed here is published in Michael F. Egan et al., 'Effect of COMT
Val[108/158] Met Genotype on Frontal Lobe Function and Risk for Schizophrenia,' *Proceedings of the National Academy of Sciences* 98 (June
5, 2001): 6917–6922.

102   **As a recent genetics book:** Jonathan Flint., Ralph J. Greenspan, and
Kenneth S. Kendler, *How Genes Influence Behaviour* (New York: Oxford University Press, 2010).

102   **Helle Larsen, a psychologist:** The study discussed here is published
in Helle Larsen et al., 'A Variable-Number-of-Tandem-Repeats Polymorphism in the Dopamine D4 Receptor Gene Affects Social Adap-

tation of Alcohol Use: Investigation of a Gene by Environment Interaction,' *Psychological Science* 21 (2010): 1064–1068.

104 **One of the most outspoken:** Jonathan Flint, along with Marcus Munafo, a psychologist at the University of Bristol, has conducted many
meta-analyses (studies of studies) to test whether personality traits such
as neuroticism can be pinned down to a specific gene. They generally
find that the results differ depending on the particular questionnaire
used by the original researchers. Some questionnaires show a link, while
others don't. Two academic papers address this issue for the interested
reader: M. R. Munafo et al., '5-HTTLPR Genotype and Anxiety-
Related Personality Traits: A Meta-Analysis and New Data,' *American
Journal of Medical Genetics B: Neuropsychiatric Genetics* 150B, no. 2
(2009): 271, and M. R. Munafo and J. Flint, 'Meta-Analysis of Genetic
Association Studies,' *Trends in Genetics* 20 (2005): 439–444.

104 **single genes have only a tiny impact:** An excellent discussion of this
issue can be found in Flint, Greenspan, and Kendler, *How Genes Influence Behaviour*.

106 **the outcome measures are often:** I should point out that I discussed
the issue of GWAS outcome measures being less sensitive than those
from candidate gene studies with the University of Virginia psychiatrist Kenneth Kendler, following a lecture he gave at the University
of Oxford in October 2011. While he broadly agrees that this is true
for many GWAS, he also makes clear that many studies 'in the field'
collect far more detailed information about people's family background and details of working and social life than do candidate gene
studies. Testing people in the lab has many advantages without all of
the messiness we find in real life. The problem is that some of the effects that are quite clear and strong in the controlled environment of
the laboratory may not be robust enough to survive when we are testing people in their home environments.

107 **The serotonin transporter gene is one:** Good academic overviews of
work on the serotonin transporter gene can be found in A. R. Hariri
and A. Holmes, 'The Serotonin Transporter and the Genetics of Affect Regulation,' *Trends in Cognitive Sciences* 10 (2006): 182–191, and
T. Canli and K.-P. Lesch, 'Long Story Short: The Serotonin Transporter in Emotion Regulation and Social Cognition,' *Nature Neuroscience* 10 (2007): 1103–1109.

108 **the very first study of how genes:** The classic study, led by Avshalom
Caspi and Terrie Moffitt, which showed a gene-environment interaction with the serotonin transporter gene and the risk of depression is

A. Caspi et al., 'Influence of Life Stress on Depression: Moderation by a Polymorphism in the 5-HTT Gene,' *Science* 301 (July 18, 2003). The relationship between the serotonin transporter gene and risk of depression has become controversial recently, with some studies finding strong effects and others not finding any relation. For example, one meta-analysis concluded that the interaction of the serotonin transporter and stressful life events did *not* increase depression. See N. Risch et al., 'Interaction Between the Serotonin Transporter Gene (5-HTTLPR), Stressful Life Events, and Risk of Depression: A Meta-Analysis,' *Journal of the American Medical Association* 23 (17 June 2009). Part of the problem is that there is wide variation in how well different studies measure stressful life events. Some studies only assess stress over a short period – say, about a year – while others measure stress over much longer periods, like the five years used in the Caspi study. These differences in study design often result in apparently conflicting outcomes. The overall evidence remains strong, however, that there are important gene–environment interactions in the risk of depression and other psychiatric disorders. For an excellent overview of how genes and environment might interact in psychiatry, see A. Caspi and T. E. Moffitt, 'Gene-Environment Interactions in Psychiatry: Joining Forces with Neuroscience,' *Nature Reviews Neuroscience* 7 (2006): 583–590.

109   **Once again, a study by Avshalom Caspi:** The study showing that abused children only developed antisocial problems if they had a specific variant of the MAOI gene is A. Caspi et al., 'Role of Genotype in the Cycle of Violence in Maltreated Children,' *Science* 297 (2002): 851.

110   **discovered a link between two genes:** The original article that reported this finding is C. M. Kuhnen and J. Y. Chiao, 'Genetic Determinants of Financial Risk Tasking,' *PLoS ONE* 4, no. 2, e4362 (2009): 1–4. A more accessible overview of this study was published online: 'Big-Time Financial Risk Taking: Blame It on Their Genes,' *Science Daily*, 11 February 2009, www.sciencedaily.com/releases/2009/02/090211082352.htm.

111   **Ahmad Hariri, a dynamic advocate:** Ahmad Hariri and his colleagues have conducted many studies on the serotonin transporter, along with several other genes, and their association with anxiety traits. The classic study showing that the amygdala reacts more in short allele carriers is published in A. R. Hariri et al., 'Serotonin Transporter Genetic Variation and the Response of the Human Amygdala,' *Science* 297 (2002): 400–403. A meta-analysis published in 2008 found support for the as-

sociation of the serotonin transporter polymorphism and amygdala activation, although this analysis also found that the effect found in the first study was probably an overestimate, which is typical of many GWAS. This meta-analysis is published in M. R. Munafo, S. M. Brown, and A. R. Hariri, 'Serotonin Transporter (5-HTTLPR) Genotype and Amygdala Activation: A Meta-Analysis,' *Biological Psychiatry* 63 (2008): 852–857.

111 **In my own lab:** Our paper on the genetic basis of optimistic and pessimistic biases in attention is Fox, Ridgewell, and Ashwin, 'Looking on the Bright Side.'

114 **a new study we had been running:** The study discussed here is published in Elaine Fox et al., 'The Serotonin Transporter Gene Alters Sensitivity to Attention Bias Modification: Evidence for a Plasticity Gene,' *Biological Psychiatry* 70 (2011): 1049–1054.

115 **a radical new theory:** These theoretical ideas are described in J. Belsky and M. Pluess, 'Beyond Diathesis-Stress: Differential Susceptibility to Environmental Influences,' *Psychological Bulletin* 135 (2009): 885–908. For a highly accessible read on the idea that people with certain genotypes may fare worse in a crisis but gain the most when times are good, see David Dobbs, 'The Science of Success,' *Atlantic* (December 2009).

116 **Kathleen Gunthert and colleagues:** The study discussed here is Kathleen Gunthert et al., 'Serotonin Transporter Gene Polymorphism (5-HTTLPR) and Anxiety Reactivity in Everyday Life: A Daily Process Approach to Gene by Environment Interaction,' *Psychosomatic Medicine* 69 (2007): 762–768.

119 **Using the meticulous Swedish:** An excellent overview of this work and epigenetics in general can be found in John Cloud, 'Why Your DNA Isn't Your Destiny,' *Time*, 6 January 2010.

120 **Bygren and Golding, working with:** The study discussed here is published in Marcus E. Pembrey et al., 'Sex-Specific, Male-Line Transgenerational Responses in Humans,' *European Journal of Human Genetics* 14 (2006): 159–166.

121 **His laboratory group discovered:** This work is described in 'Epigenetics: DNA Isn't Everything,' *Science Daily*, 12 April 2009, www.sciencedaily.com/releases/2009/04/090412081315.htm.

121 **Epigenetic inheritance is not restricted:** There are now hundreds of well-documented studies demonstrating epigenetic inheritance without changing fundamental DNA structure. A comprehensive review can be found in Eva Jablonka and Gal Raz, 'Transgenerational Epigenetic Inheritance: Prevalence, Mechanisms, and Implications for the

Study of Heredity and Evolution,' *Quarterly Review of Biology* 84, no. 2 (2009): 131–176. A less technical overview of epigenetics with an emphasis on the implications for cancer treatment can be found in Stephen S. Hall, 'Beyond the Book of Life,' *Newsweek*, July 13, 2009.

121 **In research led by:** The work of Tracy Bale and her colleagues demonstrating that a high-fat diet in pregnancy can lead to epigenetic changes in mice is published in G. A. Dunn and T. L. Bale, 'Maternal High-Fat Diet Promotes Body Length Increase and Insulin Insensitivity in Second-Generation Mice,' *Endocrinology* 150, no. 11 (2009): 4999–5009.

122 **As Frances Champagne:** The following article provides an excellent overview of the interplay between genes and the environment: F. A. Champagne and R. Mashoodh, 'Genes in Context: Gene-Environment Interplay and the Origins of Individual Differences in Behaviour,' *Current Directions in Psychological Science* 18 (2009): 127–131. The diagram presented here (Figure 4.5) is a modified version of Figure 1 from that article.

124 **A fascinating series of studies:** The empirical work conducted by Ian Weaver and his colleagues is described in I. C. Weaver et al., 'Epigenetic Programming by Maternal Behaviour,' *Nature Neuroscience* 7 (2004): 847–854. For an excellent overview of epigenetics and how differences in maternal care can have profound effects on gene expression that can be passed on from generation to generation, see Frances A. Champagne, 'Epigenetic Mechanisms and the Transgenerational Effects of Maternal Care,' *Frontiers of Neuroendocrinology* 29 (2008): 386–397.

125 **Tim Oberlander:** This work showing that maternal depression can result in the silencing of some essential genes that help us deal with stress is published in T. F. Oberlander et al., 'Prenatal Exposure to Maternal Depression, Neonatal Methylation of Human Glucocorticoid Receptor Gene (NR3C1) and Infant Cortisol Stress Responses,' *Epigenetics* 3, no. 2 (2008): 97–106.

Chapter 5: The Malleable Mind

128 **In 2000, Professor Eleanor Maguire:** This work was published in E. A. Maguire et al., 'Navigation Related Structural Change in the Hippocampi of Taxi Drivers,' *Proceedings of the National Academy of Sciences* 97 (2000): 4398–4403.

129 **Several of the brain areas:** Evidence for this claim can be found in C. Gaser and G. Schlaug, 'Brain Structures Differ Between Musicians and Non-Musicians,' *Journal of Neuroscience* 23 (2003): 9240–9245.

129 **With the discovery of neuroplasticity:** A very accessible account of the science and scientists who discovered how plastic brain processes really are is in Norman Doidge, *The Brain That Changes Itself: Stories of Personal Triumph from the Frontiers of Brain Science* (New York: Penguin Books, 2007). Another excellent book that recounts much of the same material but is centred around a conference hosted by the Dalai Lama in 2004 with some leading scientists on the topic of brain plasticity is Sharon Begley, *The Plastic Mind: New Science Reveals Our Extraordinary Potential to Transform Ourselves* (London: Constable & Robinson, 2009).

130 **Several studies now confirm:** The study showing that areas of the visual cortex were recruited to process sounds in the blind was reported by A. A. Stevens et al., 'Preparatory Activity in Occipital Cortex in Early Blind Humans Predicts Auditory Perceptual Performance,' *Journal of Neuroscience* 27 (2007): 10734–10741.

130 **Neuroscientist Helen Neville:** Neville and her colleagues have published several relevant findings. The first demonstration was in H. J. Neville, A. Schmidt, and M. Kutas, 'Altered Visual-Evoked Potentials in Congenitally Deaf Adults,' *Brain Research* 266 (1983): 127–132. Some more recent discussion is presented in D. Bavelier et al., 'Visual Attention to the Periphery Is Enhanced in Congenitally Deaf Individuals,' *Journal of Neuroscience* 20 (2000): 1–6.

131 **Ironically, William James:** William James, *The Principles of Psychology* (New York: Henry Holt, 1890).

131 **some groundbreaking experiments:** This work is described in T. G. Brown and C. S. Sherrington, 'On the Instability of a Cortical Point,' *Proceedings of the Royal Society: Biological Sciences* 85 (1912): 250–277. This work giving an early clue that the brain might be highly flexible was largely ignored. Charles Scott Sherrington went on to win the Nobel Prize in physiology and medicine in 1932 for his work on the nervous system.

132 **Shepherd Ivory Franz found something:** A good overview of the studies that led Franz to these conclusions is in S. L. Franz, 'The Functions of the Cerebrum,' *Psychological Bulletin* 13 (1916): 149–173. An excellent overview of the life of S. L. Franz and his often overlooked contribution to the history of psychology can be found in V. A.

Colotle and P. Bach-y-Rita, 'Shepherd Ivory Franz: His Contributions to Neuropsychology and Rehabilitation,' *Cognitive, Affective, & Behavioural Neuroscience* 2 (2002): 141–148.

133 **By showing that areas of motor cortex:** Karl Lashley spent many years studying and searching for the 'location' of memory in the brain. In 1950 he summarised all of this work, which ultimately failed to establish that our memories existed in a particular brain area. The article is K. S. Lashley, 'In Search of the Engram,' *Symposia for the Society of Experimental Biology* 4 (1950): 454–482. Lashley's work demonstrating brain plasticity in the motor cortex of the monkey brain is K. S. Lashley, 'Temporal Variation in the Function of the Gyrus Precentralis in Primates,' *American Journal of Physiology* 65 (1923): 585–602. An interesting overview of Lashley's life and contribution to the development of psychology can be found in N. M. Weidman, *Constructing Scientific Psychology: Karl Lashley's Mind-Brain Debate* (Cambridge, UK: Cambridge University Press, 1999).

133 **'Cells that fire together:** The principle of mass action is described in Hebb's classic book. See Donald O. Hebb, *The Organisation of Behaviour: A Neuropsychological Theory* (New York: Wiley, 1949), 60. A clear overview of Hebb's theory of neuroplasticity can be found in S. J. Cooper, 'Donald O. Hebb's Synapse and Learning Rule: A History and Commentary,' *Neuroscience and Biobehavioural Reviews* 28 (2005): 851–874.

134 **it still took more than thirty years:** Excellent overviews of the history of neuroplasticity can be found in P. R. Huttenlocher, *Neural Plasticity: The Effects of the Environment on the Development of the Cerebral Cortex* (Cambridge, MA: Harvard University Press, 2002), and Jeffrey M. Schwartz and Sharon Begley, *The Mind and the Brain: Neuroplasticity and the Power of Mental Force* (New York: HarperCollins, 2002). Somewhat more accessible discussions of this history can be found in Begley's later book *The Plastic Mind* and Norman Doidge's book *The Brain That Changes Itself*. The neurochemistry and brain mechanisms underlying Hebb's proposals were eventually worked out by Eric Kandel from Columbia University in New York; he shared the Nobel Prize in 2000 for his discoveries on the molecular basis of learning and memory.

134 **they began the series of studies:** A description of this work is available in any introductory psychology textbook or textbooks on perception. The original article is D. H. Hubel and T. N. Wiesel, 'The Period

of Susceptibility to the Physiological Effects of Unilateral Eye Closure in Kittens,' *Journal of Physiology* 206 (1970): 419–436.

135 **Teija Kujala has shown:** The key experiment demonstrating that the visual cortex is activated by *listening* in people who only became blind after the 'critical period' is T. Kujala et al., 'Electrophysiological Evidence for Cross-Modal Plasticity in Humans with Early- and Late-Onset Blindness,' *Psychophysiology* 34 (1997): 213–216.

136 **His innovative program of work:** Alvaro Pascual-Leone has conducted numerous experiments with humans showing that when a particular motor activity is repeated, over and over, the part of the cortex responsible for that activity expands. For instance, some of his early studies showed that the region of the cortex that controls the 'reading' finger is much larger in people who can read Braille compared with those who cannot. A. Pascual-Leone and F. Torres, 'Plasticity of the Sensorimotor Cortex Representation of the Reading Finger in Braille Readers,' *Brain* 116 (1993): 39–52. This reflected earlier work that had been conducted by Michael Merzenich with monkeys. At the University of Wisconsin, Merzenich and his team conducted microsurgery on a number of young monkeys and cut a crucial nerve in the hand so that the cortical areas responsible for a large part of the hand were no longer getting any signals from the hand. They waited about seven months to see what had happened in the brain of these monkeys. Much to his astonishment, Merzenich discovered that the cortical area of these monkeys' brains had completely rewired. In strong contradiction of the zeitgeist of the time in neuroscience, he had demonstrated beyond doubt that the brain was plastic. Indeed, so out of sync were his findings that the paper was only published with the proviso that no mention was made of neural plasticity! R. L. Paul, H. Goodman, and M. M. Merzenich, 'Alternations in Mechanoreceptor Input to Brodmann's Areas 1 and 3 of the Postcentral Hand Area of *Macaca Mulatta* After Nerve Section and Regeneration,' *Brain Research* 39 (1972): 1–19.

137 **Gage came to these conclusions:** Gage's first demonstration that young mice raised in enriched environments actually grew new neurons was reported in G. Gage et al., 'More Hippocampal Neurons in Adult Mice Living in an Enriched Environment,' *Nature* 386 (1997): 493–495. This team also later found that neurogenesis could also occur in much older animals. G. Kempermann, H. G. Kuhn, and F. H. Gage, 'Experience-Induced Neurogenesis in the Senescent Dentate Gyrus,' *Journal of Neuroscience* 18 (1998): 3206–3212. It is interesting to

note, however, that these were not actually the first demonstrations of neurogenesis. Just as the initial discoveries of neuroplasticity were ignored by the scientific community, the earliest reports of neurogenesis by the MIT neuroscientist Joseph Altman way back in 1962 were also ignored, in spite of being published in a leading journal. See J. Altman, 'Are New Neurons Formed in the Brains of Adult Mammals?' *Science* 135 (1962): 1127–1128. The story of the discovery of neurogenesis is beautifully told in Michael Spector, 'Rethinking the Brain: How the Songs of Canaries Upset a Fundamental Principle of Science,' *New Yorker* July 23, 2001, as well as in Begley, *The Plastic Mind*.

137   **It was already known that mice:** Mark Rosenzweig led a team at the University of California, Berkeley, in the 1960s that showed that rats, gerbils, and mice raised in more enriched environments had larger and heavier brains than those brought up in sparser surroundings. See M. R. Rosenzweig and E. L. Bennett, 'Effects of Differential Environments on Brain Weights and Enzyme Activities in Gerbils, Rats, and Mice,' *Developmental Psychobiology* 2 (1969): 87–95. A few years later, William Greenough at the University of Illinois showed that this was because rats who were raised in enriched environments developed more connections between neurons and grew more dendrites on their neurons (the part that receives signals from other neurons), leading to much denser and thicker cortical networks. F. R. Volkmar and W. T. Greenough, 'Rearing Complexity Affects Branching of Dendrites in the Visual Cortex of the Rat,' *Science* 176 (1972): 1145–1447.

139   **As Gage told a small conference:** This refers to a Mind and Life conference hosted by the Dalai Lama with a number of leading scientists held in Dharamsala in 2004 and recounted by Sharon Begley in *The Plastic Mind*, 79. The scientific paper reporting this breakthrough finding is P. S. Eriksson et al., 'Neurogenesis in the Adult Human Hippocampus,' *Nature Medicine* 4 (1998): 1313–1317.

142   **Known as *fear conditioning*:** An excellent, and highly accessible, description of fear conditioning by one of the leaders in the field can be found in Joseph E. LeDoux, *The Emotional Brain: The Mysterious Underpinnings of Emotional Life* (New York: Simon & Schuster, 1996). A clear overview of fear-conditioning procedures can also be found in Joseph E. LeDoux, 'Emotional Memory,' *Scholarpedia* 2, no. 7 (2007): 1806.

142   **In the famous 'Little Albert' experiment:** This well-known early example of what is now known as fear conditioning was published in J.

B. Watson and R. Raynor, 'Conditioned Emotional Reactions,' *Journal of Experimental Psychology* 3 (1920): 1–14.

144 **University of Vermont psychologist Mark Bouton:** Mark Bouton's work showing that extinguished fears can be reinstated is discussed in this accessible article: M. E. Bouton, 'Context, Ambiguity, and Classical Conditioning,' *Current Directions in Psychological Science* 3 (1994): 49–53.

146 **In one study conducted in my lab:** Our visual search experiments showing that contemporary threats – like guns and syringes – are found just as quickly as more ancient dangers – like snakes and spiders – are published in Elaine Fox, Laura Griggs, and Elias Mouchlianitis, 'The Detection of Fear-Relevant Stimuli: Are Guns Noticed as Quickly as Snakes?' *Emotion* 4 (2007): 691–696.

147 **classic experiment conducted by Susan Mineka:** This study is published in M. Cook and S. Mineka, 'Observational Conditioning of Fear to Fear-Relevant Versus Fear-Irrelevant Stimuli in Rhesus Monkeys,' *Journal of Abnormal Psychology* 98 (1989): 448–459.

148 **what has been called the *covariation bias*:** Many experiments in psychology labs have shown that we find it easier to associate danger with some things more than others, even when there is no actual association. The first study to demonstrate this effect is published in A. J. Tomarken, S. Mineka, and M. Cook, 'Fear-Relevant Selective Associations and Covariation Bias,' *Journal of Abnormal Psychology* 98 (1989): 381–394.

148 **The same type of thing happens:** The experiment demonstrating that people tend to overestimate the link between happiness and being thin is published in R. J. Viken et al., 'Illusory Correlation for Body Type and Happiness: Co-Variation Bias and Its Relationship to Eating Disorder Symptoms,' *International Journal of Eating Disorders* 38 (2005): 65–72.

151 **a syndrome scarily called *electrosensitivity*:** Many people believe that mobile phones can affect their health. However, the vast majority of scientific studies have shown that as long as people are not aware of whether the phone is switched on or off, they are unable to detect the phone, and their symptoms are no worse when the phone is on relative to when it is off. Public health bodies around the world have been putting large sums of money into funding scientific research to determine the veracity of the claims that mobile phone technology is negatively affecting human health. I was awarded funding from the British Mobile Telecommunications and Health Research Programme

(**MTHR**) to set up a new laboratory and lead a multidisciplinary team of scientists to find out whether the electromagnetic fields generated by mobile phones and mobile phone base stations were indeed causing the problems reported by a small but increasing number of people. Our studies, along with dozens of other placebo-controlled, double-blind trials, have now been conducted around the world testing hundreds of people, and the most consistent finding is that people are unable to detect electromagnetic fields above what we would expect by chance. Moreover, the short-term negative health symptoms reported by people who believe they are affected by mobile phone signals do not seem to be related to the presence of the electromagnetic fields in spite of what people think; instead they seem to be due to what a person believes, rightly or wrongly. The most reasonable interpretation is that the health problems that occur in so-called electrosensitivity are due to the *fear* of mobile phones and the *belief* that they are toxic, rather than the electromagnetic fields themselves. There may well be some people out there who can detect electromagnetic radiation, but so far the scientific spotlight has failed to find them. Some of our scientific papers on this topic are: S. Eltiti et al., 'Does Short-Term Exposure to Mobile Phone Base Station Signals Increase Symptoms in Individuals Who Report Sensitivity to Electromagnetic Fields? A Double-Blind Randomised Provocation Study,' *Environmental Health Perspectives* 115 (2007): 1063–1068; and R. Russo et al., 'Does Acute Exposure to Mobile Phones Affect Human Attention?' *Bioelectromagnetics* 27 (2006): 215–220. For an accessible summary of the science going on around the world on electromagnetic fields and health, see the following website created by the World Health Organization: www.who.int/peh-emf/project/en/.

152   **The characteristics of the fear system:** The experiment demonstrating that out-group members act like prepared stimuli, so that we learn to fear them far more easily, is published in A. Olsson et al., 'The Role of Social Groups in the Persistence of Learned Fear,' *Science* 309 (2005): 785–787.

153   **Brain scanning experiments:** This study is published in E. A. Phelps et al., 'Performance on Indirect Measures of Race Evaluation Predicts Amygdala Activation,' *Journal of Cognitive Neuroscience* 12 (2000): 729–738.

154   **girls with Williams syndrome:** The study showing that children with Williams syndrome, a genetic disorder leaving them with no social fear, do not learn racial stereotypes is published in A. Santos, A.

Meyer-Lindenberg, and C. Deruelle, 'Absence of Racial, but Not Gender, Stereotyping in Williams Syndrome Children,' *Current Biology* 20 (2010): 307–308. The work by Santos and colleagues seems to be strong evidence that social fear underlies racism. Get rid of social fear, and racism should go out the window. Not everyone agrees. Liz Phelps, for instance, has said that while she thinks the results are interesting, the problem is that because the children with Williams syndrome also have severe learning difficulties, their inability to pick up racist attitudes may have more to do with learning than social fear. This is a good point, but on the other hand, the fact that these kids picked up gender stereotyping with few problems argues against it. The notion that we can reduce racism and negative stereotyping by reducing fear of other groups is intriguing and worthy of further investigation.

155 **The possibility of changing entrenched:** The first papers to publish data showing that it is possible to change people's biases focused on modifying how we *interpret* ambiguous information. See A. Mathews, and B. Mackintosh, 'Induced Emotional Interpretation Bias and Anxiety,' *Journal of Abnormal Psychology* 109 (2000): 602–615, and S. Grey and A. Mathews, 'Effects of Training on Interpretation of Emotional Ambiguity,' *Quarterly Journal of Experimental Psychology* 53A (2000): 1143–1162. Colin MacLeod's first demonstration that it is possible to modify biases in attention appeared in C. MacLeod et al., 'Selective Attention and Emotional Vulnerability: Assessing the Causal Basis of Their Association Through the Experimental Manipulation of Attentional Bias,' *Journal of Abnormal Psychology* 111 (2002): 107–123. Detailed overviews of this and subsequent work are available in A. Mathews and C. MacLeod, 'Induced Processing Biases Have Causal Effects on Anxiety,' *Cognition and Emotion* 16 (2002): 331–354, and C. MacLeod, E. H. W. Koster, and E. Fox, 'Whither Cognitive Bias Modification Research? Commentary on the Special Section Articles,' *Journal of Abnormal Psychology* 118 (2009): 89–99. Several chapters in J. Yiend, ed., *Cognition, Emotion, and Psychopathology: Theoretical, Empirical and Clinical Directions* (Cambridge, UK: Cambridge University Press, 2004), discuss the development of cognitive bias modification procedures. More recently, my own textbook, *Emotion Science: Neuroscientific and Cognitive Approaches to Understanding Human Emotions* (Basingstoke, UK: Palgrave Macmillan, 2008), also contains overviews of CBM studies and detailed discussions of the links between cognitive processes and emotions.

156 **Reinout Wiers, a psychologist:** The study described here is published in Reinout W. Wiers et al., 'Retraining Automatic Action Tendencies Changes Alcoholic Patients' Approach Bias for Alcohol and Improves Treatment Outcome,' *Psychological Science* 22 (2011): 490–497.

162 **Great excitement surrounds:** Several academic overviews of this work are now available. See the special issue on cognitive bias modification, edited by Ernst Koster, Elaine Fox, and Colin MacLeod, *Journal of Abnormal Psychology* 118, no. 1 (2009). A commentary on all of the papers appearing in the special issue is available in MacLeod, Koster, and Fox, 'Whither Cognitive Bias Modification Research?' More recently, Paula Hertel from Trinity University and Andrew Mathews at UC Davis have published an overview: 'Cognitive Bias Modification: Past Perspectives, Current Findings, and Future Applications,' *Perspectives in Psychological Science* 6 (2011): 521–536.

Chapter 6: New Techniques to Reshape Our Brains

164 **OCD begins when a basic fear:** An excellent discussion of OCD and the various ways of combating it can be found in Jeffrey Schwartz, *Brain Lock: Free Yourself from Obsessive Compulsive Behaviour* (New York: Harper Perennial, 1997).

168 **D-cycloserine by itself:** D-cycloserine is one of a number of drugs known as *cognitive enhancers*. Michael Davis, a psychologist at Emory University, has found evidence that this drug can improve the benefits that come from exposure therapy in helping people to overcome phobic fears, like a fear of heights. A very accessible discussion of this work can be found here: www.dana.org/news/cerebrum/detail.aspx?id=752. One of the first academic papers showing the potential benefits of this drug alongside psychological interventions is K. J. Ressler et al., 'Cognitive Enhancers as Adjuncts to Psychotherapy: Use of D-Cycloserine in Phobias to Facilitate Extinction of Fear,' *Archives of General Psychiatry* 61 (2004): 1136–1144.

170 **The New York team discovered:** The paper reporting this study is D. Schiller et al., 'Preventing the Return of Fear in Humans Using Reconsolidation Update Mechanisms,' *Nature* 463 (2010): 49–54. A good discussion of this work can be found in Daniel Lametti, 'How to Erase Fear in Humans,' *Scientific American*, March 23, 2010, www.scientificamerican.com/article.cfm?id=how-to-erase-fear -in-humans.

171 **Support for this notion:** The study described here is R. L. Clem, and
     R. L. Huganir, 'Calcium-Permeable AMPA Receptor Dynamics Me-
     diate Fear Memory Erasure,' *Science* 330 (2010): 1108–1112.

172 **Once activated, the cortical:** The study showing that activating areas
     of the prefrontal cortex can dampen down the amygdala response to
     fear in rats is published in M. R. Milad and G. J. Quirk, 'Neurons in
     Medial Prefrontal Cortex Signal Memory for Fear Extinction,' *Nature*
     420 (2002): 70–74.

172 **It seems that people with:** An academic overview of a large number
     of brain-scanning studies that examined the activity of various brain
     areas in people with PTSD can be found in L. M. Shin et al., 'Amyg-
     dala, Medial Prefrontal Cortex, and Hippocampal Function in PTSD,'
     Annals of the New York Academy of Science 1071 (2006): 67–79.

172 **In the 1960s Richard Lazarus:** An excellent description of this work
     can be found in Richard Lazarus, *Psychological Stress and the Coping
     Process* (New York: McGraw-Hill, 1966).

173 **By merely giving a label:** Experiments demonstrating that applying
     a verbal label to emotional pictures can activate the prefrontal cortex
     and attenuate the amygdala were reported in A. R. Hariri, S. Y.
     Bookheimer, and J. C. Mazziotta, 'Modulating Emotional Re-
     sponses: Effects of a Neocortical Network on the Limbic System,'
     NeuroReport 11 (2000): 43–48. The same pattern of results was
     found in a study with a similar design that used pictures of distress-
     ing or threatening scenes; see A. R. Hariri et al., 'Neocortical Mod-
     ulation of the Amygdala Response to Fearful Stimuli,' *Biological
     Psychiatry* 53 (2003): 494–501. There is a growing literature on how
     actively reinterpreting or reappraising emotional situations can lead
     to real changes in the control centres of the brain. An excellent
     overview can be found in K. N. Ochsner and J. J. Gross, 'Cognitive
     Emotion Regulation: Insights from Social, Cognitive and Affective
     Neuroscience,' *Current Directions in Psychological Science* 17
     (2008): 153–158.

175 **Justin Kim and Paul Whalen:** The study discussed here showing that
     the strength of the uncinate fasciculus differs according to the level
     of anxiety reported is published in J. Kim and P. Whalen, 'The Struc-
     tural Integrity of an Amygdala-Prefrontal Cortex Pathway Predicts
     Trait Anxiety,' *Journal of Neuroscience* 29 (2009): 11614–11617.

176 **The classic talking therapy:** An excellent overview of the science
     behind this claim about CBT can be found in David A. Clark and
     Aaron T. Beck, 'Cognitive Theory and Therapy of Anxiety and

Depression: Convergence with Neurobiological Findings,' *Trends in Cognitive Sciences* 14 (2010): 418–424.

177   **While much more research is needed:** Much more research is needed to establish the effects that CBM procedures have on brain circuits. However, one study has indicated that these procedures might change control centres in the PFC; see M. Browning et al., 'Lateral Prefrontal Cortex Mediates the Cognitive Modification of Attentional Bias,' *Biological Psychiatry* 67 (2010): 919–925.

179   **An intriguing explanation:** An excellent overview of this work can be found in C. J. Harmer, G. M. Goodwin, and P. J. Cowen, 'Why Do Antidepressants Take So Long to Work? A Cognitive Neuropsychological Model of Antidepressant Drug Action,' *British Journal of Psychiatry* 195 (2009): 102–108.

180   **A particularly impressive demonstration:** Richard Davidson, the University of Wisconsin psychologist, was one of the first to examine the effect of meditation on mental control and regulatory functions. In a unique series of studies, he has examined the patterns of brain activity that occur when experienced Buddhist monks enter into meditative states. A good overview of this work can be found in A. Lutz et al., 'Attention Regulation and Monitoring in Meditation,' *Trends in Cognitive Sciences* 12 (2008): 163–168. This group's first demonstration of brain activity in Buddhist monks – the Olympic athletes of the meditation world, as Davidson calls them – was A. Lutz et al., 'Long-Term Meditators Self-Induce High-Amplitude Gamma Synchrony During Mental Practice,' *Proceedings of the National Academy of Sciences* 101 (2004): 16369–16373. A highly readable overview of this work is also found in Sharon Begley, *The Plastic Mind: New Science Reveals Our Extraordinary Potential to Transform Ourselves* (London: Constable & Robinson, 2009).

181   **With his colleague Julie Brefczynski-Lewis:** This work is reported in J. A. Brefczynski-Lewis et al., 'Neural Correlates of Attentional Expertise in Long-Term Meditation Practitioners,' *Proceedings of the National Academy of Sciences* 104 (2007): 11483–11488.

181   **Another common form:** An excellent discussion of mindfulness meditation and its role in helping people cope with stress can be found in Mark Williams and Danny Penman, *Mindfulness: An Eight-Week Plan for Finding Peace in a Frantic World* (Emmaus, PA: Rodale Books, 2011).

183   **Schwartz scanned people's brains:** The landmark study demonstrating that ten weeks of mindfulness-based CBT led to a reduction in ac-

tivity in the orbitofrontal cortex of OCD patients as well as a substantial clinical improvement was J. M. Schwartz et al., 'Systematic Changes in Cerebral Glucose Metabolic Rate After Successful Behaviour Modification Treatment of Obsessive-Compulsive Disorder,' *Archives of General Psychiatry* 53 (1996): 109–113. Jeffrey Schwartz's development of a mindfulness-based form of cognitive behavioural therapy is described in Jeffrey M. Schwartz and Sharon Begley, *The Mind and the Brain: Neuroplasticity and the Power of Mental Force* (New York: Harper Perennial, 2002).

183   **Mindfulness-based CBT has also been:** An excellent academic review of studies on depression can be found in K. J. Ressler and H. S. Mayberg, 'Targeting Abnormal Neural Circuits in Mood and Anxiety Disorders: From the Laboratory to the Clinic,' *Nature Neuroscience* 10 (2007): 1116–1124. For a more accessible discussion, see Williams and Penman, *Mindfulness*.

184   **Teasdale, Williams, and Segal recruited:** The study that demonstrated the effectiveness of mindfulness-based cognitive behaviour therapy in preventing relapse in major depression was published in J. D. Teasdale et al., 'Prevention of Relapse/Recurrence in Major Depression by Mindfulness-Based Cognitive Therapy,' *Journal of Consulting and Clinical Psychology* 68 (2000): 615–623. A book by Z. V. Segal, J. M. G. Williams, and J. D. Teasdale, *Mindfulness-Based Cognitive Therapy for Depression: A New Approach to Preventing Relapse* (New York: Guilford Press, 2002), also provides an excellent overview of mindfulness approaches to cognitive therapy.

185   **Not long after this landmark study:** The study that showed that Jon Kabat-Zinn's eight-week mindfulness-based stress reduction technique can improve immune system function and lead to a shift in the frontal asymmetry of the brain to a more positive (left-sided) pattern was R. J. Davidson et al., 'Alterations in Brain and Immune Function Produced by Mindfulness Meditation,' *Psychosomatic Medicine* 65 (2003): 564–570. Excellent overviews of the scientific evidence that a relative left-sided asymmetry in the activity of parts of the PFC is associated with experience of positive emotions, whereas a relative right-sided asymmetry in PFC activation is associated with negative emotions can be found in R. J. Davidson, 'Emotion and Affective Style: Hemispheric Substrates,' *Psychological Science* 3 (1992): 39–43, and in R. J. Davidson and W. Irwin, 'The Functional Neuroanatomy of Emotion and Affective Style,' *Trends in Cognitive Sciences* 3 (1999): 11–21.

186 **While lying in an fMRI brain scanner:** The study using fMRI to show that people who scored higher on a 'mindfulness' questionnaire had stronger activity in the PFC and reduced amygdala activation (i.e., fear response) was J. D. Creswell et al., 'Neural Correlates of Dispositional Mindfulness During Affect Labelling,' *Psychosomatic Medicine* 69 (2007): 560–565.

187 **The MBSR program had reduced:** The study described here can be found in K. Britta et al., 'Mindfulness Practice Leads to Increases in Brain Grey Matter Density,' *Psychiatry Research: Neuroimaging* 191, no. 1 (2011): 36–43.

187 **Given that there are individual:** The study showing that people differ in their ability to regulate their emotions and that this relates to real-life differences in well-being and financial success is published in S. Côté, A. Gyurak, and R. W. Levenson, 'The Ability to Regulate Emotion Is Associated with Greater Well-Being, Income, and Socioeconomic Status,' *Emotion* 10 (2010): 923–933.

189 **George Bonanno, a psychologist:** An accessible overview of the scientific research showing that most people are highly resilient after trauma can be found in George A. Bonanno, *The Other Side of Sadness: What the New Science of Bereavement Tells Us About Life After Loss* (New York: Basic Books, 2009). For an accessible account of how people can grow and even experience 'post-traumatic growth' after major trauma, see Stephen Joseph, *What Doesn't Kill Us: The New Psychology of Posttraumatic Growth* (New York: Basic Books, 2011). An excellent overview can also be found in Gary Stix, 'The Neuroscience of True Grit,' *Scientific American* (March 2011): 28–33.

189 **In his original experiments, Seligman:** The original discovery of learned helplessness in dogs was made by Martin Seligman and colleagues and published in M. E. P. Seligman, S. F. Maier, and J. Geer, 'The Alleviation of Learned Helplessness in Dogs,' *Journal of Abnormal Psychology* 73 (1968): 256–262. One of the interesting things to note is that approximately one-third of the 150 dogs who received inescapable shock did not become helpless – they never gave up. While most developed a depressive coping style and became helpless, some remained resilient and maintained a more optimistic style. There is little doubt that these differences are also reflected in the patterns of pessimistic and optimistic thinking we see in people.

190 **The development of this psychological immunity:** This research is published in J. P. E. Amat et al., 'Previous Experience with Behavioural Control over Stress Blocks the Behavioural and Dorsal Raphe

Activating Effects of Later Uncontrollable Stress: Role of the Ventral Medial Prefrontal Cortex,' *Journal of Neuroscience* 26 (2006): 13264–13272.

190   **Studies with rats have even:** The experiment reported here was published in J. M. Weiss, 'Effects of Coping Behaviour in Different Warning Signal Conditions on Stress Pathology in Rats,' *Journal of Comparative and Physiological Psychology* 77, no. 1 (1971): 1–13. It's worth noting that an earlier study published by Joseph Brady with monkeys found the exact opposite results. In what became known as the 'executive monkey' studies, Brady reported that the monkey that had control, the 'executive,' developed *more* ulcers than the yoked monkey, who received the same number of shocks but had no control. However, it is now widely acknowledged that there was a serious problem with the design of Brady's study. The problem was that monkeys were not randomly assigned to the different conditions. Instead, the monkeys who learned fastest were given the 'executive' role, while the slower monkeys were put in the 'no control over shock' group. Subsequent work by Jay Weiss found that fast responders were more prone to developing ulcers in the first place (with or without shock), which meant that Brady's study was seriously flawed. Subsequent work has found the pattern reported by Jay Weiss, that having control actually leads to a *decrease* in ulcers. Brady's study was published in J. V. Brady et al., 'Avoidance Behaviour and the Development of Gastroduodenal Ulcers,' *Journal of the Experimental Analysis of Behaviour* 1 (1958): 69–72.

190   **elderly residents of a New England:** The studies with elderly nursing home residents by Ellen Langer and Judith Rodin referred to here have been published in two articles: E. J. Langer and J. Rodin, 'The Effects of Choice and Enhanced Personal Behaviourality for the Aged: A Field Experiment in an Institutional Setting,' *Journal of Personality and Social Psychology* 34 (1976): 191–198, and J. Rodin and E. J. Langer, 'Long-Term Effects of a Control-Relevant Intervention with the Institutionalised Aged,' *Journal of Personality and Social Psychology* 35 (1977): 897–902.

191   **A classic study by psychologists Lauren Alloy:** The original study on depressive realism was published in L. B. Alloy and L. Y. Abramson, 'Judgement of Contingency in Depressed and Non-Depressed Students: Sadder but Wiser?' *Journal of Experimental Psychology: General* 108 (1979): 441–485. Subsequent studies have shown that it is not really the case that depressed or pessimistic people are sadder

but wiser; instead it seems that depression is associated with more accurate estimates of one's *own* lack of control, but interestingly a tendency to *overestimate* the amount of control other people have. This work was published in D. Martin, L. Y. Abramson, and L. B. Alloy, 'The Illusion of Control for Self and Others in Depressed and Non-Depressed College Students,' *Journal of Personality and Social Psychology* 46 (1984): 125–136.

192   **we have a better chance of winning:** A comprehensive overview of the effects of the illusion of control can be found in E. J. Langer, 'The Illusion of Control,' *Journal of Personality and Social Psychology* 32 (1975): 311–328.

193   **the 'Paradox of Progress.':** In his book *The Paradox of Progress: How Life Gets Better While People Feel Worse* (New York: Random House, 2003), George Easterbrook presents many fascinating facts and figures about how the wealth of the developed world has increased dramatically over a fifty-year period. For instance, he points out that in the 1950s a cheeseburger at McDonald's cost the equivalent of half an hour's wage, whereas in 2003 the cost was equivalent to about nine minutes of work. Yet people surveyed in 2003 say that they were worse off than their parents and they expect their children to inherit an even worse world. It's not all McDonald's fault! There are lots of other examples of how things have improved (e.g., having space and warmth in one's home) while feelings of well-being have not budged.

193   **science has found that genuine:** Martin Seligman has been at the forefront of the 'positive psychology' movement, which tries to discover what it is that can lead to a life filled with joy and meaning, especially trying to uncover the factors that allow people to flourish. His findings are explained in his book *Authentic Happiness: Using the New Positive Psychology to Realise Your Potential for Lasting Fulfillment* (New York: Free Press, 2002). For a more academic description of positive psychology, see M. E. P. Seligman and M. Csikszentmihalyi, 'Positive Psychology: An Introduction,' *American Psychologist* 55 (2000): 5–14. Mihaly Csikszentmihalyi has also written widely on positive psychology, especially on the concept of 'flow' or 'optimal experience.' This work is beautifully described in his now classic book *Flow: The Psychology of Optimal Experience* (New York: Harper-Collins, 1990).

195   **Psychologist Barbara Fredrickson:** The study on flourishing and positivity ratios described here can be found in B. L. Fredrickson and M. F. Losada, 'Positive Affect and the Complex Dynamics of Human

Flourishing,' *American Psychologist* 60 (2005): 678–686. Barbara Fredrickson's work is described in her inspiring book, *Positivity: Groundbreaking Research Reveals How to Embrace the Hidden Strength of Positive Emotions, Overcome Negativity, and Thrive* (New York: Crown, 2009). You can also work out your own positivity ratio on her website: www.positivityratio.com. It is worth noting that, while it is important for flourishing to maintain our positivity ratio above 3, it is also possible to have too much of a good thing. In her book, Fredrickson points out that the positive experiences have to be genuine and if the positivity ratio gets very high, that might actually be a bad thing.

197 **Positivity ratios are also important:** John Gottman's research has identified several things that are important for a happy marriage, including a positivity ratio of more than 5 to 1. You can read about this work in John Gottman, *Why Marriages Succeed or Fail: And How You Can Make Yours Last* (New York: Fireside, 1994).

197 **Having a healthy and responsive:** The work showing that parts of our brain that respond to fear, such as the amygdala, are also important in pushing us towards an optimistic bias is published in T. Sharot et al., 'Neural Mechanisms Mediating Optimism Bias,' *Nature* 450 (2007): 102–105. Anthony Ong's work demonstrating that resilient people tend to experience more positive *and* negative emotions in a crisis can be found in A. D. Ong, C. S. Bergeman, and T. L. Bisconti, 'The Role of Daily Positive Emotions During Conjugal Bereavement,' *Journal of Gerontology: Psychological Sciences* 59B (2004): 158–167.

INDEX